“Thirty-one years ago, Catholic thinker Charles Rice wrote 50 *Questions on the Natural Law: What It Is and Why We Need It.* Although Daryl Charles doesn’t comment, his new book, *The Idea and Importance of Natural Law: Fifty Questions and Answers*, can be read as a sympathetic Evangelical Protestant engagement with many of the same issues. Such a thing would have been much less likely a generation ago, but Catholic-Protestant conversation about natural law has changed a great deal since then, and Daryl Charles has been active in the discussion.”

J. Budziszewski, Ph.D.,
Professor of Government and Philosophy,
University of Texas at Austin,
author of *What We Can’t Not Know: A Guide*

“No one has done more than J. Daryl Charles over the past two decades to educate Christians of all persuasions about the value of natural law as a reliable guide to our moral reasoning. No one has done more to convince skeptics of the pressing need to retrieve natural law after many years of neglect, and deepen our understanding of it. In this latest book, Charles continues this great project, with a text that is as crystal-clear and cogent as it is sharply reasoned and beautifully organized—and withal a delightful read. All those who value careful and theologically informed moral reasoning, while appreciating the author’s crisp and accessible formulation of guiding concepts, will want to have this book on their shelf.”

Wilfred M. McClay, Ph.D.
Victor Davis Hanson Chair in Classical History
and Western Civilization, and Professor of History
Hillsdale College

“This concise but multifaceted primer on natural law—attentive to its historical, philosophical, theological, and political dimensions—will be much appreciated by those engaged in the important work of retrieving and reclaiming the intellectual riches of the classical and Christian traditions. It is especially recommended to those Protestants still (wrongly) convinced that the natural law is not part of their own tradition.”

Korey D. Maas, D.Phil.
Department. of History
Hillsdale College

"J. Daryl Charles observes in this valuable volume, 'Every generation finds a new reason to rediscover natural law.' Such rediscovery requires reliable guides, however, and Charles demonstrates in this book what he has shown throughout his previous works: he is an accomplished advocate and expositor of the natural law. Reckoning with the moral order is perhaps both the preeminent challenge and the most significant opportunity of our day. Charles not only helps us to ask the right questions, but he also provides worthy and worthwhile answers. This is no small achievement and I am grateful for his diligent labors to help us rediscover anew the ancient truths of the natural law."

Jordan J. Ballor, D. theol., Ph.D.
Director of Research,
Center for Religion, Culture & Democracy

"In this time of war and rumors of war, natural law is no dusty old concept, but a living, breathing idea that profoundly affects our 21st century lives. Daryl Charles' latest book, "The idea and importance of natural Law, fifty questions and answers" explains it in a practical, pithy, way. Charles should be commended for making it accessible and relevant to our times. Be it just war or criminal justice, this book holds the golden key to understanding."

David C. Iglesias, J.D.
Captain, JAG Corps, U.S. Navy (ret.)
Director, Center for Faith, Politics & Economics
Jean & E. Floyd Kvamme Associate
Professor of Politics and Law, Wheaton College

"Daryl Charles is an illustrious and long-standing contributor to revitalizing the philosophical, theological, and cultural importance of the natural law tradition. In this book, he admirably answers with insight every question that pertains to natural law. His answers do not fail to persuade. Charles's book deserves a wide readership."

Eduardo Echeverria, Ph.D.
Professor of Philosophy and Theology
Sacred Heart Major Seminary

“Daryl Charles offers a very helpful resource on natural law that should appeal to all morally serious Americans especially curious Christians. While often intuited or unstated, most American Christians are unaware of the natural law tradition and its rich interaction with Christian teaching across millennia. As Dr. Charles explains, natural law is a boost to faith and ethics by explaining how the deity has inscribed his law into all that we see around us, if we will take notice. The implications are enormous.”

Mark Tooley
President, Institute on Democracy and Religion
Editor, *Providence–A Journal of Christianity & American Foreign Policy*

“In this volume Daryl Charles provides us with a masterful, memorable, and reliable guide to help us understand what natural law is, how it reveals universal values, and the ways it should shape our thinking about everything from abortion to euthanasia, from criminal justice to capital punishment, from revenge to war, and beyond. We tip our hats to Daryl, a careful thinker, seasoned teacher, and a skillful author.”

C. Ben Mitchell, Ph.D.
(University of Tennessee at Knoxville), professor of moral philosophy and author of *Ethics and Moral Reasoning: A Student's Guide* (Crossway, 2013) and *Bioethics and Medicine: A Short Companion* (B&H Academic 2025).

“What an exciting time it is that Protestants are seeing the return of the natural law tradition in its ranks. J. Daryl Charles is one of the most important voices responsible for this resurgence. The new primer you hold in your hands is a wonderful distillation of the most important facets of the natural law tradition. Readers will come away deepened by the coherence of the Christian natural law tradition.”

Andrew T. Walker, Ph.D.,
Associate Professor of Christian Ethics and Public Theology, The Southern Baptist Theological Seminary and Fellow, The Ethics and Public Policy Center.

THE IDEA & IMPORTANCE OF NATURAL LAW

FIFTY QUESTIONS AND ANSWERS

J. DARYL CHARLES

STONE TOWER PRESS

The Idea and Importance of Natural Law:
Fifty Questions and Answers

Special thanks to Jacob Alexander for his copyediting and proofreading assistance.

Stone Tower Press
7 Ellen Rd.
Middletown, RI 02842
stonetowerpress.com

Paperback ISBN: 979-8-9919831-1-2

Cover and text design by Amy Cole, JPL Design Solutions

Printed in the United States of America

Table of Contents

1

How is natural law defined?

The idea of natural law proceeds on the baseline assumption of a shared nature in all human beings, irrespective of culture or location, and a shared knowledge of this nature by all human beings based on human intuition and reasoning. This metaphysical reality (common human design) and epistemological reality (common human awareness and knowledge) lead to the assumption of common ethical standards that are normative for human behavior. The Roman statesman Cicero (106–143 BCE) defined natural law as "right reason" which is "in accordance with [human] nature." He believed it to be universal, applying to "all men," and "unchangeable and eternal." "By its commands this law summons men to the performance of their duties; by its prohibitions it restrains them from doing wrong."[1] Closer to our time, German legal philosopher Heinrich Rommen (1897–1967) describes the natural law as "a judgment of reason which presents actions as commanded or forbidden by the Author of reason because the light of reason shows them to be in agreement or disagreement with man's essential nature."[2]

John Locke (1632–1704), in distinguishing between "natural right" and "natural law," offers this definition: "This law of nature can...be so described [as a law] because it is the command of the divine will, knowable by the light of nature, indicating what is and what is not consonant with a rational nature."[3] While acknowledging the role that reason plays in perceiving the natural law, Locke hesitates to call it "a dictate of reason," as some have done.[4] His rationale for this hesitation is threefold. First, reason cannot lay down a decree or command; it can only *discover and investigate* a law that has been ordained by a higher authority—a law, he acknowledges, which has been "implanted in our hearts." Second, reason is not the source of this law, but, rather, its *interpreter*. Third, reason cannot give us moral laws; that is, reason is not, at bottom, a moral faculty, and hence, the source of what human actions *ought* to be done.[5]

Traditional religious thinking, at least in the Judeo-Christian tradition, distinguishes between a general and a more particularized mode of revealed knowledge operative among human beings ("general revelation" versus "special revelation"). Accordingly, what unites all people is the former, a knowledge of moral "first things" or moral predicates that is prior to any knowledge that they might acquire. This "prior" knowledge—"what we can't not know," in the words of one social philosopher,[6] or the "unwritten law" (*lex non scripta*)[7]—is precisely what one New Testament writer describes when he refers, in his letter to Christian believers in the imperial seat of Rome, to a moral law "written on the heart."[8]

In strictly practical terms, we might define natural law in terms similar to those of Locke above: natural law is an order that is (1) perceived by reason but not created by reason; (2) brought to light by reflection and recognized by moral and legal deliberation; and (3) in some way normative for human conduct and thus for law.[9] The reality and awareness of the natural law—a reality that, summarily, is perceived by, applied by, and normative for human beings—are not dependent on religious belief, given human beings' shared nature and shared intuition of basic moral reality.[10] Rather, they are in accordance with practical reason.[11] It is called "law" because it both commands and forbids; it is called "natural" because it is implanted in human nature.

Deep within human consciousness people discover a "law" to be at work. It is a law that they themselves did not create yet which they are constrained to obey, even when in theory they might reject it. In universal terms, external *and* interior witnesses—i.e., all of the cosmos *and* human conscience—work together in harmony, by which human beings intuit what is good and evil, just and unjust, acceptable and unacceptable. This moral "law," though intuited by all, can of course be ignored, discarded, or rejected, since every human being wills, chooses, and acts for the sake of an intended end. While an awareness of this "law" comes to full expression through the Judeo-Christian framework of faith,[12] it is not relegated purely to the realm of religious faith. All people possess this moral sense—this "law of oughtness" or "law of nature"[13]—and thus are "without excuse" and morally accountable,[14] just as the virtue of wisdom is universal and accessible to all who seek it, regardless of their social location in human history and circumstances. The objective measure of right action, which transcends the human mind yet remains accessible to it, is the natural law.[15]

Throughout history this phenomenon has been described variously by philosophers, theorists, and theologians and in diverse cultural contexts. What the Chinese wisdom tradition calls the *Tao*, what has been called the "perennial philosophy," what has been depicted in Plato and Jesus's teaching as the "Golden Rule," what Aristotle called the "first principles of practical reason," what is embodied in the "Ten Commandments" as well as in Hebrew wisdom literature, what Paul the apostle to the Gentiles described as the "law written on the heart," what the founders of the American republic referred to as the "law of nature" (mirroring "nature's God") and that which is "self-evident," and what acclaimed writer C. S. Lewis described as "the reality beyond all predicates"[16]—all refer to what we may call "natural law." Strangely then, natural law can be said to belong in our day to "the lost world of common truths."[17] But because it belongs to "common truth," it is not "a theory which we are asked to adopt," but rather "the claim that there are certain judgments we have already made and *could not help* making."[18] Natural law, "present in the heart of each man and established by reason, is universal in its precepts and its authority extends to all men."[19] Even when it is not universally acknowledged or obeyed, its reality and authority are universally binding.

2

What is the essence of the natural law?

Natural law reasoning proceeds on the assumption that human nature is comprised of body and spirit, the material and non-material, and thus serves as a norm for guiding the morality of human behavior. There exists an objective order that is defined by natural law, and this order issues from—and is intuited by—human nature. Because the natural law is "the voice of nature,"[1] it presupposes "human nature" to be a *shared* nature. Therefore, a common sense of morality—what *ought* and *ought not* to be done—can be found among all human beings. Natural law, thus, points human beings to an order of nature, a universal and shared reality, that informs us of the substantive moral content of what it means for humans to flourish. And what is the essence of human flourishing? It is to develop the human virtues. In the words of Thomas Aquinas, the natural law "as to general principles" is "the same for all, both as to rectitude and as to knowledge."[2] That is to say, natural law principles are *right* for everyone and *known* by everyone.[3] And if they are *right* for everyone as well as *known* by everyone, then they are *binding* on everyone. Hence, Locke concludes: "if the law of nature is not binding on men, neither can any human positive law bind them"; and "if you would abolish the law of nature, you overturn at one blow all government among men, [all] authority, rank, and society." This, of course, "would be to establish the power of tyrants, thieves, and pirates."[4]

In its essence, natural law guides human beings as moral agents. It enables and protects human freedom insofar as it shields humans from making choices that undermine human well-being while directing them in the direction of the good, which accords with their fundamental nature. The efficacy of natural law, it needs stating, does *not* depend on a knowledge of God.[5] All human beings are to some degree aware of human moral obligation. The natural law expresses itself at the most elementary level in the common moral intuition of good and evil, right and wrong, justice and injustice, acceptable and unacceptable. All humans intuit that we *ought* to do good and *ought* to avoid harm or evil. That good is to be done and evil avoided, however, is not some sort of nebulous or vacuous principle, void of content. All people sense that murder, theft, greed, sexually defrauding others, dishonesty, malfeasance, and disrespect are wrong, violating our fundamental nature and design. "Criminal justice," as most civilized societies understand it, confirms this basic and shared universal intuition.[6] By "criminal justice" we understand that a moral equilibrium and balance in our communities must be restored following human behavior that is unjust and evil. Punishment helps to restore that balance in temporal affairs. Punishment belongs to the classical definition of justice, namely, *what is due another*. Justice, then, based on human design and the common good, has a reciprocal character.[7]

Aristotle's emphasis on an ordered community, as well as his distinguishing between human and non-human animals, has many confirmations in the Western philosophical and theological traditions.[8] Humans possess a "prior" knowledge and awareness of moral "first things." At the most basic level, for example, cannibalism is sensed by human beings as evil and everywhere unacceptable; such would not be the case among animal creatures. Murder, rape, and thievery as well produce the same response among humans regardless of socio-cultural location. While moral "first things" do not inform us as to whether to drive, fly, or bus to New York City, they do "guide" us—and "condemn" us—if the reason for our journey is to partake in a Mafia hit squad.

Given the aforementioned shared nature of all human beings and hence the presence of an internal moral guide—a "law" that is inscribed on the human heart and a common fund of knowledge—one need not be of any particular religious persuasion or outlook to acknowledge the reality of the natural law; this awareness is what unites all people. The human propensity for an ordered community, for reasoning and moral reflection, and for distinguishing "right" from "wrong" sets human beings apart from non-human animals. There exists no people-group, no human society, no culture that does *not* discriminate between acceptable and unacceptable, between "right" and "wrong," between just and unjust (even when these distinctions are defined or measured in different ways by different individuals, people-groups, or cultures). In the first century, Paul the apostle to the Gentiles could note that Gentiles—that is, those who had not received particularized "special revelation" as Jews had received in the form of the Mosaic Law—still did "by nature the things required by the law." And thereby "they show that the requirements of the law are written on their hearts."[9]

To employ the language and logic of morality—i.e., to insinuate "ought" or "ought not"—is to presuppose *of necessity* that (1) there exist "good" and "evil," and hence a right and wrong, and that (2) humans exercise a moral "freedom" with respect to the choices they make. This freedom, in turn, means that (3) people can be held responsible for their actions; they choose to act virtuously or viciously. Thus, for example, when people are rewarded or punished not for the moral quality of their acts but for the "accident" of their ethnic or racial background, it must be said that ethnic and racial discrimination is wrong *of necessity* and not merely on the basis of personal perspective, circumstance, or social location.[10] The natural law, then, is the starting point of moral realism—a starting point that predisposes the human person to do good and avoid doing evil or harm.[11]

Natural law is part of our "nature" neither in the sense that it is a biological instinct nor in the sense of being social or cultural habit or custom. Rather, it is "natural" insofar as it corresponds with our fundamental design; human beings possess a basic awareness of moral norms and the moral character of their actions.[12] The moral norms of the natural law are neither opinions, which can be doubted, agreed upon or rejected; nor are they incomprehensible judgments that cannot be perceived.[13] Locke expresses human moral knowledge in this way:

> if man were creator of himself, someone who could give himself being, who could bring himself into the world, he would also have granted himself an eternal duration for his existence (not to mention a perfect knowledge of all things and a greater power over natural things).[14]

The natural law, thus, serves as a guide—a "common sense" guide—whereby human actions are directed toward a highest good. That "good," moreover, is not merely personal; nor is it mere self-interest. Rather, it is communal as well (hence, we speak of the "common social good"). For this reason *tradition* is important. We human beings do not simply "figure out" moral truth and reality individually as we stumble along in life. We learn to align ourselves with moral truth which exists and endures outside of our experience, our awareness, and our acknowledgment; as a "tradition," it transcends us. The natural law tradition is like a river. It applies to different contexts and different locations, just as a river is characterized by eddies, lakes, streams, and tributaries. Yet the water—the "tradition"—is one in substance, regardless of where one is located and how far removed from other people-groups one is located. Moral traditions are important precisely for this reason: in their continuity they inform us, they encourage us, they warn and admonish us.

3

Where do we find evidence of the natural law?

In his work *Questions concerning the Law of Nature* (1664), Locke expresses the reality of natural law in the following way:

> without the law of nature there would be no virtue or vice, no praise for probity or punishment for wickedness; where there is no law [there would be] no wrong, no guilt...The words "upright" and "decent" would perish as meaningless, or nothing would remain of them except an empty name. None could act against the law, since no law would make either commands or prohibitions. Man would be the supreme and absolutely free judge of his own actions.[1]

Because of this "law" that is rooted in "common sense" and human "nature" and is antecedent to human culture, all peoples' consciences "bear witness" to basic reality and what is true, with their thoughts both "accusing" and "defending" them in their actions.[2] The language of conscience, accusation, guilt and culpability, justification, and rationalization points to the realm of moral reality—a realm that transcends self-interest and individual experience—and the natural law. It is "nature" because it describes *the way things are* and how humans function normally[3]; the fact that not everyone gives assent to the natural law does not assail its universal reality.[4] It is a "law" because *nothing can change our essential design*, and our design entails behavior that is to be normative for all humans.[5] Proper use of something—indeed *anything*—that has been "designed" requires on our part an understanding of its function. Design, then, constitutes a natural source of moral knowledge.[6] At the same time, since human moral depravity is universal in its extent yet restrained and varied in terms of degree, the potential in humans to express depravity, devastating as it may be, neither eliminates our ability to choose to do good (moral freedom) nor releases us from the sense of moral obligation (culpability, the common good).

Moral predilection characterizes all people everywhere and at all times, even when individuals and people-groups ignore or refuse to acknowledge and honor it or when people morally "draw the line" differently. Of course, a standard objection will be raised, as Locke notes: "If the moral law is implanted within and known by the light of nature, why are so many people 'blind' when illuminated by it?" Locke's response is that even granting the presence of our intellectual and moral faculties, "not all men necessarily make right use of these faculties."[7] "Knowledge of it [the natural law]," he insists, "can be hidden to no one except to the lover of blindness and darkness, who, to escape his duty, would cast off his nature."[8]

Moral "first principles," it should be emphasized, cannot be "proven" or "demonstrated" like mathematics through experiment or evaluation since they are anterior to the human experience. Nevertheless, we may acknowledge as true everywhere and at all times the proposition that "all men are created equal." Such cannot be "demonstrated" or "proven" in laboratory; it is a "necessary truth," a "first principle," based on the reality of a shared human nature. For this reason, as one political philosopher observes of the moral skeptic:

> The person who seeks to deny the existence of morals will spend most of his days trying to flee from the perils of contradiction

> and the tangle of his own argument. He will discover, again, that for the man of reason the existence of morals must hold the place of a *necessary assumption* or a *first principle* in the ground of his understanding.[9]

In the words of writer C. S. Lewis, the moral sceptic "attacks traditional values (the *Tao*) in defence of what he at first supposes to be (in some special sense) 'rational' or 'biological' values. But...all the values which he uses in attacking the *Tao*, and even claims to be substituting for it, are themselves derived from the *Tao*." The conclusion: "If the *Tao* falls, all his own conceptions of value fall with it."[10]

On what basis, we might ask, could the founders and framers of the American experiment—indeed, could *anyone*—speak of "self-evident truths"? Such language, two centuries removed, strikes us today as outmoded and quaint at best and oppressive and "intolerant" at worst. For many of our contemporaries it is "self-evident" that there are *no* self-evident truths.[11] But, in addition to the inherent contradiction herein—it is *self-evident* that there are *no* "self-evident truths"—we are faced with a conundrum that is not only ethical but social-political in nature; hence, the presumption of the founders needs some measure of honesty on our part, even though we might balk at such. The very assumption of "self-evident truths" carries with it eminent and political consequences. At the very least, it means that there *are* human goods—goods that (a) determine human flourishing, (b) are intrinsic in nature, and thus (c) need to be protected and preserved. This, of course, forces upon us the weight of a moral "law"—what *ought* to be done in the human experience and in the context of human relations. This "oughtness" corresponds to the so-called "Golden Rule" ethic—loving our neighbor as ourselves—which is found in the teaching of both Plato and Jesus. *No one* anywhere does *not* believe in the "Golden Rule." Stated differently, *some* principle of virtue and vice is recognized among all people and all societies. In the words of Locke, "there is no race so barbarous, so removed from all humanity, that it does not have some notion of virtue and vice, some consciousness of praise or censure."[12] Human nature, he concludes, would have to be abolished before anyone could be free of moral obligation. *Whence comes that awareness of obligation?* Locke persists in asking.

All people, it needs reiterating, feel the weight and sense the effects of this moral law in terms of what we call "conscience."[13] We might say that it is a law not unlike the "law of gravity." Few have captured the reality of natural law's evidence as compellingly as the writer C. S. Lewis. In his essay "Right and Wrong as a Clue to the Meaning of the Universe,"[14] Lewis argues that all people exhibit moral sentiments; all seem to intuit the presence of justice and injustice in their lives. This awareness, he notes, is mostly keenly and practically evident in the case of *injustice*. What is striking, as Lewis well observes, is the fact that all people protest the presence of unjust treatment when it visits them personally. And even when they do not publicly complain or protest (which they usually do), they are convinced that *something is not right*, that *justice has somehow alluded them*. To his readers Lewis poses the question *Why this reflex*? His response is meant to give us pause: it is as if there is a "law"—indeed, a *moral* law—in existence in the universe, a law that we did not create but which we are forced to acknowledge and affirm, even when we deny its theoretical reality. Indeed, we affirm this law every time we protest injustice.

Lewis's observation and intuition—*Why do we sense and react to injustice?*—is worth pondering. Worth pondering because it is a *universal* predisposition, and a predilection that is unique to the human species. The great apes, with whom we are often compared by biologists and social psychologists, alas do *not* wrestle with issues of fairness, justice, indignity, or the problem of evil.[15] How does one arrive at an awareness of moral principle? Whence comes the "moral sense"? While human behavior is surely complex, it is foremost intuitive, rational and reflective, perceiving, and—in the end—conceiving. Hence, we do not as humans concern ourselves solely with our rawest of physical needs, like the animals, but rather with our soulish, moral-spiritual, as well as mental-psychological and intellectual needs. In fact, human beings tend—though not always—to prioritize their moral-spiritual over physical needs. Philosophers are inclined to speak of this tendency in terms of human flourishing.

Natural law theorists are proponents of human flourishing for this very reason. They view human nature to be moral-spiritual and not merely physical-material in its constitution. Moreover, they affirm the reality of moral principles—universal in scope—that govern the behavior of all human beings, regardless of time, culture, and location. Thus, what is important—indeed telling—is *not* what differences we may find in moral codes characterizing various people-groups and cultures but rather *what is shared in common* by these diverse people-groups. Why is it that murder and fraud and thievery and incest and disrespect toward elders are unacceptable by human beings, and universally so? Why is it that both Plato and Jesus, in addition to other cultural versions of the same,[16] teach a moral principle (the aforementioned "Golden Rule" ethic) which is universally recognized and admired? As it turns out, this moral principle is known to all: *Do unto others as you would have them do unto you*, with its corollary, *Don't do unto others what you would not want them to do unto you.* Again, it needs emphasizing that no one does *not* affirm this moral principle.

4

How broad or narrow is the content of the natural law, and is there agreement on its content?

NATURAL LAW REASONING DOES NOT operate on the assumption that humans know *everything* there is to know about human nature and about moral values and moral principle, only about what *fundamentally distinguishes* the human creature—namely, rationality and moral reflection. It would seem fairly clear, based on human experience and observation, that most humans do not arrive at a comprehensive or detailed awareness of specific moral laws through cognitive reasoning. For this reason, for example, a moral code such as the "Ten Commandments" (the Decalogue) mirrors a more general awareness of good and evil, just and unjust, morally acceptable and unacceptable among the human species. The Decalogue, it needs emphasizing, is not an exhaustive summary of all moral truth; it simply captures the most prominent features of social morality—features that we might describe as "self-evident." All people intuit the evil, wrong, and debilitating effects that arise from idolatry, murder, theft, dishonoring one's parents, defrauding one's neighbor, false testimony, and coveting, even when human beings find it difficult to obey those very general moral principles. For this reason, Thomas Aquinas writes that it is from the precepts of natural law, that is, from *general and indemonstrable principles*,[1] that human reason then proceeds to a more particularized understanding of specific matters.[2] Aquinas observes: "in matters of action, truth or practical rightness is not the same for all" as it applies to "matters of detail," but "only as to the general [moral] principles."[3]

In introducing his work *Politics*, Aristotle makes the very basic observation that "everyone does every action for the sake of what seems to be good."[4] And when we reflect on those things that are viewed universally as good or bad, right or wrong, as we do *every day of our lives*, we stand in the domain of ethics; we hereby show ourselves to be moral creatures.[5] At the same time, the sphere of ethics remains irreducibly *practical*, as political philosopher Hadley Arkes well reminds us.[6] Ethics involves an intuition of moral standards that guides our actions and activities in everyday life. Following Aristotle's basic line of reasoning, Thomas Aquinas famously summarized the "bottom line" of natural law reasoning: human beings are to *do good and avoid doing evil/harm*. This, he observes, is "in accord with reason"; it is "a dictate of practical reason."[7] We may hereby define the "good" as a fulfilling or realizing of the very ends for which humans exist—ends that subsist in human "nature" and are guided by right intention.

We may, then, argue on the basis of "self-evident" moral principles that two (classically formulated) moral norms govern the content of natural law reasoning. These two baseline criteria are as follows: (1) do good and avoid doing evil/harm (or, with other words, do what is just and avoid what is unjust) and (2) render to all what is due (or, with other words, give to everyone what is deserved). Because these are rational and self-evident, they demonstrate themselves to be universal in character. They are thus immutable, just as the moral precepts of the Decalogue—"Thou shalt not murder," "Thou shalt not steal," "Thou shalt not defraud others," etc.—are universal and binding in nature. There is no situation or circumstance among human beings and human cultures in which such moral norms are not binding.

5

Why is the natural law important?

There is a veritable host of reasons why the concept of natural law is important. These reasons, moreover, are central to human existence and civil society as we know it; they are not mere embellishments. Many of these, upon closer inspection, tend to fall into three general categories: (1) serving as a bridge between all people, given a shared human nature and hence our commonality; (2) establishing human dignity that accords with our basic nature; and (3) underpinning basic moral regulations and obligations in society through the fabric of law, thereby facilitating human flourishing and the common social good.[1] A bit of commentary on each of these three is in order.

A primary function of natural law is to furnish a bridge between people, based on human nature and what they share in common. In this way, it has an "apologetic" function. That is to say, it serves as justification or explanation of particular beliefs or practices.[2] "Apologetics," defined as such, may be seen to have three varieties or uses—religious, moral and political.[3] The religious value of natural law is that it establishes a point of contact between people of differing belief systems and cultural traditions. In theological terms, this point of contact is part of what we call general revelation and is established by God himself. The moral application of natural law is at work when we engage in ethical discourse and persuasion, as this entire volume attempts to do. And the political use of natural law reasoning allows people of differing outlooks and belief systems to agree to work together toward law and social policy in a way that is just and contributing toward the common good.[4]

While it may be useful to distinguish between the three aforementioned uses or applications of natural law reasoning, they should not be viewed as isolated or unrelated; rather, they are interrelated, in the same way that all of human life is integrated. Thus, from a religious standpoint, unbelievers (or non-religious persons) typically don't begin with the Judeo-Christian scriptures, for example, and then reason their way to affirming the faith. Not infrequently the process moves in the opposite direction. Traditionally, Christian "apologetics" has often assumed a process whereby the Christian engages the non-Christian initially at the place of moral first things, in the interest of introducing people to the faith. This is not to say that the scriptures have no place in communicating fundamental moral reality; it is only to illustrate that we must engage people *where they are located* in terms of their outlook on life. After all, everyone has a guiding set of presuppositions about ultimate reality, whether spoken or unspoken, that must be identified and properly understood.[5]

The concept of natural law is also important because it underpins human dignity, in accord with our basic nature. Human dignity, which is discussed more fully below,[6] expresses itself characteristically in specific non-material human faculties of reason, free will, and moral reflection.[7] In our day it has become increasingly evident that most—if not all—of our culture's pressing ethical issues hinge in some way on the matter of personhood and human dignity. Among other things, what has generally distinguished the character of Western cultural values over the centuries has been its ability to agonize over what it means to be "human." This, we may readily grant, has not always been the case; nonetheless, those values that helped shape Western cultural values have their roots, broadly speaking, in natural law moral reasoning. This commitment has decided effects in terms of human dignity. We might well consider, less than a generation after the devastations of World War II, the words of the Second Vatican Council (1962–1965), which retain their relevance insofar as they condemn with supreme clarity various crimes and attacks against human life that cry out for a response by people of good will:

> [W]hatever is opposed to life itself such as any type of murder, genocide, abortion, whatever violates the integrity of the human person such as mutilation, torments inflicted on body or mind, attempts to coerce the will itself; whatever insults human dignity such as subhuman living conditions, arbitrary imprisonment, deportation, slavery, prostitution, euthanasia or willful self-destruction; the selling of women and children, as well as disgraceful working conditions, where people are treated as mere instruments of gain rather than as free and responsible persons; all these things and others like them are infamies indeed. They poison human society...Moreover, they are a supreme dishonor to the Creator.[8]

Compounding the challenges of our day, given the aforementioned scourges that have visited the 20th and 21st centuries, is the role that leading ethical thinkers play in our own cultural tradition. We might illustrate by one supremely visible representative, a professor of bioethics at an Ivy League university "Center for Human Values" and one of the world's most famous and influential philosophers, who has argued categorically that membership of the human species is not "morally relevant."[9] It follows that "some nonhuman animals whose lives, by any standard, are more valuable than the lives of some humans," the latter being lives not worth living.[10] In consequence, "[a] chimpanzee, a dog, or pig, for instance will have a higher degree of self-awareness and a greater capacity for meaningful relations with others than a severely retarded infant or someone in a state of advanced senility."[11] How this ethicist knows this to be true we cannot know; nor can he. And whether he is *genuinely* convinced that membership in the human species is not "morally relevant" is doubtful.[12] In any case, by what moral standard or code can he—or *any* theorist, for that matter—make such a declaration?[13] And what are the implications of such a view?

If human personhood, however, *is* a morally relevant matter, then our task is to identify the nature of what a person is. Of course, to identify and amplify human nature is to identify and underscore an abiding consensus about human personhood. If such pronouncements by the aforementioned bioethicist are found to be outside of the human and cultural consensus, we are justified in rejecting them in the interest of both intellectual honesty and the common social good.

An authentic understanding of human personhood lays hold of the nature of what is characteristically and uniquely "human." When philosophers and scientists speak of the human being as a "rational animal," they invite qualification, inasmuch as rationality conveys sentience, self-awareness, self-responsibility, and the ability to reflect. Human life, thus, transcends physical matter and other "animal" life in its creativity, its aspiration, its moral imagination, and its pursuit of the good. This "consensual" understanding of human nature did not arrive yesterday. It is affirmed by both ancients and moderns and transcends different cultures. What science "discovers" tomorrow will not alter this truth.

Aristotle's well-known example of the oak helps to illustrate this consensus regarding human nature. Resident within the acorn is all the potential that distinguishes the genus oak. This potential, moreover, furnishes a sufficient explanation of both the diversity and the sameness within that genus, offering an adequate description of the nature of the oak, at whatever stage of the oak's development along the way. Several observations, applicable to human nature, may be made. The acorn is dependent on the oak tree for its existence. Conversely, the oak tree is dependent on the acorn for its continued existence. What's more, the acorn may or may not grow sufficiently, but this possibility does not bear on its essential nature, just as the oak tree itself may or may not grow to the size of other oaks, with this fact in no way affecting its essential nature. The truth of the essential nature of the genus oak does not vary, nor is it subject to debate.

Thomas Aquinas offers a definition of human personhood that accords with the consensus of classical philosophy yet is distinctly Christian.[14] "Person" signifies the individual substance of a rational nature. "Personhood" thus denotes what is distinct about the human being, implying a fundamental *dignity*. For Aquinas, dignity is what distinguishes human nature through its design—a design that is utterly unique to anything in the cosmos.[15] And were this not the case, one's value would then rise and fall according to the development or deterioration of one's functions, utility, and "usefulness." As it turns out, human sanctity and human rights are meaningless apart from the notion of inherent dignity and what we are by nature. Animals possess no "rights" in the proper sense of the term.[16] The great apes do not agonize over justice, wrestle with inequities, or search for meaning and purpose. In the language of Locke, "Is the law of nature binding on brutes? It is not."[17] As not a few philosophers have observed, when non-human animals run out of biological opportunities and activities—for example, seeking food and shelter, reproducing, playing and avoiding predators—they sleep. When humans, by contrast, run out of biological opportunities and activities, they ask questions. Significantly, the nature of this questioning always and again returns to *what it means to be human*. Who am I? Where am I headed? Is there a knowable truth? Why do I suffer? What are the consequences of my actions? To what or whom am I morally accountable? Do I have intrinsic worth?

The nature of human dignity is such that, all too often, it is taken for granted. Only when it is threatened do we find ourselves contemplating it with a measure of seriousness. We see what becomes of "human dignity" when it disappears in the context of tyrannical regimes. And if we do not allow the natural law to master or rule us, then something else will—something that becomes an oppressor and a destroyer of humanity. In recent generations, two things stand out as supreme distorters of human dignity: totalitarianism and science misused.[18]

But if we reject transcendent moral standards, if we deny accountability to a higher moral law (the natural law), where then do moral principles—if in fact they exist—originate by which to affirm human worth? It is implausible to understand them other than as secular materialists, for whom the soulish, non-material, and thus moral dimension of life is inexplicable and fluid.[19] As such, "moral principle" becomes a shifting entity—a matter of taste, if not of power. Nevertheless, in our post-consensus cultural climate, despite our insistence on denying civilizational consensus, our *knowing*—recall Aquinas's definition: moral principle is the same for all, both in rectitude and knowledge—is not based on subjective, private, or inaccessible data. It is a common fund accessible to all—to Kansans, Canadians, Kenyans, and Kazakhstanis—and a historical consensus around which there has been considerable agreement.

Finally, affirming objective moral truth, underpinned by natural law, not only leads us to affirm an intrinsic human dignity, but it yields an awareness of basic moral obligations to others. That awareness also entails a common moral judgment to protect and dignify human life, particularly human life that is vulnerable. This moral-philosophical commitment results in a moral line that connects beginning-of-life issues with end-of-life issues but also with atrocities that manifest themselves under totalitarian rule—for example, slavery, genocide, and mass human rights violations. To eliminate human life at the margins, on the one hand, and to fail to protect human lives who are oppressed and persecuted, on the other, are both *always* wrong. They are wrong not only because Christianity or Western culture or religion in general teaches such but also because the moral law "written on the heart" (Rom. 2:15) of every human being witnesses to their wrongness.

With the universal declarations on human rights and human dignity that proceeded in the aftermath of the Second World War, one might conclude that natural law thinking was pressed upon human civilization in an unprecedented way.[20] The hallmark of our era, to the present day, is most assuredly its accent on rights.[21] However, "rights" have moral meaning when—and *only* when—they issue out of a particular understanding of human nature—a nature that is inalienable and unchanging. What's more, we cannot conceptualize human "rights" properly unless we are willing to attach thereto an equal commitment to duties. The relationship of the two is reciprocal. And if duties are obligatory, most people will demand to know, *On what authority?* This is the real question, in the end. On what authority? The most plausible answer is *an authority that transcends* people and societies.[22]

Upholding human dignity and honoring basic moral obligations or duties require that both elements be anchored in a transcendent view of human nature. This understanding of human nature means that we are endowed with a twofold sense of motivation in our actions toward others: to do justice and to express charity. This twofold sense of moral obligation can be summed up in the so-called "Golden Rule" (about which we have more to say below[23]).

Those who reflect seriously on history or human affairs are conscious of the sobering truth that when and where the principles of natural law are ignored or rejected, human culture is subject to decline and—if that decline is not mitigated—collapse. The atrocities not only of the 20th century but the 21st remind us of the infinitely tragic consequences of failing to live according to moral "first principles" based on our fundamental design. Natural lawyers, against the spirit of the age, insist that morality is discovered, not constructed, and that reality is apprehended, not created. Therefore, natural law "moments" in human history—which is to say, a renewal or rebirth of the moral truths of natural law—are to be expected in history's ebb and flow, particularly against the backdrop of human history's darkest moments. Someone has said that every generation finds a new reason to rediscover natural law. Ours is no different, particularly given its pressing challenges. Historically, renewed interest in natural law and its principles has frequently emerged from the excesses and atrocities accompanying totalitarianism.[24] The doctrine of natural law, after all, provides the lone ideological and moral basis for countering the totalitarian spirit.[25] However, the danger in relatively free societies subsists in the illusion that legal institutions are a sufficient bulwark against "government by raw power."[26] The question, then, is what ideals and values will end up informing lawyers, judges, the courts, and gate-keepers of the land, if we deny the moral foundations of law and politics. Historically, the notion of natural law is obscured or lost when morality and law are separated.

6

Where do we find the idea of natural law being taught in human history, and who have been some of the major proponents of natural law in Western thought?

THE HISTORIAN (AND ANY INTERESTED reader) discovers that the idea of universal moral truths dates as far back as Socrates and Aristotle. In fact, several generations prior, Heraclitus (ca. 536–470 BCE) had argued that wisdom points to a wider "law" in the universe, a transcending *logos* or reason, to which human nature and human ethical striving are ordered. "Wisdom is the foremost virtue," according to Heraclitus, and "wisdom consists in speaking the truth, and in lending an ear to nature and acting according to her. Wisdom is common to all."[1] Heraclitus's attempt to understand a "natural moral law" as unchangeable stands in notable contrast both to the demagoguery of the Sophists and the capriciousness of the general population. The Sophists of his day, like the sophists of any era, refused to venerate the "natural moral law," since they viewed laws as artificial constructs that merely serve the interests of those in power.

Natural law thinking in Plato and Aristotle will be characterized by a high regard for the *polis*, the political community. All of life, for them, is "political" insofar as the city-state[2] subsists in rightly ordered relationships. Both reject a subjectivism about what constitutes the "good," which they hold to be self-evident. Aristotle differs, however, on one point. He holds the good to be understood in terms of human nature. Despite this difference of opinion, both care to preserve the social order, placing a strong emphasis on justice and how human laws should reflect enduring moral norms. Significantly, both recognize that what is *legally* just may or may not be what is *naturally* just.

In *Nicomachean Ethics*, Aristotle acknowledges some human behaviors to be intrinsically wrong—for example, murder, theft, and adultery. What is by nature just, based on natural law, "has the same validity everywhere" and does not depend on personal opinion; true justice, then, is universal and non-fluid.[3] In fact, Aristotle believes in and defends the "legislating" of morality. That is, laws—whether they are *written or unwritten*—are part of our moral education, helping to shape character, since human beings are not born virtuous.[4] Virtuous character, of course, is not inborn; rather, it is acquired. At the same time it is part of human nature that we have the ability to acquire virtue. Thus, discipline, moral reflection, wisdom, and yes, a particular environment—one which can be enhanced by good laws—all help in the shaping of good character, as any parent realizes.

Roman writers from Cicero to Marcus Aurelius also offer commentary on laws that issue out of human nature. Perhaps the most important early Roman commentary on natural law comes from the Stoic Cicero, who in *De Republica* ("On the Commonwealth") writes:

> To invalidate this law by human legislation is never morally right, nor is it permissible ever to restrict its operation, and to annul it wholly is impossible. Neither the Senate nor the people can absolve us from our obligation to obey this Law…It will not lay down one rule at Rome and another at Athens, nor will it be

> one rule today and another tomorrow. But there will be one law, eternal and unchangeable, binding at all times upon all peoples...[5]

The New Testament stands in general agreement with this perspective, even with certain necessary qualifications and when its writers would acknowledge that classical philosophers' intuition of the natural law was incomplete. One natural lawyer writes, with some justification, that while Greek thought anticipated various truths of Christianity, it was nonetheless insufficient. The reason for this is that "it saw the world only in terms of patterns—forms—rather than in terms of a personal Logos through whom these patterns are manifest."[6] The New Testament, in continuity with the Old Testament, presupposes rather than negates the natural law. In the words of Matthew Hale, the noted 17th-century jurist in the common law tradition, "the great scope of the Gospel of Christ is to reimprint and reinforce...this Natural Law upon human Nature."[7] And indeed we find Jesus teaching the permanence of the moral law, both directly[8] and indirectly.[9] In the words of the apostle Paul ("apostle to the Gentiles"), "Ever since the creation of the world his eternal power and divine nature, invisible though they are, have been understood and seen through the things he has made. So they [all people] are without excuse."[10] This, for the apostle, constitutes "the law written on the heart."[11] The same apostle's speech in the city of Lystra in the first century confirms the idea of the world being governed providentially through natural phenomena.[12] A similar speech and tactic occurs in Athens, first-century center of intellectual thought, where the apostle is invited to address Epicureans and Stoics who comprise the famed Council of the Areopagus.[13] Here Paul touches on core philosophical assumptions of his audience, emphasizing (a) what can be known and is known by all people and (b) that the universe is both material and non-material in its constitution.[14]

The notion of natural law was central to—and presupposed by—the church's social teaching through the centuries. The great champion of natural law, in the thirteenth century, was Thomas Aquinas, for whom moral law was "natural" insofar as it mirrored the very order of creation and human design and for whom philosophy and theology were in dialogue.[15] For Aquinas, a corrective to the Augustinian view of total (human) depravity was necessary: he countered that human design, though marred through our tendency toward evil, was nevertheless still intact. Notwithstanding the ravages of human fallenness and our propensity for doing evil, Aquinas insisted that natural law remains self-evident, and this by means of two evidences: reason and revelation. Aquinas reasons:

> So it is clear that as far as the general principles of reason are concerned, whether speculative or practical, there is one standard of truth or rightness for everybody... So we must conclude that the law of nature, as far as first principles are concerned, is the same for all as the norm of right conduct and is equally well known to all.[16]

While the Protestant reformers of the 16th century do not systematically treat natural law in their writings, they nevertheless presuppose it, in fundamental agreement with their Roman Catholic counterparts.[17] This is true even when they generally tended to be more distrustful of human reason. Martin Luther affirms an innate awareness of right and wrong, alluding to the so-called "Golden Rule" in all people. Agreeing with Aquinas, he writes: "Natural law is a practical first principle in the sphere of morality; it forbids evil and commands good."[18] Everyone, observes Luther, must acknowledge that what the natural law dictates in the human heart is right and true. There is no one, he insists, who does not sense the effects of the natural law, since nature and "the law written on the heart" (Rom. 2:14–15) attest to it.[19] Luther's colleague Philip Melanchthon, as well as John Calvin, understood natural law similarly. For Melanchthon, natural law represents a common fund of knowledge to which all people assent, and therefore one which God has "implanted" upon the soul of all human beings, "grafted into the nature of man" as a result of our design.[20] This implanted knowledge in the minds and hearts of human beings Melanchthon compares to light that can be seen by human eyes. The voice of the natural law, Melanchthon notes, has sounded "from the beginning of the world," even "before the time of Moses," and it remains "in force forever."[21] For Calvin, the natural law is dictated to us by "that inner law," which is "written, even engraved, upon the hearts of all."[22] A "rule for the right conduct of life," natural law "can lead them [all people] toward the goal of reason and truth" and is therefore a common law among nations.[23] The purpose of natural law, according to Calvin, is "that apprehension of the conscience which distinguishes sufficiently between just and unjust, and which deprives apprehension men of the excuse of ignorance, while it proves them guilty by their own testimony."[24]

Matthew Hale, the above-noted legal historian, and Hugo Grotius, considered by many the father of international law, are roughly contemporary and important voices invoking the place of natural law in common law. Hale joined a longstanding tradition in legal culture in which lawyers were trained to understand natural law as both the *source* of and *guide* for developing positive law.[25] Grotius continues to advance the natural law tradition in the early 16th century in the context of just war moral reasoning against the backdrop of Europe's religious wars. (In his application of natural law reasoning to the just war idea, Grotius is joined by the two important early-modern theorists Francisco de Vitoria and Francisco Suárez.[26]) Unlike medievalists who would have grounded natural law theologically in the divine nature and in the church's teaching, Grotius acknowledges the "secular" evidence of the natural law; it is grounded in and attested to by human nature. Perhaps somewhat unfairly, Grotius is remembered for having remarked that *even if there were no God*, natural law would exist, as all of human experience bears witness. At the same time, he acknowledges that

> even the Law of Nature itself, whether it be that which consists in the Maintenance of Society, or that which in a looser Sense is so called, though it flows from the internal Principles of Man, may notwithstanding be justly ascribed to God; because it was his Pleasure that these Principles should be in us.[27]

In his *Of the Laws of Ecclesiastical Polity*, penned in 1594, Richard Hooker observes of the law of nature: "Her seat is the bosom of God and her voice the harmony of the world."[28] Similarly, Nathaniel Culverwell, in 1652, writes: "By this great and glorious Law every good action was commanded, and all evill was discountenanc'd, and forbidden from everlasting."[29] As it happened, Culverwel would exercise direct influence on the thinking of a significant political philosopher to come, John Locke.

As a result of the writings of Locke, the 18th century would witness the application of natural law to political philosophy in particular. In Locke's work there is a notable shift in emphasis away from the ethical authority of the church and Scripture toward reason as the means by which moral norms are established. Locke's writings, as it turns out, undergird the American "experiment in ordered liberty," and his definition of natural law is presumed by America's founders in order to ground the new nation's establishment:

> By the foundation of natural law we understand that which supports and upon which are erected, as upon a foundation, all other precepts of this law, even the less obvious, and that from which [these precepts] can be deduced in some manner. As a consequence, these derive their entire force and their binding power from this [foundation] because they are in agreement with primary and, as it were, fundamental law, which is the rule and measure of all other laws which depend upon it.[30]

The founders' and framers' appeals to "Laws of Nature and Nature's God" are mirrored in those "self-evident truths" spelled out in the

Declaration of Independence. The framers of America's charter documents speak of human beings possessing certain inalienable rights, an emphasis that is owing to Locke.[31]

Over the last one hundred years, there has been a tendency among judges and legal experts to *make* law rather than *discover* it, thereby constructing law and policy for the purpose of progress (so-called) and social reform. This has generally been the consequence of (a) skepticism and agnosticism over against the idea of constitutional democracy and (b) the at times militantly secular approach to law, politics, and political philosophy operative in Western culture and notably in the U.S. Where an emphasis on natural law has been found, it has generally been anchored in Roman Catholic social thought and advanced by Roman Catholic theorists.[32] Many of the more prominent natural law theorists of the 20th century were writing between the late 1930s and 1950, and notably in the aftermath of the Second World War, at a time when questions of human dignity and human rights were once more critically important. If nothing else, the effects of World War II reminded human beings of the danger of philosophy without metaphysics and epistemology without truth's certainty.

7

What is the relationship between law as a basic concept and natural law?

Classically, law has been defined as the rule and measure of human behavior, whereby humans are induced to act or restrained from acting in accordance with reason. In short, law seeks to regulate human behavior toward a particular end, and natural law points in the direction (and end) of "the good." Law should uphold the common weal. As noted by Aquinas, who reflected much on the nature and character of law, "it belongs to the reason to direct [behavior] to the end," which is the "first principle in all matters of action."[1] Law, then, is proper to rational creatures alone, for it mirrors human rationality and a tendency toward order. Moreover, given human beings' social nature, law is an instrument of facilitating human flourishing and preserving the common good. Its effects extend beyond the individual to the community and society.

Within the historic Christian tradition, which has largely informed the Western cultural heritage, law has been understood at three levels—divine, natural, and civil law[2]—under the assumption that lower forms of law derive from a higher form. Many approaches to law in our era—whether utilitarianism, functionalism, subjectivism, etc.—fail to acknowledge this larger derivative framework that affirms interlocking categories of law. According to Aquinas, divine law—that "eternal and immovable" judgment "impressed on human minds"—is given with the purpose that it "directs what we are to be like, what we are to do, [and] what we must omit." Human law, by contrast, only "demands or forbids external works." Humans, Aquinas insists, participate in "divine" law, and they do so in two essential ways: (a) we are inclined always and everywhere toward behavior that is characteristically "human," and (b) this inclination is indicative of a moral order that transcends human beings themselves. This inclination, due to natural law, is not mere habit.[3] Based on reason, moral "first principles" are self-evident.[4]

The natural law, for Aquinas, is "the natural knowledge" and "governance of our conduct," originating outside ourselves—a knowledge and governance that are "grafted into the nature of man." In understanding human law, which should derive from the natural law, we must reflect on our very nature, which is oriented toward order and regulations and the good. The purpose of law, according to Aquinas, is "to lead men to virtue, not suddenly but gradually."[5] In its essence and at its base, humans' awareness of moral reality has a self-evident character, informing all of the difference between what is honorable and shameful, good and evil, just and unjust. The voice of the natural law, one might say with Aquinas, has sounded from the beginning of the world; in Christian terms, this awareness is based on the "divine image" implanted within.[6] The fundamental structure of human nature does not change. This explains why responses to and prohibitions of murder, theft, slavery, incest, defrauding others, etc. are immutable and non-fluid. Hence, the natural law is the basis for law in any human society.[7]

Aquinas is helpful not only in helping define the essence of law but underscoring its consequences as it affects society. "The chief and main concern of law properly so called is the plan for the common good," and such is the task of all people and their political representatives, Aquinas observes.[8] The "good" is not private but public or "common" in nature, benefitting both the communities in which we live and the wider community or nation of which we are a part. Every law, he insists (and echoing classical definitions), is shaped according to the *common good.* In truth, law is designed, as "a kind of dictate of the practical reason," to protect and preserve the wider community. What, then, are the effects of this "practical reason"? The chief end of this process is that we arrive at human laws, "provided that they fulfill the essential conditions of law."[9]

The focus of Aquinas's discussion of law and the natural law, then, is the common good, a focus that perhaps is lost on us in our day, as evidenced by the following observations:

> law is ordained to the common good, and consequently there is no virtue of which some activity cannot be enjoined by law. Nevertheless human law does not enjoin every act of every virtue, but those acts only which serve the common good, either immediately, as when the social order is directly involved from the nature of things, or mediately, as when measures of good discipline are passed by the legislator to train citizens to maintain justice and peace in the community.[10]

If the common good is our goal (and it should be the aim of *all* law), then reliance on natural law wisdom as it affects contemporary social-legal controversies and our deliberations over legislation is desperately needed. It can assist us in mitigating naked appeals to social and political power, in preventing the "construction" or creation of law, in preserving just social conditions in our communities, and in moderating sectarian or damaging social-political interests.

Objective moral norms—in law and in the social fabric of any culture—distinguish relatively free societies from rogue nations and totalitarian regimes. If there is no ultimate truth to guide and direct society and political activity justly, then "ideas and convictions can easily be manipulated for reasons of power. As history demonstrates, a democracy without values easily turns into open or thinly disguised totalitarianism."[11]

8

What is moral realism?

What we may call "moral realism" is a view of human existence that is grounded on moral absolutes, which is to say, moral principles that are non-fluid and universal in their applicability. It is to affirm that there exists a truth that transcends all human inventions, manipulations, and rationalizations. And to that truth all human beings are answerable. The trademark of all totalitarian regimes is their fundamental denial of a higher truth; rather, they determine what is "true," and any binding ties—for example, religious freedom and convictions issuing out of the sacred rights of conscience—are not to be tolerated.

To adopt a conviction of moral realism is to affirm that there are no other ("new") moral realities. The categories of good and evil, right and wrong, and just and unjust, as well as the notions of guilt, culpability, rationalization, and justification arising from issues of human conscience, simply mirror interior and exterior moral realities that transcend self-interest, circumstance, and individual experience.

Moral realism assumes that the good, the right, and the proper can be known; therefore, the (natural) moral law serves as the foundation for human actions and endeavor. At the same time, a realist perspective assumes that in our post-consensus age, we shall need to learn how to think about metaphysics—to which we are, quite frankly, unaccustomed. Why? To think "metaphysically" is to think about—and wrestle with—*ultimate* things. Among other things, this will inform our view of justice, which is integral to our understanding the character of law. But Enlightenment thinking and the presuppositions of modernity, and now those of postmodernity, have trained us to expose and throw off "uncritical" assumptions that were long held. Law, as understood in our day, is perceived to have no enduring basis. We are incapable of explaining why, with Aquinas and before him Augustine, that "an unjust law is no law at all." Utterly incapable.

However, the natural lawyer will respond—as this volume attempts to do—that it is not possible to be free from certain metaphysical assumptions, i.e., assumptions about what is real. The real issue is the degree to which people are aware of the metaphysical assumptions that lie behind their choices and their philosophy of life. Thus, viewed philosophically, a shift to modernity is not a shift away from metaphysics and toward "neutrality" but a shift from one set of metaphysical assumptions to another. The same can be said of the postmodern turn as well. Natural law reasoning finds it thus necessary to shed light on the uncritical operating assumptions of both modernity and postmodernity—assumptions that are by no means "neutral" but metaphysical in their own right. Such examination inevitably requires, at the most basic level, that we provide a compelling answer to the question *What is the good?*[1]

As numerous questions in this volume suggest, we must wrestle—in any age but especially in the present one—with the meaning of "the good." This, after all, is the basis of what we call morality. If there is no transcending concept of the good and "oughtness" which provides a measurement and baseline for "law," then we shall have to admit that "might makes right," and that in the end power will determine what is acceptable and unacceptable. To acknowledge such is to be a moral realist. At the same time, the moral realist will assert that the good is both universal and knowable to all, and that it is not the possession of any particular culture, people-group, or society. The good, therefore, we may call an end in itself, to be distinguished from self-interest, happiness, or other circumstantially- or culturally-determined "virtues."

There are, of course, various attempts historically to avoid connecting law and the good. Two in particular command our attention, for they are intertwined. One of these is perennial, always with us; it is the attempt to understand law as the enforcement of power and authority. Not moral reality but political power determines the "good"; as was previously noted, "might makes right." Not only totalitarian regimes—ever present and a particular menace in our day—but decaying democratic regimes lead inevitably to this end. Mere power, however, cannot impose an inner duty of obedience.

Another factor, an ideological secularism leading to relativism and positivism, represents the fruit of broader Enlightenment thinking and modernity, whether in its logical, moral, or legal form. Enlightenment thought—not all of it but a significant portion thereof—not only rejected revealed religion, and hence the authority of the church, but denied the capacity of human reason to know objective moral truth. This, of course, has led in our era to a denial of the *very possibility* of objective "truth." Over time, we find that relativism leads to various forms of positivism. Inasmuch as moral absolutes are denied, positivism—whether in its logical or legal form—takes on a utilitarian cast, resting on assumptions informed either by empirical data or by social-cultural trends and rejecting all other sources of explanation as an impediment to human knowledge. Empiricists limit explanations to efficient causes. Thus, laws as they concern human conduct are measured by and reduced to physical and material measurements, with the legal profession at large assuming supremely utilitarian perspectives. Any appeal to God or the transcendent is unhelpful at best and irrelevant and anachronistic at worst in terms of showing "how things work," since it is cannot be verified. Positivists, of course, are guided by their own dogmas; these, alas, are not testable or provable by any sort of empirical means.[2]

The moral realist, in the end, will affirm human freedom and human flourishing, given the reality of human design. But he will also affirm a transcending and guiding concept of the good as well as a concept of moral responsibility and accountability to that good, whereby the common social good is protected and preserved. Where a person chooses against the good, in spite of all accessible data and knowledge, there is then no excuse. Guilt or culpability ensues. Guilt and culpability, it needs emphasizing, are a problem of the will, not the lack of knowledge. Evidence that we indeed have sufficient moral knowledge is the fact of conscience. Conscience exhibits itself through guilt, remorse, atonement, and reconciliation on the one hand, as well as excusing-making and justification on the other.[3] The function of law at that point, if in fact it is just, is to render *what is due*, in accordance with the laws of a universe that require that "what goes up must come down."[4] Natural law cannot be removed, eliminated, or blotted out, even when it can be forgotten, ignored, or denied. Moral laws are neither extrinsic to human nature nor arbitrary in their formulation. Because human beings are inclined by nature to know the truth about themselves and their surrounding world, they cannot escape its influence, any more than they can escape the effects of the law of gravity.

9

Is objective moral truth possible without the natural law?

In his introductory chapter to *What We Can't Not Know*, J. Budziszewski makes the following observation: "Once upon a time it was possible for a philosopher to write that the foundational moral principles are 'the same for all, both as to rectitude and as to knowledge'[[1]]—and expect everyone to agree."[2] Alas, this was "once upon a time"; that age is long past. The challenge before us—socially, politically, and culturally—is quite simply that we live in a post-consensus era. Sixty years ago John Courtney Murray titled the book for which he is best known *We Hold These Truths*.[3] Today the fact is that we hold *no* truths; we profess *nothing* as a society (I write as an American)—that is, other than unbridled individual freedom. And those who would dare inject moral principle into the public sphere are routinely accused of being "hate-filled," "bigoted," and "intolerant." The questions confronting us, then, are these: What language should we use as we live and move in a post-consensus society? How do we engage in moral reasoning with our contemporaries, and in this endeavor how do we even get to first base in terms of ethical understanding?

But *how* did we arrive at this stage of "holding no truths"? The postmodern challenge before us may well be understood as an extension of the modernist challenge, and that challenge came to us in the following way:

> If we cannot know the metaphysical absolute, we cannot know the moral absolute, and if we cannot know the moral absolute, we cannot be held responsible for failing to be good. Modernity did not simply claim that we cannot know God; as it progressed, it encountered many competing views of the metaphysical absolute.[4]

In response to the wider cultural trend and contemporary challenges, a former U.S. Court of Appeals judge asks (rhetorically), "Who can deny the reality of natural law?" After all, he observes, "all law derives from a bedrock in humanity"; hence, "[n]atural law must be part of the enterprise of human law."[5] At bottom, in his opinion, two principal categories of deniers need identifying: positivists and individualists. A hidden bond unites these two camps: some are either *explicit* deniers of transcendence as a metaphysical reality while others are *practical* deniers, rejecting and resenting what they perceive as a "brooding omnipresence" of the divine over culture that would transcend (and quash) individual desires while ordaining law.[6]

In more academic and theoretical circles of our post-consensus era, one of the most widely held and disseminated fallacies—if not, *the* most widely held and disseminated fallacy—is the assumption that there are no neutral or universal principles of reason to which we might appeal. In this light, therefore, our disagreements on ethical matters demonstrate the lack of universally valid moral truths.[7] But *do* they? And what undergirds this belief? Here it is helpful—indeed, *necessary*—to distinguish between moral principle and self-interest.[8] It should be self-evident that any moral principle will eventually come into conflict with self-interest. As one social critic has noted, precisely this is the perennial problem for politics, for the polity will face the need to legislate on *any* matter—whether that legislation concerns the many current controversies relating to abortion, sexuality, education, and racial preferences or whether it agonizes over foreign policy.[9]

The broader point is that moral principle will eventually come into conflict with self-interest. And *all* people make moral judgments; all draw the line at some place and by reason of some view of ultimacy (even when that "ultimacy" is self-interest). Properly construed, moral judgments require the connection between moral reasoning and the very notion of law (i.e., the regulation of people's moral choices). Human rationality presumes that people are free to choose how to act and why, but also that they are held accountable in human community for the consequences and effects of those choices. This, of course, forces upon us the realization that law—i.e., moral rule or guidelines—can be, and not infrequently will be, in opposition to self-interest. Without the undergirding of moral law (i.e., natural law), objective moral principle is impossible. All that is left is self-interest and power. Over time, "might," where it is not mediated and intercepted by the authority of moral law, inevitably and irreducibly becomes "right."

Totalitarian regimes demonstrate this reality most excruciatingly and perennially. John Paul II, who was intimately acquainted with totalitarianism, frames the reality of this tragedy in the following way:

> Totalitarianism arises out of a denial of truth in the objective sense. If there is no transcendent truth, in obedience to which man achieves his full identity, then there is no sure principle for guaranteeing just relations between people. Their self-interest as a class, group or nation would inevitably set them in opposition to one another. If one does not acknowledge transcendent truth, then the force of power takes over…[10]

In the end, once the force of power takes over, not even the majority of the people may violate those "laws" which those in power have set in place. And in fact, previously "free" states, in which the underpinnings of that freedom have been forgotten or disavowed over time, prepare themselves for the very same tragic end.

During his lifetime, John Paul was burdened by a grave danger which he called "an alliance between democracy and ethical relativism." This, he insisted, would undermine political and social life in catastrophic ways. There can be "no freedom apart from or in opposition to the truth," since honoring moral norms alone establishes the foundation of genuine democracy. And regarding those norms that prohibit intrinsic evil, "there are no privileges or exceptions for anyone. It makes no difference whether one is the master of the world or the 'poorest of the poor' on the face of the earth. Before the demands of morality, we are all absolutely equal."[11]

It is surely a sign—a tragic sign, indeed—of the West's moral erosion that the connection between moral law and human law has dissipated. Most of our leading educational institutions aggressively deny this connection in our day. Thus, it should come as no surprise that neither in law, nor in politics or policy analysis, nor in any gatekeeping institutions are the moral foundations of law, politics, or "civil society" to be acknowledged and promoted. This a far cry from America's founding. And it presages the collapse of "civil society" as we know it.

10

Why is reason important, and what is the relationship between reason and revelation?

NATURAL LAW REASONING PRESUPPOSES COMMON ground between reason and religious faith, based on the assumption that the two realms are *integrated*—rather than *divorced*—in accordance with human design. Moreover, it needs emphasizing that *all people* have a view of *ultimate things* and hence accept on "good faith" what they cannot prove yet accept as "real." The fact that *all* people adopt a view of *ultimacy*, even when this view remains unstated (or even undefined), negates any idea of "neutrality" as it concerns the public square.[1] Of course, many people operate on the assumption that belief in God is not rational, and that to bracket theistic assumptions from the public sphere is to be "neutral." This, as it happens, is a fairly recent development in the history of philosophical and social thinking and merits some discussion, given the error upon which it feeds.

It is broadly assumed that philosophical, social-scientific, and political endeavor must appeal solely to reason (so-called)—a consensus that comes from aggressively secular voices. Therefore, it is thought, the injection of any religious or theistic considerations into public and political discussions is an imposition of the irrational. This false stereotype needs continual refutation, if for no other reason, the mainstream of the historic Christian tradition has *always* affirmed the rationality of the faith. The epistemological awareness that reason and faith work in symbiosis facilitates a rich and very much needed dialogue, especially in a militantly secular cultural climate. Such dialogue is exemplified in an exchange in 2004 between renowned German philosopher Jürgen Habermas and Joseph Cardinal Ratzinger (a year before becoming Pope Benedict XVI) that focused on the intersection of reason and religion in a "post-secular" age. Both men address the social and political ramifications of this intersection.

To the surprise of many, Habermas called for secularized society to welcome a fresh tolerance and understanding of religious conviction. In this challenge, Habermas raises the question of whether secular reason in fact is capable of providing adequate grounds for a democratic constitutional state. Benedict argues for the importance of reason properly understood as well as the necessity of moral principles that derive from and are anchored in religious faith. Wedded together and purged of their respective "pathologies," reason and religion are observed to support the foundation of a free society. Habermas and Benedict are in fundamental agreement that reason and religious conviction benefit from one another and thus need interaction.[2] In our day, this tolerance and interaction, which underpins basic notions of religious freedom, become increasingly important, given the degree to which persecuted minorities around the world are suffering and the manner in which militant secularism in the West has driven religious conviction from the public sphere.

Few have articulated the symbiotic relationship between reason and religious faith more thoroughly than Benedict's predecessor, John Paul II, in his final encyclical *Fides et Ratio* (1998). Instructively, the first line of this important document reads, "Faith and reason are like two wings on which the human spirit rises to the contemplation of truth."[3] The notion of truth *per se* is typically met in our day with deep-seated suspicion and resistance. John Paul senses this stark contradiction, and thus emphasizes the unity of thought and being, which have become divided and alienated. In a previous encyclical, *Veritatis Splendor* (1993), the pontiff had drawn attention to "certain fundamental truths" of Christian doctrine which, "in present circumstances, risk being distorted or denied."[4] In *Fides et Ratio* John Paul wishes to examine the theme of truth in relationship to both reason and faith. The fundamental assumption that undergirds this document—that faith and reason, while distinct, are harmonious, given their grounding in a common truth—is both intellectually sustainable and faithful to the historic Christian intellectual tradition. People of faith of any era must wrestle with the implications of a "faith that seeks understanding" (*fides quaerens intellectum*). *Fides et Ratio* takes up and continues this centuries-long discussion. Human beings have been given access to the knowledge of a self-revealing Creator-God.

The encyclical reminds us that truth attained by philosophy and the truth of revelation are neither identical nor mutually exclusive; each realm has its own "autonomy," yet it is an autonomy that is not absolute but integrated. Philosophy and theology, and hence reason and faith, serve as partners "in dialogue, in order to confirm the intelligibility and universal truth" of claims that are made.[5] Faith, predicated upon what has been revealed, functions differently than natural reason, of which philosophy and the sciences are primary expressions. But because divine revelation occurs within the context and fabric of human history, it is thus the object and "point of reference" for both philosophy and theology.[6]

Underlying *Fides et Ratio* is the fundamental conviction of the unity and symbiosis of faith and reason. It is because of this presumed unity that from the patristic period onward philosophy was called the *ancilla theologiae*. This title, it should be emphasized, was not intended to suggest philosophy's "servile submission" to theology; rather, it was to underscore "the necessity of the link between the two sciences and the impossibility of their separation."[7] Given the essential unity of reason and faith, the effects of severing the two are not only lamentable but catastrophic—for contemporary society as well as for the church. Theological distortions of the unity of faith and reason may express themselves in equal and opposite ways. They may take the form of fideism (i.e., faith without foundation or faith in faith itself), on the one hand, or they may manifest themselves in the form of rationalism, on the other hand, by falsely attributing to natural reason a knowledge that only the light of faith can confer. Theologically speaking, it is possible to place faith in things that are illusory, without foundation, biblically untenable, or inconsonant with the character of God. Such faith (i.e., fideism) "runs the grave risk of withering into myth or superstition"; deprived of reason, faith stresses feeling and personal experience and so "runs the risk of no longer being a universal proposition."[8] Without rational support, faith collapses into sloppy sentimentalism.

But there exists an equal and opposite danger when the unity of faith and reason is severed. From the standpoint of philosophy, the end result of a divorce of faith and reason is rationalism, and in our present day, nihilism. The latter is noted by John Paul as having "a certain attraction for people of our time, inasmuch as its adherents claim that the search is an end in itself, without any hope or possibility of ever attaining the goal of truth."[9] The fruit of such thinking, however, is by no means benign. Just as faith deprived of reason degenerates into fideism, sentimentalism, or superstition, reason divorced from revelation and faith breeds rationalism, which over time sinks into nihilism and despair (hence the oft-lamented "crisis of meaning" in our day). Against the temptations toward either fideism or rationalism, it is necessary to stress the unity of truth and thus "the positive contribution which rational knowledge can and must make to faith's knowledge," and vice versa.[10] Illustrating how deep-seated and widespread the distrust of reason and revelation together is in contemporary philosophical discourse, some theorists even speak of "the end of metaphysics."[11]

It needs emphasizing that over the last 2000 years much of Western history—certainly not all, but much of it—has been characterized by the assumption of the unity of reason and revelation.

It is a relatively recent—i.e., modern and postmodern—development that a divorce has occurred between the two. The human search for truth, which is part of our essential *nature*, points to their unity—a unity that leaves both enriched and allows both to stand in harmony.

11

What is the nature of general revelation?

IN THE PRIOR QUESTION WE argued that reason and faith are integrated rather than divorced, and this based on human design. And as we observed, this has been the position of the historic Christian tradition through the ages. Reason and revelation, though distinct, are continually in dialogue. This position, of course, rejects the radical dichotomy between the two that rationalists of the Enlightenment and militant secularists would assume. But God by definition transcends the empirical realm; hence, knowledge of God cannot be limited to reason unaided. The historic Christian tradition teaches that God has revealed himself through what is often referred to as "special revelation"—namely, through the person of Christ and through the scriptures—as well as through the medium of "general revelation."

When we speak of general revelation we are referring to what God has revealed to all of humanity by means of the created order. It is to this realm that our nature—our fundamental design—belongs and can be understood. According to the biblical doctrine of general revelation, all people in all places and at all times have some knowledge of the Creator. Theologians have traditionally understood this general knowledge according to two categories: the cosmos and conscience. That is, human beings have an inner knowledge or awareness as well as an external awareness based on the world around them.

The same apostle to the Gentiles who writes that that all people have a law "written on the heart, with their consciences bearing witness to this knowledge and at times accusing them and at times excusing them" (Rom. 2:15), also pens these words: "Since the creation of the world God's invisible qualities—his eternal power and divine nature—have been clearly seen, being understood from what has been made" (Rom. 1:20). Just as a work of art reveals something about the artist who created it, in the same way all of creation—the cosmos and human nature—mirror the one who designed it. This is the sense in which the Psalmist proclaims "The heavens declare the glory of God…There is no speech or language where their voice is not heard" (Ps. 19:1-3). When Paul is engaging his audience at the Council of the Areopagus in Athens (Acts 17), he is utilizing a natural-law argument while citing two well-known poets as witnesses.[1] Several elements are worthy of note:

1. God made every nation and determined the times for them and the exact places where they should live.
2. He did this so that human beings would seek him, reach out, and find him.
3. He is not far from each one of us as human beings.
4. In him we live and move and have our beings.
5. We are his offspring.

Here the apostle is utilizing general revelation in order to build a bridge to his audience, most all of whom have a Stoic or an Epicurean world- and life-view.[2]

Conscience and creation, the interior and the external, combine in their witness to the knowledge of God. Notice what the apostle says concerning the operation of the human conscience: by the "accusing" and "excusing" voice of conscience human beings demonstrate that they have this moral law "imprinted on the heart" (Rom. 2:15). The apostle's argument is not that this inner guide is infallible; rather, it is that the conscience is able both to condemn as well as condone.[3] At the same time, the apostle elsewhere observes that some people have consciences which "have been seared as with a hot iron."[4] The image here is graphic: a person who has suffered a severe burn and is left with little or no feeling on that part of the skin or the body. That process of moral "dulling," however, is learned. As free moral agents, people make choices and they possess a will; they choose to be attentive to or ignore the voice of conscience, which by nature reminds them of the moral law.

In a series of radio broadcasts that would become the well-known writer C.S. Lewis's most famous book, *Mere Christianity*, Lewis begins with the essay "Right and Wrong as a Clue to the Meaning of the Universe," which we noted in Question 3. His argument is essentially that our moral sentiments, which cause human beings to seek justice and protest injustice, are a chief witness to the presence of a supreme "Lawgiver." These sentiments give expression to more than mere social custom, more than mere personal preference or individual taste. They cry out that there *does* exist the reality of right and wrong. In this regard Lewis is particularly struck by human reaction to injustice. *Why* do we protest when we have been *wronged*? It is as if a *moral law* exists in the universe, and we are forced to acknowledge it.

In response to the cultural relativist,[5] who argues that moral sentiments are simply expressions of particular values and not universal in nature, Lewis notes the presence of certain moral facts that stubbornly refuse to disappear from human existence, thereby undermining the relativist's argument. One is the fact of human hypocrisy. Human beings, at some point, and in assorted ways, tend not to live in accordance with their professed beliefs. Why is this? Deep within, all people know that they should act in a certain way; all people are aware that they fall short of their own moral standards.

Another stubborn fact confounding the relativist (at least the theoretical relativist) is that common elements—*numerous* common elements—are found in various moral codes around the globe and in different cultures. All moral codes, Lewis observes, share in common many of these foundational norms. There is *no* moral code, he insists, that is *entirely different* from all other codes. And as to what a so-called "entirely different morality" might look like, he speculates in this manner:

> Think of a country where people were admired for running away in battle, or where a man felt proud of doublecrossing all of the people who had been kindest to him. You might just as well try to imagine a country where two and two made five. Men have differed as regards what people you ought to be unselfish to—whether it was only your family, or your fellow countrymen, or everyone. But they have always agreed that you ought not to put yourself first. Selfishness has never been admired.[6]

In the end, the implications of general revelation are wide-reaching and significant. General revelation serves to provide human beings with a basic knowledge both of God and of ourselves. Relatedly, general revelation is a source of human wisdom. Wisdom is a universal entity, accessible to all, regardless of time, place, and social location. Wisdom arises out of observations made about both the cosmos and conscience, about physical nature and human nature.[7] Further, general revelation makes us aware of our basic moral obligations and reminds us that as moral creatures we are accountable—to the Creator and to others. Finally, and no less importantly, general revelation provides common ground between peoples, given our common humanity. All of these implications are anchored in the reality of natural law.[8]

12

What is the relationship between Christianity and the natural law, and how does Christianity affirm the natural law?

WHAT DISTINGUISHES REVELATION IN THE wider Judeo-Christian tradition is its accent on creation in general and the human creature in particular. This religious tradition, thus, presupposes the order of creation (nature). While order was important to the ancients, particularly to classical philosophers, order and law undergird the entirety of both the Old and New Testaments. The theological assumption informing the writers of the New Testament is that the "new covenant" does not abolish or eliminate nature but rather *builds* upon it. For the biblical writers, natural law is the outcome—the consequence—of the doctrine of creation. Not coincidentally, then, have most of the proponents of natural law reasoning tended to be associated with the Judeo-Christian tradition. Moreover, these proponents represent a considerable variety, both philosophers and theologians, including people as diverse and far removed as the Jewish medievalist Moses Maimonides, the early church fathers, Thomas Aquinas, the magisterial Protestant reformers,[1] Hugo Grotius, and John Locke.

Already in this volume we have noted statements by Paul, the apostle to the Gentiles, whose philosophical-theological declarations to the Christians in Rome and elsewhere reinforce the implications of the natural law: (a) all people everywhere have basic knowledge of moral reality, based on the law "written on the heart," and therefore, (b) all people are without excuse in terms of moral knowledge and moral culpability.[2] This assumption undergirds the writings of the New Testament, alongside (c) the consistent and prevailing emphasis on grace, (d) the need for forgiveness, and (e) the overarching reality of divine sovereignty. The moral law finds its completion and fullest expression in the person of Christ. For this reason Paul also reminds the Romans, "For Christ is the end [*telos*] of the law, that everyone who has faith may be justified."[3] That is to say, Christ is the *goal* or the *fullest expression* of the moral law.[4]

Further evidences of the natural law surface in Romans 13. Here we find teaching reminding the community that even pagan, unbelieving governing authorities can discern basic justice, reward those who do right, and punish those who do wrong.[5] Despite human imperfections and the reality of imperfect justice, the governing authority is described by the apostle in this context as a divine "servant" (*diakonos* and *leitourgos*).[6] Hence, believers are admonished to obey, not only because of the threat of civil punishment but because of conscience.[7]

Several times the New Testament records Jesus's teaching on the abiding nature of the moral law and its permanent influence. Often the context of these statements is found to be debate with Pharisaical Judaism, with its emphasis on "the jot and the tittle" and the finer points of Levitical law. The Gospel of Matthew is particularly instructive, insofar as it attempts to narrate Jesus's interaction with—and frequent denunciation of—first-century Pharisaical Judaism. While scribes and Pharisees demonstrate a preoccupation with keeping the "letter of the law," Jesus's intention is essentially twofold: (1) to alter contemporary understanding and application of Jewish law and (2) to affirm the moral law, which is lodged at the heart of those laws given to Israel of old.[8] The problem with Pharisaism is that it misses the moral and internal meaning of the law while focusing on the external and legalistic. For this reason, Jesus warns: "Do not think that I have come to abolish the Law or the Prophets. I have not come to abolish but to fulfill..." (Matt. 5:17).[9]

In addition to elements of Jesus's teaching recorded in the gospel narratives, particular themes are recurring in the other New Testament documents that verify abiding moral norms. Among the more frequent are warnings against sexual immorality and idolatry (i.e., misplaced affections and values). Recurring associated exhortations and warnings regarding sexual purity that surface—and these occur in virtually all of Paul's epistles as well as in 1 and 2 Peter, Jude, and the Revelation[10]—confirm the "design" of the creation model. Human nature is meant to conform to this pattern; this is the natural law. Sexual immorality contravenes the *natural* purposes of the sexes. Moreover, marriage, from the beginning of human civilization, has been normative, divinely ordained by the Creator, and in the New Testament it is represented as an enduring institution. Jesus, unequivocally, affirms its permanence.[11]

Taken as a whole, the teaching of the New Testament is univocal in its affirmation that *love fulfills the law*. This is another way of saying that charity and justice are one and cannot be divorced, as the next Question will attempt to argue.[12] To contend that love "fulfills" the law (Matt. 5:17 = Rom. 13:8, 10 = James 2:8) is to insist that love is the *meaning* of the law. Another way of saying this is that law provides the content and structure of the love.[13] Justice, therefore, becomes the instrument of charity. In this regard the Romans 13 and James 2 texts are instructive. In the former text, according to the apostle's rationale retributive justice and individual conscience are necessarily linked because of the debt of charity, which "fulfills the [moral] law." In the latter text, the author is responding to tensions within the emergent Christian community in which the role of law is being hotly debated. He finds it necessary, utilizing techniques from wisdom literature, to admonish and exhort on the basis of the conviction that *authentic* faith will be *verified* by deeds. Neighbor-love, according to James, will do justly.[14] The moral law remains.

For most of Christian history the notion of natural law has served as a bridge to connect Christian belief and the surrounding culture. Natural law is part of the ebb and flow of early and later patristic writings as the fathers interact with the surrounding world.[15] For the early church father Tertullian, writing in the late second century, the Christian God is the God of all of nature:

> Demanding then a law of God, you have that common one prevailing all over the world, engraven on the natural tables to which the apostle too is wont to appeal, as when in respect of the woman's veil he says, Does not even Nature teach you?...as when to the Romans, affirming that the heathen do by nature those things which the law requires, he suggests both natural law and a law-revealing nature.[16]

Irenaeus underscores the abiding nature and significance of the Decalogue for Christians: "The words of the Decalogue remain likewise for us Christians. Far from being abolished, they have received amplification and development from the fact of the coming of the Lord in the flesh."[17] With Tertullian and Irenaeus, Origen understands one moral code to unite the Old and New Testaments. Therefore, "it is not a matter of surprise that the same God should set in the hearts of all men those truths he taught by the prophets and the Savior."[18] Ambrose (late fourth century) writes that humankind needed Mosaic law, given its forgetfulness of the natural law. He reiterates the argument of the apostle Paul in the letter to the Romans, observing that an awareness of the natural law is inborn, "springing up in the breast" of every person.[19] Jerome as well recognizes the awareness of the natural law that resides within the human heart, given to the entire human race. He acknowledges, as Ambrose, that Mosaic law is the result of humans' inability to live according to the *ius natural*. In the words of Augustine, the natural law places its imprint on the human heart, much "like a seal on a ring that passes into wax."[20]

In most discussions of natural law it is assumed that Aquinas, in the thirteenth century, best represents the tradition both in its theological grounding and in its application to the matter of virtue as well as social ethics. Aquinas concerns himself with the perennial questions that affect the moral life. For this reason among others, any study of the natural law must be conversant with Aquinas. Aquinas's work can be understood *inter alia* as a response to challenges to the faith arising from Aristotelian thought as it reemerged in the thirteenth century as well as from Muslim influences. Many commentators tend to view Aquinas's system of thought as a fusion of Aristotelian, Stoic, and Christian thought. While this is not inaccurate as far as it goes, it needs qualification. Thomas does not merely wish to view reason as some vague source of "natural law"; rather, he attempts to identify and underscore the manner in which human "nature" fulfills the divinely intended purpose for which it was created. In parlance familiar to some contemporary readers, he understood that "all truth is God's truth."

Most discussions of the natural law down to the present day take their general orientation from Aquinas. And there are good reasons for this. As noted above, he reflects on the perennial questions that concern the moral life. In addition, he refuses to pit philosophy and theology against one another, fully aware that these two "disciplines" are—or should be—in continual dialogue with each other in the pursuit of truth. Finally, he is adept at understanding the implications of the natural law as it concerns virtue, character-building, and wider social ethics.

Natural law is by no means the sole account of a Christian view of morality. However, the present volume wishes to argue that natural law is the necessary starting point for (a) distinguishing between good and evil, between justice and injustice; (b) measuring and advancing the common good in a pluralistic society; and (c) requiring a basic level of moral accountability for all. Moral norms in broader society are impossible apart from a presumption of natural law; otherwise, moral norms are fluid and constantly changing. Natural law presumes—and respects—individual autonomy and thus distinguishes itself from "divine command" ethical theory in that it does not deny secondary causality. Humans, as Thomas Aquinas insisted, "participate" in divine law, and they do so in two essential ways. First, human nature inclines us to act in particular ways—ways that are characteristically human. Second, human nature—i.e., ordered human nature—presupposes the existence of a transcending moral order, an order whose existence and authority lie outside of personal experience and inclinations.

From the Christian standpoint, divine sovereignty and human moral freedom coexist.

To speak in terms of preserving the common good of society, Christians of every age must be able both to conceptualize and to articulate a "shared" or common understanding of human nature that unites all people. Natural law reasoning does not pretend to offer an exhaustive account of ethics with a set of detailed prescriptions. Rather, it presupposes basic inclinations, i.e., cognitive foundations of the moral life that must be cultivated in the direction of virtue. One moral theologian is surely correct to argue that by rejecting the natural law as the foundation for moral reflection theologians neglect one of the richest resources in our tradition for developing a distinctly Christian account of the moral life.[21] Ethicists and theorists who reject natural law thinking are wholly unable to give an account of morality in the public sphere; they have cut themselves off at the knees, as it were.

It is the position of classical Christian theology and moral philosophy that the natural law is an enduring and concrete expression of Providence. As a common fund of moral knowledge it is the basis on which all people may be held morally accountable in the public arena for their actions, regardless of their particular world- or life-view. As a shared and public standard, natural law reasoning furnishes the basis for a common code of morality in a pluralistic environment. It is the basis of what we call "criminal justice" in particular and "civil society" in general. It provides basic orientation in a world that mixes belief and unbelief, virtue and vice, agreement and sharp disagreement. At its most rudimentary level, it allows us to praise or commend what is good and not merely what is religious. By the same token, it allows us to condemn what is evil or repulsive. For this reason, we can promote "justice" in society, without which there is no such thing as "civil society" as we know it, since justice in its essence is not a fluid concept; justice remains immutable with the passage of time.[22]

The relationship between Christianity and natural law, then, can be summarized in the following way:

- The natural law states the first and essential precepts which govern the moral life.
- The natural law is nothing other than the light of understanding placed in us by God; through it we know what we must do and what we must avoid. God has given us this light or law at creation.
- The natural law is present in the heart of each human being, is established by reason, and is universal both in its precepts and its authority. The moral duties of life do not conflict with one another.
- The natural law is immutable and permanent through the variations of history. A Christian view of natural law is not that what we know through reason is replaced by supernatural revelation, but rather that its essence is confirmed thereby.
- The natural law represents an important way in which God graciously preserves and orders the world, even when human awareness thereof does not bring human beings into a right relationship with their Creator.

- The natural law provides the indispensable moral foundation for social relations, for building the human community, and for providing the necessary basis for civil law to which it is connected.[23]

In the words of one esteemed theologian, natural law serves as "a bridge category on ethical and social questions between church and world, between those with *a priori* commitment to sacred Scripture and the Christian creed and those outside the community of faith," namely, to people of all races, classes, cultures, and religions.[24]

13

Why is Thomas Aquinas central to any discussion of natural law?

As suggested in the previous question, Aquinas represents a high point in terms of defining natural law, understanding the symbiosis between reason and faith, and deriving natural law's ethical implications for both the individual and the community. In his examination of law he distinguishes between three types—moral, ceremonial, and judicial[1]—a distinction that has been followed by most interpreters operating in the Christian tradition to the present day. The moral law, he reiterates, was not abolished according to any particular dispensation or era, because it *cannot* be abolished; it remains as true and abiding as the sun. Moral principles reflect the natural law and therefore are unchangeable: "The natural law is altogether unchangeable in its first principles."[2] Fundamental to Aquinas's perspective is the belief that grace (*gratia*: that which is given to us) builds upon or completes human nature. In Christian theological terms, this is to say that despite human fallenness and the human propensity for doing evil, our basic nature—our design, based on the image of God—remains intact, based on our design and our basic orientation toward the good. This means for Thomas that human nature and human virtues—for example, the "cardinal" virtues of justice, wisdom, courage, and temperance—are fully realized through faith. All of this is in accordance with the natural law.

By way of "natural reason," human beings "discern what is good and what is evil." As Aquinas sees it, this is a self-evident premise and "habit" of all peoples. It is "nothing else than an imprint on us of divine light." In this light it is "evident," he concludes, that the natural law is "nothing else than the rational creature's participation" in the "eternal law."[3] For Aquinas, the natural law mirrors the very order and structure of creation, and notwithstanding the ravages of human fallenness, this order and structure remain self-evident through both reason *and* revelation.

> So it is clear that as far as the general principles of reason are concerned whether speculative or practical, there is one standard of truth or rightness for everybody... So we must conclude that the law of nature, as far as first principles are concerned, is the same for all as the norm of right conduct is well known to all.[4]

Where humans depart from or reject right use of reason, "it has the quality not of a law but of an act of violence," which is to be viewed as "unnatural."[5] In fact, Aquinas believes that human reason *cannot fail* to grasp *some* knowledge of the truth; basic moral principles, he insists, are knowable, "inscribed on the human heart."[6]

What is significant is that Aquinas does not insist that our awareness of the natural law is dependent on religion *per se*, even when as a Christian he personally acknowledges Christ to be the fullest expression of divine revelation. "We cannot know the things that are of God as they are in themselves," he concedes; rather, these things come to us on the basis of what is known by all people through general revelation.[7] Human rationality is *by nature* directed toward the good of human beings and the good of society. This permits every human act to be measured as right or wrong, morally acceptable or unacceptable, to the extent that it *fulfills or undermines* human nature and the divine intention. Reason is the chief means by which we determine the moral quality of our actions, and reason operates to apply this natural law moral standard—pursue the good and avoid doing evil—in specific situations as it affects the common good of all.[8]

A further significant feature that is indebted to Aquinas's natural law understanding is his conjoining of justice and charity. In his *Summa Theologica* the nature and character of both justice and charity are examined in considerable depth, along with their ethical consequences. Charity, according to Aquinas, must be developed through habit and thus is "a principle of action."[9] Here we observe the extent to which Augustine had influenced Aquinas's thought. For Augustine, charity must motivate all that we do, including even the application of coercive force. Not the external act but the internal motivation determines the morality of our deeds.[10] As a social force, this "rightly ordered love" is foremost concerned with what is good, particularly as it concerns justice.[11] Charity thus is expressed toward the perpetrator of criminal acts when wrong is done, it is expressed toward society at large when wrong is prevented or punished, and it is expressed toward future or potential criminals who might be tempted to act in malicious and unjust ways. Justice, for Augustine, is the love of God diffused through other virtues.

To read Aquinas's treatment of both justice and charity in the *Summa* is to witness the extent to which Augustinian thinking influenced his own. Questions 23–46 of the *Summa*'s *secunda secundae* are devoted to the nature of charity, its priorities, its moral dimensions, and its consequences. In Aquinas's understanding, charity is the *form* of all the virtues, whether theological or moral.[12] Why is it the "form" of all virtues? Because, he reasons, every virtue and the general good depend on it, and for this reason charity is commanded. Someone might ask, "Is a command to love really necessary?" Aquinas answers, yes, any moral obligation requires a command, given the human propensity for hatred or strife. In fact, the command to love is implicit in all ten commands of the Decalogue. Indeed, it may be argued that the "Golden Rule" underpins the entire "second tablet," since no one does to another what he does not wish to be done to himself.[13] In any case, the virtues, to which charity belongs, are developed habitually, and therefore must be both commanded and practiced. It is for this reason that Aquinas describes charity as "a principle of action."

What is noteworthy in Aquinas's discussion is the fact that the problem of war is contextualized in the middle of his treatment of *caritas* (charity), a fact that is not infrequently ignored in modern commentary. Therefore, it falls to Aquinas to show how coercive force can be just as well as true to the demands of charity. In fact, he argues that where the public good is at stake and wrongdoers fail to mend their ways, they are to be slain. This, he reasons, is done not out of hatred but out of charity.[14] In Thomistic thought the guiding principle of loving one's neighbor is linked to numerous virtues, with each virtue being opposed to a corresponding vice and war standing in opposition to peace. Because war seems such an extreme form of vice, it is natural to wonder whether war is not *always* wrong. Precisely for this reason Aquinas begins his commentary with the words *utrum aliquod bellum sit licitum* ("whether some kind of war is ever lawful"). After all, war would seem contrary to the precept expressed in Matthew 5:39: "Do not resist the one who is evil." Therefore, one might reasonably conclude, war is evil. Period. But this is precisely the reason why Aquinas's discussion of war in Question 40 of the *Summa* begins with the question of whether war is *always* a sin.

Although Aquinas's debt to Augustine is evident throughout his discussion of war, he accomplishes something that neither Augustine himself nor those who subsequently drew from Augustinian thought achieved. He places the problem of war within a coherent framework of human virtues—and specifically charity—in order to illuminate its proper and improper manifestations more clearly. Charity and justice meet and are to guide us in applying coercive force. And one of the three classic criteria for a war to be considered "just" is right intention. Right intention concerns itself with proper motives in undertaking intervention. It is measured by the presence of both charity—which desires the best for the neighbor—and justice—which is protective of the basic rights of the innocent neighbor. Because "justice directs a man in his relations with others,"[15] justice and charity meld in Thomistic thought.

As Aquinas understands it, by means of our design (creation) and divine image-bearing we respond to the moral impulse, manifesting a justice that is motivated by charity in our social relations. Such can be summarized by the so-called "Golden Rule" ethic, in which justice and charity embrace and combine to give tangible embodiment to the natural law and its "first principles" of doing good and avoiding evil.

14

What is the relationship between justice and the natural law?

THE CLASSIC NOTION OF JUSTICE that extends from antiquity is that human beings render *what is due*. In its measurement of human behavior, justice reconciles freedom and responsibility. To be "free" is to be human, but being what it is, human nature will need restraints inasmuch as liberties will compete and collide. The nature of justice, moreover, is that it is communal; it is concerned to guard the common good. For this reason, justice is mediating (i.e., distributive), rectifying, and reciprocal in character.[1] In his *Nicomachean Ethics*, Aristotle writes that "what we call just is whatever produces and maintains well-being and its parts for a political community." A rule of justice is "natural," moreover, that has "the same validity everywhere," independent of our accepting it or not.[2] Similarly, Aquinas famously states that justice "directs man in his relations with other men."[3] Others, such as English jurist Matthew Hale, define justice as *regula iuncta cum imperio* (a rule conjoined with authority).[4]

Undergirding each of these voices is the basic assumption that natural law is *antecedent* to human law, and therefore, to civil government; it is *preparatory* to civil society and government. True justice, and hence just law, transcends human attempts to manufacture any sense of justice in a given social-cultural context. Human beings, rather, acknowledge an enduring standard of justice; they do not create it.[5] Moreover, only that which transcends human experience can demand obligation and therefore *obedience* to what is (properly) law. Human conscience—whether in obedience, complacency, or denial—confirms the reality of natural law requirements as they touch human experience. Hereby we are bound to—and reminded of—our basic "nature."

Therefore, the force of law depends on the extent of its justice. Every human law can be measured according to its justice or injustice, and hence to the extent that it derives from the natural law, according to which humans are obliged to do good and avoid evil. Because of its universal, non-fluid character, justice cannot be one thing for Kansans but another for Kenyans, one thing for Uruguayians and another for Ukrainians. If and where law of any type deflects from the natural law, says Aquinas, it is "a perversion of law" and hence unjust.[6] After all, laws are designed to preserve the good and guide human action in community. Aquinas seems to be restating what Augustine had insisted: that which is not just is, in truth, "no law at all."[7] Thus, we can begin to appreciate the social chaos that ensues when law and morality are divorced.[8]

Here it is useful to compare the classical notion of justice, with its basic natural law assumptions, and contemporary theorizing about justice. Few have exerted greater influence in this regard than John Rawls,[9] whose widely accepted understanding of justice, the common good, and the public sphere are predicated on a utilitarian scheme supported by the notions of "fairness," "mutual disinterestedness," "efficiency," "average utility," "a veil of ignorance," as well as definitions of "reason" and "reasonable consensus." Rawls's approach effectively bleaches the public sphere of any religious viewpoint—what Rawls calls a "comprehensive doctrine." The Rawlsian concept of society and political life dons a mantle of "moral neutrality" which, at bottom, is anything but "neutral," as the natural lawyer well intuits.

Although an extended discussion of Rawls's ideas lies well beyond the scope of this question and the present volume, several qualifications are necessary, given the version of "political liberalism" and "justice" being set forth by Rawls and his wider influence. By all measurements, Rawls is formulating a *comprehensive* view, and yet it is a view that excludes "comprehensive doctrines" (his term) from political life and consideration. Rawls's understanding of "public reason" and "reasonable pluralism" needs severe qualification, for it assumes that the "truth" of a secularized political regime is greater—and more "reasonable"—than "truths" that issue out of religious beliefs. Rawls's view of political liberalism reduces religious belief and conviction to the *private* sphere, where it cannot intrude and create controversy on ethically sensitive matters (for example, abortion). This view perpetuates the false, "irrational" stereotype of religion that secularists, with considerable success, have advanced. For the natural lawyer, this view is deficient to the extent that "neutrality" on moral matters is neither possible nor desirable.[10] In the end, hereby justice loses its transcendent character.

In our own day, we are constantly reminded through the daily news of the desperate need for (and lack of) justice both in the domestic context and in foreign affairs. Let us for the moment leave aside the breakdown of "criminal justice" as it applies to our own domestic context and focus on foreign affairs. Three decades ago, with the supposed end of the Cold War, we were caught by surprise and witness to the bloodbath in Rwanda in which anywhere between 750,000 and 1.25 million people were macheted or clubbed to death due to tribal warfare.[11] About this time ethnic cleansing and terror, civil war, war crimes, genocide, and untold crimes against humanity exploded in Croatia, Slovenia, Serbia, Montenegro, Macedonia, and Bosnia-Herzegovina, despite international intervention and attempts at peace. In the years since we have been witnesses to an explosion of Islamic terrorist activity on most continents around the globe. As I write we are three years into Russia's unjust invasion of Ukraine, in which the unthinkable has been perpetrated against a largely defenseless people whose territorial integrity and boundaries had been agreed upon by not only Russia but the U.K. and the United States in 1994.[12]

I raise the following question: how might relatively free nations—particularly those which serve in important political, humanitarian, or military capacities—propose to deal with the scale of humanitarian need in our day that is massive and frequently the result of either unstable or unjust regimes? In previous questions I have argued that moral "neutrality" in life is an impossibility and thus untenable. Most mainstream debates about foreign policy and humanitarian intervention proceed from questionable—and surely contestable—assumptions about state sovereignty, human rights, and cultural relativism that, alas, are anything but "neutral." But for our present purposes I will assume the durability and applicability of natural law thinking as it informs the "just war" idea. The tradition of just war thinking—and it is a *tradition* that spans several millennia—represents a moral framework for thinking about the dilemma of humanitarian or military intervention.[13] Based on this tradition, those nations which have the wherewithal to prevent or retard socio-political evil in other nations have both a right and a duty, for the sake of justice and charity, to intervene. The aim thereof is to help bring about a just peace through protecting and securing basic human rights for the defenseless or oppressed.[14] This tradition and way of thinking about justice insists that *some*—though not *all*—interventions are morally justified.[15]

Just war moral reasoning is necessarily anchored in moral realism, by which it is assumed that due to our common humanity we have moral duties and responsibilities to those who stand in need. Those needs, moreover, are not limited to family, ethnicity, or politics but extend to our "neighbor," which is to say, *whoever stands in gross need* in the community of nations. Such duties, again, can be described as "pre-political" inasmuch as they are anchored in an awareness of a higher law, the natural law. Only in this way are we able to posit any sort of grounding for "universal human rights." If that were not so, then "Nuremberg was nothing but victors' vengeance dressed up in a fiction of 'justice.'"[16] Just war moral reasoning allows us to conceptualize the assistance of a "neighbor" in need through its severe moral justification and morally guided application of limited force.

Even when "humanitarian intervention" in general has found little support in modern international law, an older tradition, anchored in just war thinking, justifies force not only to correct wrongs but also to protect the innocent. At the heart of this tradition is the conjoining of two "cardinal" virtues, justice and charity.[17] To divorce justice and charity, as is common both in theoretical understandings of justice as well as in our practice, is to do irreparable damage to the character of both virtues. Both justice and charity are non-fluid in character. As quintessential *human* virtues, they are deemed universally binding, and hence, "owed" to all people. As already noted in several of the above Questions, evidence of this universality is the transcultural "Golden Rule" ethic surfacing in the teaching of both Plato and Jesus. This ethic, wherein justice and charity embrace, gives tangible embodiment to the natural law.

In the words of ethicist Paul Ramsey, who speaks of a "preferential ethics of protection" for the innocent neighbor or third party in view,[18] "no authority on earth can withdraw from 'social charity' and 'social justice' their intrinsic and justifiable tendencies to rescue from dereliction and oppression all whom it is possible to rescue."[19] In an important address at the U.S. Holocaust Museum, South African Justice Richard Goldstone, who had previously been chief prosecutor of the International Criminal Tribunals for the former Yugoslavia and Rwanda, had this to say:

> The one thing that I have learned in my travels to the former Yugoslavia and in Rwanda and in my own country is that where there have been egregiously human rights violations that have been unaccounted for, where there has been no justice, where the

> victims have not received any acknowledgment, where they have been forgotten, where there's been a national amnesia, the effect is a cancer in the society. It is the reason that explains, in my respectful opinion, spirals of violence in the former Yugoslavia for centuries and in Rwanda for decades.[20]

In his address Goldstone identified four specific elements that justice requires in the context of international tragedy: (1) exposing the truth of specific guilt and avoiding general guilt; (2) recording the truth of moral atrocity for the historical record in order to prevent attempts by the guilty to avoid guilt; (3) publicly acknowledging the loss of victims, who, as terrified people, need justice; and (4) applying the deterrent of criminal justice and punishment.

By its very nature, justice fulfills the first precept of natural law thinking: to do good and to avoid doing evil. The good is that which corresponds to our essential nature. Only in such an environment can human beings live and flourish. In the words of Cicero, only a madman would conclude that justice and injustice are matters of opinion and not fixed by nature.[21]

15

What is the relationship between the Ten Commandments (the Decalogue) and the natural law?

THE THREE SYNOPTIC GOSPELS RECORD an encounter between Jesus and a man of considerable wealth.[1] He came with the question, "Good Master, what must I do to have eternal life?" Jesus's response contains several noteworthy elements. Jesus affirms "the good," the natural law, which is rooted in God's character, and he then cites various of the Ten Commandments—for example, those addressing murder, adultery, theft, false witness, defrauding others, and parental honor. Added on in Matthew's account is the admonition to keep the "Golden Rule": "you must love your neighbor as yourself."[2] To this the man responds that he has kept all of these commandments since his youth, suggesting that he has led an ethical life. Jesus's final admonition, however, catches the man off guard: he is to go, sell what he has, and give to the poor. This, Jesus says, will result in great "spiritual treasure." Such, however, was not the advice that the man was hoping for, and the gospel narratives inform us that he went away sad because of his considerable wealth.

For our present purposes, the point of referencing this encounter is to underscore the natural law reasoning employed by Jesus. He affirms the Ten Commandments and the "Golden Rule" as foundational to an ethical life. The point of the story, quite clearly, is *not* that wealth or the lack of it is the basis for an ethical life; both poor and rich can lead honorable lives. It is only that in the case of this particular individual, wealth seems to have become idolized. "Golden Rule" ethics expresses the natural law, and at its core is the motivation to "do unto others as we would have them do to us." Hence, "the good" is not mere external action; it is an interior reality.

Because the human person is "by nature a social animal,"[3] the social order depends on humans' commitment to preserve the good and resist what is evil. To fail to do so is to pervert justice and invite moral anarchy. Society's laws, therefore, out of necessity must intentionally seek to affirm and reinforce moral principle, anchored in the natural law. The Decalogue, properly understood, provides the broader ethical contours of the natural law. The moral norms expressed through the Decalogue protect and sanctify critical social elements such as marriage, family, parental authority, human life, material property, truthfulness, and respect for others; these govern the essential relationships of the human person as a social creature. As moral obligations they are self-evident and unchanging with time and culture. In the language of Aquinas, "the precepts of the Decalogue admit of no dispensation whatever."[4] Without these necessary social structures, no society can survive.

In fact, these moral laws promulgated at Sinai "were but the concrete and practical form of enunciating principles which did not then for the first time come to have relevance but were relevant from the beginning." And as they "did not begin to have relevance at Sinai, so they did not cease to have relevance when the Sinaitic economy had passed away." Rather, "they embody principles which belong to the order which God established for man at the beginning, as also to the order of redemption."[5] There is no disagreement or discord between the Ten Commandments and the natural law.

In recent decades, we have been witness to the removal of the Ten Commandments from public places—often schools—based on the argument from militant secularists that these religious symbols are supposedly in violation of church-state separation. Very little reflection is needed by reasonable people to perceive the irrationality of such arguments. Consider this basic line of reasoning: "The Ten Commandments are a religious symbol," or, "The Ten commandments are too 'religious.'" We are forced to ask, *What culture or society condones murder, thievery, lying, defrauding others, and coveting some else's spouse or belongings?* And even within a militantly secular cultural context, *are people who don't consider themselves religious accepting of murder, theft, lying, and coveting?* A cursory review of the wide sweep of human history reveals that all civilizations have had an understanding of moral law that has translated into social obligation and political law. *No* society has ever affirmed murder, rape, thievery, defrauding one's neighbor, parental dishonor or coveting and survived to record or tell of it.[6]

The natural law reminds human beings that moral obligation has a transcendent source. This, of course, is the rub for the atheist and secular materialist. We might ask: If the Creator-God is not the ultimate lawgiver, then what ultimacy does moral law have? And can *any* moral principle then, at bottom, be obligatory? Whence come penalties, sanctions, and punishment for disobeying moral principle? Two possibilities emerge. Either freedom unbound—i.e., license—governs people's actions, by which people in essence are saying that *all* moral opinions are valid and at which point chaos and anarchy are regnant. Or, might determines what is "right," as in the totalitarian state, whereby the state becomes and remains the ultimate arbiter of acceptable and unacceptable, "right" and "wrong," applying various punishments—usually draconian in nature—to enforce what is "law."

Natural law reasoning, by contrast, insists that right and wrong have *intrinsic* value and are known through reason; they are pre-political, transcending the state, a society's "elite," personal preference, and social custom. Regardless of the spurious argument against the so-called "religious" character of the Ten Commandments, the consequences of ignoring or violating them is disaster—to both individuals who court that view and to societies which refuse their efficacy in the communal, public sphere. To deny or ignore the moral realities behind these "commandments" is to guarantee the "abolition of man."[7] The moral law, after all, is like the law of gravity; it remains, regardless of human attempts to ignore or deny it.[8]

16

How does the natural law inform human dignity and thus human moral obligation?[1]

THE HEART OF THIS QUESTION arises from intrinsic human nature and the character of human *obligation*. Obligation, according to Locke, arises from "the bond of law," and thus "duty"—that is, that which is "incumbent on each individual as something which must be performed by reason of one's own nature."[2] As Locke admits, this bond or duty arises from an authority or power that is superior to human beings and their actions—an awareness that includes the debt of punishment, which assumes an unwillingness by some human beings to recognize such authority.[3] Every form of obligation binds our conscience, Locke notes; therefore, he concludes, the natural law is binding on all men, before any other law.

Locke helpfully reasons toward the fact of the natural law. If the law of nature is *not* binding on all persons, he observes, then *positive law cannot be binding*, since any and all laws from the civil magistrate only have moral authority to the extent that they are anchored in transcending moral principle. To illustrate, Locke writes that we need not obey a king (or political authority) out of fear simply "because he is more powerful and can compel us." For if we did, this "would be to establish the power of tyrants" (as well as thieves and pirates). We do this, rather, freely "out of conscience." Thus, for Locke, "the obligation of civil law depends on the law of nature."[4]

The foundations of a "free" society—a decent society—require a commitment to common moral principles and to supporting institutions that embody that commitment. Among the basic of these principles is a respect for human life, protection of the family and marriage as bedrock institutions of society, and just laws enacted by a (relatively) just political authority. Each of these reinforces the other, facilitating a social environment in which human beings can flourish.[5] At the most basic level, this begins with a view of human personhood that fosters human dignity and the sanctity of life. One of the "self-evident truths" on which the founders and framers constructed their understanding of a "good society" was the conviction that *all people* are *created equal* and that *all* are endowed by the Creator with *certain inalienable rights*. This they knew based on "nature and nature's God"—which is to say, the natural moral law. As "natural lawyers," the founders acknowledged a broad and exceedingly rich tradition of moral truth as it applied to the social and political order. This tradition, it needs reiterating, united people as diverse as Aristotle, Aquinas, the Protestant reformers, Grotius, and Locke.

A belief in the intrinsic dignity of every person turns out to anchor the most important aspects of civil polity and public policy that a democratic regime might enact. In theological terms, an understanding of "religious freedom" proceeds from an awareness of human beings as mirroring "the image of God." Justice, at bottom, needs such a foundation in which to inhere. Equality and justice are "rootless human preferences" apart from something that transcends human experience.[6] Without the transcendent, "inalienable rights" become "alienable" and shift according to trends, the social climate, or a person's functionality and utility.

We do well to be reminded of 20th-century atrocities. Fundamentally, where there is no presumed human dignity and sanctity, there can be no justice. Human dignity alone furnishes the basis for all freedoms and "rights." Illustrating this foundational truth is the language of Article 1 of the Universal Declaration of Human Rights, adopted and proclaimed on December 10, 1948, by the General Assembly of the United Nations: "All humans are born free and equal in dignity and rights. They are endowed with reason and conscience and should act towards one another in a spirit of brotherhood." In its preamble, the UDHR refers to "the inherent dignity" of "all members of the human family."[7]

If we fast-forward from 1948 to March of 2008, we encounter another pronouncement, published by the (U.S.) President's Council on Bioethics under the title *Human Dignity and Bioethics*. This volume is remarkable in several ways. For one, it is a massive collection of essays on the concept of human dignity.[8] For another, it displays a wide range of understandings as to the meaning of human dignity. And indeed, five years earlier, writing in the *British Medical Journal*, one observer had criticized the work of the Council for this very reason.[9] Two months after the publication of *Human Dignity and Bioethics*, Harvard University evolutionary psychologist (and academic celebrity) Steven Pinker published an extensive review of the volume. Under the title "The Stupidity of Dignity," Pinker's essay argues for the priority of autonomy and consent in bioethical decision-making. Pinker worries that appeals to "human dignity" might in the end bring about "wrong" to those who are "free" to shape or control their own destiny. But as Gilbert Meilaender writes in reaction, "One [sadly] feels at this point a certain need to introduce Pinker to the history of the second half of the twentieth century." In any case, Pinker's response to the work of the Council—i.e., that wrestling with the concept of human dignity is "stupid"—while being misguided at best and intemperate at worst is nevertheless telling. Human societies are always one step removed from descending into inhumanity.

In the end, apart from the concept of intrinsic human dignity, our aspirations and our commitment to higher goals and virtuous conduct—goals that transcend mere self-interest—are meaningless and without purpose. Alas, we are left unable to answer *why* we *ought* to act as we should. And most assuredly, we will be unable to respond to catastrophic geopolitical events in the world—events that require the intervention and assistance of people of good will to rescue the helpless and defenseless. We thereby fail in the most basic of human obligation—namely, to treat others as we ourselves would wish to be treated—an obligation rooted in the natural law and in which justice and charity are wed.

17

What about the natural law as it pertains to cultural relativism and pluralism?

LET US BEGIN ANSWERING THIS question with a focus on pluralism. In order to respond, it is necessary to distinguish between genuine pluralism—what has been called "principled pluralism"—and cultural relativism.[1] The former is the fruit of a society in which moral standards are not fluid but affirmed as enduring, in continuity with previous generations and supporting a common ground (and thus natural law-generated), with genuine diversity and debate being tolerated in a manner that is not mandated or coerced.[2] Such an understanding of pluralism tolerates and encourages the interaction of all voices—"secular" or "religious"—in the public sphere, creating space in society for persons and institutions of diverse belief systems. At bottom, its concern is not mere "diversity" but the protection of the common good.

A "principled" pluralism operates under the natural law assumptions, consciously or unconsciously, that while (a) there is no morally neutral ground of existence and (b) people cannot be coerced to act against their deepest convictions, (c) there are baseline moral convictions that unite all people.[3] Its goal is to work for the common good, which serves to unite its many parts; hence, it is grounded not on mere individualism but moral law (and thus something approximating the Ten Commandments). For this reason, a derivative aspect of guarding the common good, the principle of subsidiarity, assists in delineating and limiting the ability of the state in social and cultural affairs.[4] The correspondence between natural law and the notion of subsidiarity can be seen in their commitment to guard the community of a higher order, in order that it might not interfere with or obstruct social life at a lower order. Rather, aiming to build the common social good, it should encourage the activities of the rest of society, thereby fostering human freedoms.[5]

If the state forbids its citizens to form associations, it contradicts the very reason for which it exists.

A truly "plural" societal structure requires that different institutional authorities bear different kinds of restricted or limited authority. In another context, this principle has been referred to as "spheres of creation" or "sphere sovereignty," given its commitment to guard and protect the relative autonomy of various spheres comprising the wider culture.[6] Whether we refer to this mediating social-political quality as "subsidiarity" or "sphere sovereignty," the principle assists human beings in avoiding the tendency toward political totalitarianism because of its acknowledgement of different institutions or organs, at different levels, that constitute "civil society."[7]

A principled pluralism, at its philosophical base, recognizes that all of life—and most importantly, *public* life—is "religious" in nature to the extent that all people bring "religious" or comprehensive assumptions into the public square. Thus, all voices—confessionally religious *and* secular—are to be welcomed in the public arena. At the same time, it acknowledges that apart from the freedom that issues from "the sacred rights of conscience," and hence the freedom to act on our deepest convictions, *there is no freedom whatsoever*. For this reason, a "principled" pluralist perspective is committed to defend not only our own convictions but those of others, provided that the beliefs of others do not threaten or undermine the common social good. Hence, the principled pluralist will encourage discussion, debate, and persuasion where there is disagreement in the public square. Correlatively, a principled pluralist (and natural law) view of government is that it should encourage an ordered liberty and protect citizens from mob rule or revolutionary activism.[8] The role of government is neither to compel all that is right or moral nor to punish all that is wrong or immoral. Government's primary role is to guard and advance justice.

The relativist approach to "pluralism," however, diverges in significant ways and thus requires severe qualification. This view should give us pause, not only because of its widespread acceptance in our day but because of its faulty presuppositions and the tragedy of its end-effects.[9] In theory, relativists posit either (a) that "the good" cannot be known (or identified in an ultimate sense), thereby rendering everyone's view as equally valid, or (b) that "the good" is not the same for all (and hence fluid). The issue from the standpoint of the cultural relativist, then, is whether there are moral truths that are *universal* in character and scope. For the relativist, the answer is no. Morality is a social-cultural construct. At a theoretical level, of course, in order for this position to be consistent it must deny that there can be any *natural and inalienable* rights, i.e., endowments that are self-evident and universal in scope, based on reason and intrinsic human dignity. In response, we are thus justified in asking the obvious—for example: do Armenians, Jews, Rwandans, Sudanese, Burmese, and Kurds, not to mention other beleaguered people-groups such as Ukrainians, who (as I write) are caught in an unjust war that they themselves did not choose, have a *right* not to be slaughtered? Why not? Do nations and people-groups have the *right* not to be victimized by terrorist groups? Why not? Do individuals and people-groups have a *right* not to be carried off into modern-day forms of slavery—whether in the form of sex-trafficking or forced labor? *Why not and on what basis?* But *if so*, then wherein is this fundamental "right" lodged? Here, one is tempted—in fact, forced—to deduce that the cultural relativist is guilty of supporting social-public policy that borders on evil.

Based on diametrically opposed assumptions, we are forced to conclude that natural law reasoning and relativism cannot *both* be true. Both cannot be valid since their claims about human nature and about "the good" are at fundamental odds.[10] In the words of one social theorist:

> If morality is created, not discovered, then surely different groups and individuals will create *different* moralities…There will be no common standard by which to adjudicate the conflicts among these invented moralities. The clashes among them will be like clashes of clothing styles, with this strange difference—that the stakes are who lives and who dies.[11]

And yet, despite the relativist's theoretical resistance to moral absolutes, certain seemingly universal obstacles stubbornly refuse to disappear. To illustrate, there is *no* virtuous person alive who would accept the proposition that slavery for some people—depending on the culture—is a good thing. Moreover, all societies operate on some presupposition of justice, whereby they demarcate between behaviors deemed acceptable and unacceptable. Simply stated, there is no human society, past or present, that has tolerated *any and all* behaviors. Indeed, the first Neanderthal who was hit on the head by a neighbor and uttered a version of *Why did you do that?* mirrors not only an awareness of the moral world but also the fact that there exist "necessary truths."[12]

These intuited truths, as it happens, comprise justice, behavioral justification, moral discernment, and the very distinction between "acceptable" and "unacceptable." The temper of our moral reflex when we are slighted reflects the fact that the ability to make moral judgments is already in place; it is part of our nature.

Strangely, yet tellingly, relativism in its theoretical form exudes a dogmatism that is truly stunning, despite its self-contradiction: it is so intractable, so absolutely certain of itself, that it must be *imposed* on all who disagree with it. *Why* is this, and what is a *reasonable* response from the standpoint of common sense?

The alternative to the relativist position, the natural law position, is typically rejected in our day because "it reeks of metaphysics." This rejection of anything *transcending human evaluation* is the sole means by which to maintain a consistent relativism at the theoretical level. The reason for this has been described thusly: "there is ultimately no other principle governing political activity than the decision of the majority, which occupies the position of 'truth' in the life of the state."[13] If morals are indeed fluid, varying, and "majoritarian," we (and different people-groups around us) will make them up as we go. In the end, there is no such thing as *intrinsic* human dignity; there is no human sanctity. In time, then, for varying reasons, the unborn can be killed, infanticide can be justified, while the aged and infirm can be euthanized. In a pre-totalitarian anarchy, it is "my morality versus yours," and in a totalitarian context it is the state versus both mine and yours. In an atheistic society, if political authority rather than God and transcendent moral norms determines human "rights," those rights can vanish; they can be taken away, as they inevitably are. In the end, given human nature and human tendencies where unchecked by the natural law, "might makes right." Gone is any common good and common standard. Gone are "the sacred rights of conscience." Gone is "civil society" as we know it.

One might describe the "postmodern turn" in our midst as sort of return of "Sophism," the fifth-century BCE rhetorical phenomenon that found language as an instrument not for discovering truth but for changing or constructing it. In our day this trend, of course, goes by the name of "postmodernism" or "antifoundationalism"; in its essence, it is suspicious of "metanarratives." Accordingly, *no one* gets "the Big Story" right, since there is no Truth with a capital "T"; truth is merely perspectival.[14] What, then, are the consequences in relatively free societies of this sort of thinking?

While Western nations are not yet at the point of totalitarian rule, the distance between moral anarchy and political tyranny is less than people imagine. The common mantra heard in relatively free societies that *you can't impose your morality* is both true and false. It is true insofar as human nature is such that people are rational, free agents. Inner convictions are discovered and grow on us over time because we think, reflect, question, reject, and affirm as volitional beings; we do not arrive at them as a result of coercion. Ultimate truths are discovered; they are not created. But the mantra is patently false as employed in our current cultural context insofar as *all morality*, in the end, *will be enforced* by someone or something. There is no such thing as a neutral public square, for the simple reason that there are no neutral "worldviews"[15]; all people and all regimes make basic assumptions about ultimacy.[16] There exists no morally "neutral" ground, since both religious and non-religious, Christian and non-Christian, people hold to ultimate assumptions about life and reality. These "ultimate assumptions" (which, at bottom, we may call "religious") will inevitably be brought into the public square and become law.[17]

The problems with relativism are both logical and practical in nature.[18] Theoretically, the relativist will typically object that moral objectivists are wrong to impose their moral values on everyone else. But here we encounter a contradiction. It cannot be morally "wrong" to impose one's values if in reality there are *no objective moral values*. To claim—or believe—that something is "wrong" is in truth to affirm that there *are* moral values that transcend a person's experience or way of thinking. The contradiction consists in relativists' insistence that no objective moral values exist and yet their claim that another person's position is objectively wrong. Thus, moral relativism shows itself practically to be impossible to live out. It is impossible to live our lives without making moral judgments. In fact, it is hardly an exaggeration to insist that *no one* is a moral relativist; all people utilize the grammar of "right" and "wrong." The differences between people are lodged in where they insist on drawing the moral line.

At bottom, it needs emphasizing that the claim (or variant of the claim) *There is no truth!* fails its own test. At minimum, it begs the question *How can anyone know* (and therefore say) that this claim is *true*?! What's more, the fact is that most people who claim to be relativists still view murder, slavery, rape, theft, lying, and defrauding others as wrong. The perennial question remains: On *what* basis? If there are not moral absolutes, if there is no such thing as objective truth, then we may *not* applaud Socrates or Jesus or Gandhi or Martin Luther King or Mother Teresa or any other virtuous figure, since such people were simply misguided, thinking that there are objective moral values that apply to all people. To applaud such people in history would be utter hypocrisy.

18

How does natural law reasoning view the issue of tolerance?

Along with its sibling "diversity," "tolerance" has achieved the status of being our culture's reigning virtue. Given its omnipresence, it is incumbent upon us to be morally serious about its definition and its character when applied in the public sphere. Originally, tolerance—a foremost political virtue—denoted a policy of forbearance in the presence of something not acceptable to all. At bottom, it demonstrated a government's readiness to permit a variety of religious beliefs.[1] The notion that government should not enforce a specific religion comes to expression in John Locke's *Letter on Tolerance* (1688) and *Two Treatises of Government* (1690). Removed from its political context and understanding, however, tolerance ceases to be a virtue. Indeed, it becomes a vice if and where it ceases to care for truth, ignores what is good, and disdains the values that uphold a community. The culture in which we Americans presently find ourselves is one in which almost everything is tolerated. It is a culture in which people believe nothing, possess no clear concept of right and wrong and, ultimately, are indifferent to this precarious state of affairs. The challenge before us, then, is learning how to purify tolerance so that it remains a virtue, without succumbing to the centripetal forces of relativism.

Any discussion of the notion of tolerance must presuppose a context of pluralism properly understood. On the one hand, pluralism can simply signify the phenomenological reality of differing cultures, ethnic groups, social customs, and traditions. In this sense, pluralism is a social-cultural fact. It is out of this form of pluralism that the American experiment emerged; hence, our nation's motto *E pluribus unum* ("out of many, one"). Herein different communities, different identities, and different ethnic traditions agree to coexist; they do so because of a commitment to an overarching common cause.

On the other hand, pluralism can operate under the spoken or unspoken assumption that among competing religious viewpoints or worldviews, none has (or is permitted to have) a privileged place as a framework for interpreting reality. On this view, all religious positions possess an essential unity, and all religious viewpoints stand on equal terms. Therefore, we are told, to argue for the presence or authority of any one of those—say, Christianity—amounts to religious and cultural "imperialism." In response, then, it is crucial to distinguish between pluralism as a fact of life and pluralism as an ideology, since the term is employed in both contexts. On the former, tolerance is a genuine virtue. Social and cultural pluralism is to be welcomed and celebrated; it is the soil in which "civil society" can flourish. At stake in this form of pluralism are negotiable issues: for example, language, cultural customs, ethnic and group preferences. On the latter view, by contrast, citizens are asked to tolerate alternative explanations of reality, while at the same time being pressured to negotiate and abdicate claims to ultimate moral truth in public. The result, alas, is the normalizing and legalizing of behaviors and practices that genuinely undermine the common social good. American culture has shifted in its understanding of tolerance—a shift that calls for vigilance. It has devolved into an indifference toward truth, often belligerently and intolerably so.[2] The result is a permissiveness toward all manner of social evil that undermines the common social good.[3]

Tolerance, properly conceived, has private as well as public or communal dimensions. While we may disagree with another's opinion, vice, or lifestyle, we extend (in principle) that person's "right" to a specific opinion or behavior that we may find objectionable. Religious and non-religious people of *all* varieties tolerate one another's differences because of what they *all* share in common—the laws of nature, an acknowledgement of what is acceptable and unacceptable (i.e., basic good and evil), and a desire for humans in community to flourish. When, however, someone in the name of "tolerance" is making claims on the public square that lie outside these bounds, we do *not* tolerate those views.[4] Why? Because those views *undermine the common good.* This distinction is by no means owing to Christian or religious insight. Locke himself makes this basic observation—especially important for contemporary Americans—that a great deal of difference can be tolerated *provided that it does not endanger social cohesion.*

Hence, moral honesty requires that we not divorce charity and forbearance from the moral-social bedrock of truth. It will not compromise the moral consequences—very *public* consequences—of ultimate reality. Truth and charity are not mutually exclusive, despite the flawed views of both that are regnant in contemporary society. Charity will *not* sacrifice what is true and real in order to underpin compassion and empathy, while truth will *always* attempt to clothe itself in ways that dignify fellow human beings. Rightly construed, tolerance will insist on the unity of both charity and truth. To operate out of a false or perverted sense of "tolerance" is to "make the world safe for moral dereliction."[5] Where they are not rooted in moral principle, "tolerance" and "compassion" end up corrupting both the practitioner *and* the object. Disengaging tolerance and compassion from truth has multiple corrosive effects. It encourages "not self-sufficiency, but dependence…; not strength, but weakness; not honesty and integrity, but shamelessness and vicious exploitation of others; not cheerfulness in adversity, but whining; not acceptance of life's vicissitudes, but a readiness to find fault."[6]

Where, then, should responsible citizens draw the moral line as it affects social-public policy and the wider common good? How should "tolerance" be measured? Our answer must be this: we draw the line where private preferences that undermine the communal good make claims in the public sphere for normalizing through law. Are we as citizens—and I write as a confessing Christian—called to tolerate an individual or group whose sexual behavior differs from our own and the vast majority of citizens? Indeed. Are we called to tolerate the theoretical and practical promotion of their ethic in the form of law and social policy? By no means. Thus, whatever the cost and inconvenience, not only are we as engaged citizens—including religiously-informed citizens—free to contend in the public arena, we are *required* to do so for the express purposes of *preserving social cohesion, the moral order, and the common good.*[7]

We must recapitulate: tolerance as an authentic virtue is anchored in a commitment to what is true and good for society, based on natural law assumptions. As a vice, it is indifferent at best and hostile at worst to these realities. Therefore, tolerance properly understood must not—indeed, cannot—be "neutral" toward that which affects society. In its character, tolerance as a virtue will avoid the extremes of both soft-headedness and narrow-mindedness; the former encourages the excesses of indulgence, while the latter bespeaks an inability to engage people at the social level.[8] What we are prepared to tolerate, then, pivots on what is ultimate—in our personal lives and in our society. And let us be clear: there is something "ultimate" before which every person and every society will bow. Modern and postmodern idolatries abound, but there is no escaping the fact that everyone—and every society—has a hierarchy of values. What we tolerate is predicated on this hierarchy. Social consensus is possible where there are overlapping realms of agreed-upon moral-social capital. Where there is no overlapping agreement, consensus is impossible, and anarchy is invited.[9]

But we must go one step further. By contending that there is no such thing as moral neutrality, we are also declaring that *someone's morality will be imposed*. Someone's morality *will* be ascendant and, in time, become law. Thus, the public nature of the marketplace (of both ideas and goods) as well as social institutions compels us to work for the common good by using any and all means, so long as democratic pluralism resists the centripetal slide into a soft form of totalitarian statism. The hard truth is this: a society

> cannot function well, cannot survive and cannot protect the innocent...from harm and evil, without a large measure of intolerance. Yes, intolerance—of theft, burglary, cruelty, classroom hooliganism, disrespect for parental authority, and violent crime of all sorts; of substance abuse, infidelity, illegitimacy, perversion, pornography, rape, and child molestation; of fraud, envy, covetousness, and knavery; of sloth, mediocrity, incompetence, maleducation, improvidence, irresponsibility and fecklessness. A society tolerant of those things would soon find itself in serious trouble, even facing dissolution, and many people in that society would be in peril of their lives.[10]

Intolerance, it should be honestly acknowledged, is a universal and manifestly human problem and not the provenance of Western (or non-Western) cultures. It is imperative that we be reminded of this fact, given the presence, even in the West, of multiple ideologies that are blatantly anti-Western and choose to ignore the humane achievements of the Western cultural heritage.

Everyone has claims on the public square—most notably, people of Christian conviction who, with the founders and framers of the "American experiment," believe that the public square is in fact "public," and therefore needing the influence of religion to reinforce moral principles. It is not, however, a "given" today that all views will be tolerated in the public sphere.[11] Can claims to normative truth and ultimate reality—claims that offend ancient, modern, and ultra-modern sensibilities alike—still be made? To deny such, which are anchored in natural-law reasoning, in our social and political life is to prepare the way for totalitarianism.[12]

19

What is the relationship between the natural law and Scripture?

SIMPLY STATED, NATURAL LAW IS presupposed by Scripture based on the doctrine of creation and the reality of human nature based on design. Both the Old and the New Testament affirm this foundation. The Genesis 1 narrative, moreover, ascribes to this creation the pronouncement that it was "good," indeed "very good."[1] The post-flood covenant made with Noah (Genesis 9) confirms the reality of natural law in a manner that governs human relations: any shedding of human blood by another human is said to demand an accounting—an accounting that is reciprocal in nature.[2] The reason stated for this reciprocity is human design: the human person is said to be made "in the image of God."[3] Thus, the image of God was not lost because of the fall[4]; human nature remains the same.

It is noteworthy that the concept of "law" (*torah*) permeates the entirety of the Old Testament. It is central to much of the Pentateuch, in which considerable focus is devoted to both Mosaic law and Levitical law, but it is also prominent in the "Writings"—i.e., in the Psalms[5] and in the wisdom literature of Proverbs[6] and Ecclesiastes[7]—as well as in the prophetic books.[8] Upon examination, both Testaments distinguish between ceremonial law and moral law, with Jesus and the writers of the New Testament being quite clear that the one is enduring while the other is temporary, serving as but a shadow of the permanent.[9] More than once does Jesus insist on the enduring nature of "the Law and the Prophets."[10] Relatedly, throughout the entire New Testament—in the gospel narratives and the various epistles—the foundation of moral law is presented as the very ethical core of Christian faith: loving God and loving one's neighbor (as oneself).[11]

A high point in Israel's history, and thus the writings of the Pentateuch, is the giving and receiving of the "Ten Words," i.e., the Ten Commandments (the Decalogue),[12] as recorded in Exodus, Leviticus, and Deuteronomy. While these do not address all moral matters, nor do they address in detail particular issues, they encompass in a general manner foundational regulations on human relations that are timeless for all people, everywhere, and at all times. This, in its essence, expresses the natural law. The good is mirrored in general though significant ways, while prohibitions of violating this good are stated categorically. The writings of the New Testament remain in clear continuity with this moral framework, and natural law's enduring quality is exhibited at virtually every turn in a reading of the New Testament documents. Already noted in previous questions were Jesus's affirmation of the creation account and marriage as part of creation's design, his reiteration of the continuity of the "Law and the prophets," and his affirmation of the "Golden Rule." A supremely noteworthy—and eminently practical—application of the "Golden Rule" principle, mirroring the natural law, comes to expression in the parable of the "Good Samaritan."[13] The context of this teaching is Jesus's reiteration of the double command—loving God and "loving your neighbor as yourself."[14]

Previous Questions above identify recurring themes in the New Testament that demonstrate the unity of the Old and New Testament scriptures, chief among these being issues of human identity, marriage and sexual morality. No "new" ethical standard appears in the New Testament scriptures. The moral law has not changed, and this because of human nature and human design. For this reason, the *Catechism of the Catholic Church* notes:

The natural law, the Creator's very good work, provides the solid foundation on which man can build the structure of moral rules to guide his choices. It also provides the indispensable moral foundation for building the human community. Finally, it provides the necessary basis for the civil law with which it is connected, whether by a reflection that draws conclusions from its principles, or by additions of a positive and juridical nature.[15]

20

Does Jesus affirm or set aside the natural law in favor of a new ethic?

One means of identifying Jesus's attitude toward moral law, and hence the natural law, is to take note of his statements on the nature and indissolubility of marriage.[1] The qualification of his pronouncement is instructive: it has been so "from the beginning" (Matt. 19:4; Mark 10:6). Thus, he speaks of a natural order, based on creation and human nature. On this foundational assumption, then, Jesus builds teaching that addresses subjects such as divorce, adultery, and basic sexual matters.

In addition to the created order, an important theme in the Gospel according to Matthew is Jesus's ongoing debate with Pharisaical Judaism and its preoccupations with the finer points of Levitical law.[2] In light of scribal and Pharisaical preoccupancy with keeping the "letter of the law" (as well as popular notions that would mirrored scribal tendencies), Jesus's aim is to alter contemporary understanding and application of Jewish law and affirm the moral law, which is abiding and thus lodged at the heart of all laws given to Israel of old. A chief fault of Pharisaism was (and remains) its focus on what is legal and external, thereby missing the moral and internal meaning of the law. It is in this light that we should read Jesus's warning in Matthew 5: "Do not think that I have come to abolish the Law or the Prophets. I have not come to abolish but to fulfill..."[3] Jesus is affirming the moral law, and the case illustrations contained in Matthew 5 show him to be emphasizing the spirit of the law while condemning misappropriations of the law (whether popular or rabbinic).

Contextually, what then follows in Jesus's teaching is a six-fold illustration of how *moral law remains* while skewed or false interpretations and applications of the law are in need of being exposed and thus set aside.[4] The six areas of illustration concern (1) murder, (2) adultery, (3) divorce, (4) making oaths, (5) retaliation, and (6) response to one's enemies. Each of these contains an aspect of moral law, revealed in the old covenant and abiding in nature. But each has been reinterpreted, or misapplied, by Jesus's day to such an extent that the moral core is scarcely identifiable.[5] While murder, adultery, and divorce may strike the average reader as non-controversial (or, at least, less controversial), the fifth example calls for discernment. It well illustrates the presence of natural law moral reasoning in Jesus's teaching, and yet it is quite frequently misunderstood not merely by the average reader but by professional scholars and even Christian interpreters. It concerns the *lex talionis*—"an eye for an eye and a tooth for a tooth"—as recorded in Matt. 5:38–42. Of the six situations—commonly referred to by biblical scholars as "antitheses"—illustrating a proper or improper understanding of moral law, none is more perplexing than Jesus's teaching on the "talion principle," the *lex talionis*.

This law is widely viewed in our day, whether by secular or religious people, as barbaric and retaliatory, and hence no more applicable. However understandable, this viewpoint is based on a misconstrual of the principle.[6] In the Old Testament, the *lex talionis* marked a turning point in ancient understanding of punishment. This "turning point" was the result of introducing restraints and proportionality; punishment, properly and morally conceived, has both upper and lower limits. This accords with the classic notion of justice, underpinned by the natural moral law, whereby humans render to everyone *what is due*. The law's teaching on reciprocity is taught plainly in the Old Testament,[7] and to the rabbis the *talion* was a divine, not human, principle. In its pure essence, the *talion* principle may be rendered "like for like" or "measure for measure." Thus, given modern notions of "retaliation," *lex talionis* is best translated "the law of retribution." An interpretive key in the Old Testament to understanding the *lex* is found in Lev. 24:18 and 24:21, both of which contain the explicit reference to restitution.[8]

While many interpreters understand Jesus, as recorded in Matthew 5, as repudiating the *lex*, this is emphatically not the case. What he *is* doing is repudiating false notions and perverse applications of the *lex* in his day. As a measurement of justice, the *lex talionis* is a legal principle, anchored in natural law reasoning that exists both to *levy proportionality* in society's response to specific crimes as well as to *limit the upper reaches* of that response. For punishment to be "proportionate" and therefore just, both upper and lower limits are presupposed. Punishment is "just" to the extent that it "fits the crime"[9]; a just response requires no more but no less. The two aspects of proportionality and limitation inhere in the abiding character of justice—a cardinal virtue that is universal and therefore uniform, extending to the teaching of the New Testament and Christianity and informing the very foundations of Western legal theory and practice. Summarizing the Old Testament background of the *lex talionis*, one noted Hebrew scholar observes,

> the compensatory aspect of the *lex talionis* under the Mosaic Code favours its characterization as a *measured and proportionate* response to punishable conduct by a member of the community. At the very least, it may be seen to have introduced restraint and rationality as the defining features of lawful punishment *in place of the unbridled and unchecked vengeance* that had earlier prevailed.[10]

The evidence indicates overwhelmingly that, in the ancient Near Eastern context, the *lex* introduced an ennobling and just measurement of punishment that was enacted.[11] An important part of its contribution was to put an end to the vendetta. Evidence of this from the Pentateuch is found, for example, in Lev. 24:22, in which Israel of old is instructed, "You shall have one law, the same for alien as for native-born."

The important point to be made here is that Jesus is *not* questioning or negating the legitimacy of moral retribution or reciprocity as a principle of justice. Rather, two things are in play: (a) by Jesus's day the *lex* was understood or applied in distorted and illegitimate ways, and (b) the *lex* may not be applied in the realm of *private relations*, only by governing authorities.[12] This is confirmed by the context of Matt. 5:38–42. Herein Jesus's teaching consists of five admonitions, all of which are meant to illustrate the matter of reciprocity: (1) not resisting an evil person,[13] (2) turning the other cheek; (3) allowing a person to have your cloak; (4) going an extra mile; and (5) giving and lending. All five are private matters, matters of insult or private "injury," *not* issues of assault or social policy.[14] The context here is not unlike that of the material in Rom. 12:–13:1–7. Justice is *proscribed* in Romans 12—individuals do not take justice into their own hands, which we call "vigilante justice"—but prescribed in Romans 13—in the hands of the governing authorities.[15]

Not insignificantly, Augustine is one of several church fathers who concluded that there was no opposition between the *lex talionis* and Jesus's teaching. Rather, the issues at hand concerned proportionality and compensation; hence, its abiding relevance. After all, "who will of his own accord be satisfied with a revenge equal to the injury? Do we not see men, only slightly hurt, eager for slaughter, thirsting for blood, as if they could never make their enemy suffer enough?"[16] At its core, Augustine insists, the *lex* was intended "to check the vehemence of hatred" and "to curb the impetuosity of angry passion." Accordingly, because of the lack of restraint expressed in revenge, which is "unjust from its excess," the law

> established the principle of compensation, that the penalty should correspond to the injury inflicted. So the precept, "an eye

> for an eye, a tooth for a tooth," instead of being a brand to kindle a fire that was quenched, was rather a covering to prevent the fire already kindled from spreading... It is sin to demand more than is due, though it is no sin to demand a debt.[17]

By his own words, Christ came not to destroy or abolish but to fulfill the moral law. This declaration, significantly, is recorded only in the Gospel of Matthew, which in contrast to the other three New Testament Gospel narratives is focused heavily on Jewish attitudes toward "the law." Specifically, it follows directly on the heels of an exhortation to his followers that they are "the salt of the earth" and the light of the world" (Matt. 5:13–17). Only the moral law—that which is abiding and anchored in creation and human design—will ground them as they live in the present world.

21

What is the relationship between the natural law and human rights?

As several of the previous Questions have intimated, the modern understanding of human rights is indebted to natural law thinking.[1] Many modern theorists would deny (a) that there is any such thing as a universal human nature, and correlatively, (b) that there is universal objective moral truth expressed in the natural law.[2] Nevertheless, one discovers a rich—if often unmined in our day—source of natural law reflection on human rights/natural rights that extends through thinkers such as Thomas Aquinas, early-modern natural lawyers such as Francisco de Vitoria, Francisco Súarez, and Hugo Grotius, to John Locke and the founders of the American "experiment in ordered liberty" and to 20th-century writers such as Jacques Maritain and John Finnis.[3]

Human rights—or, more precisely, universal human rights (i.e., "natural rights")—have no foundation, no legitimate grounding, apart from natural law and the fact of human beings' intrinsic nature. (In truth, a "religious" worldview best explains the commitment to "human rights" for the simple reason that human beings have a design, a constitution, having been created in the "image of God." Moreover, this worldview supports an objective moral order in the universe.) Because these rights issue out of the sacred rights of conscience and human dignity, human rights are pre-political.

The notion of inalienable rights originates in the nature of man, not the state, legality, political authority, or any human construct. Those rights are pre-political, originating in the natural law; they are recognized by the state but not created by the state. Locke's observations clearly assisted the founders and framers of the American experiment as they wrestled with the foundational premise of "natural rights." Any political power exerted in violation of a human being's natural rights, as they saw it, constitutes tyranny, which is necessarily illegitimate. Americans, of course, should recognize Locke's ideas in the Declaration of Independence: "We hold these Truths to be self-evident, that all Men are created equal, that they are endowed by their Creator [not the state] with certain inalienable Rights, that among these are Life, Liberty, and the Pursuit of Happiness."[4]

To affirm objective moral truth that is underpinned by natural law not only leads us to affirm an intrinsic human dignity and universal rights, but it yields an awareness of basic moral obligations and *duties* to others. The consequence of such an awareness leads to a common (which is to say, universal) moral judgment to *protect and dignify human* life, especially human life that is vulnerable. This moral-philosophical (and, in the end, political) commitment results in a way of thinking that connects beginning-of-life issues with end-of-life issues, but also with atrocities that manifest themselves under totalitarian rule—for example, slavery, genocide, and mass human rights violations. To eliminate human life at the margins, on the one hand, and to fail to protect human lives who are oppressed and persecuted, on the other, are both *always and everywhere* wrong.

As already noted, many of the more prominent natural law theorists of the 20th century were writing between the late 1930s and 1950 and in the aftermath of the Second World War, at a time when questions of human dignity and universal human rights were once more understood to be critically important. With the universal declarations on human rights and human dignity that proceeded in the aftermath of the War, renewal of natural law thinking was pressed upon human civilization in a remarkable and unprecedented way.[5]

The hallmark of our present era is without question its accent on rights. However, "rights" have moral meaning when (and *only* when) they issue out of a particular understanding of human nature—a nature that is inalienable and unchanging. What's more, we cannot conceptualize human "rights" properly unless we are willing to attach thereto an equal commitment to duties, as noted above. The relationship of the two is reciprocal. And if duties are obligatory, most people will demand to know *On what authority?* This is the real question, in the end. On what authority? The most plausible answer is *an authority that transcends* people, culture, and societies. As it is, the weakening—and in some respects collapse—of Christianity in most Western cultures challenges this formerly inherited understanding of human rights. More and more, we have come to understand "rights" in largely economic or social terms.

Alas, in the current cultural climate the distinction between "inalienable" rights and personal wants or "needs" has been largely obscured. Contemporary rights-talk tends to enshrine the self at the center of the moral universe, unencumbered by moral-social obligations. Forgotten or ignored is the role of duties, the foundation upon which any decent culture survives. This strain of amnesia and loss, however, is far from innocent. It has a darker side that in its purest form calls into question the most elementary assumptions about human nature and life. The volatile mix of moral relativism, advances in medical and scientific technology, and the disintegration of the family as a caring and cohesive social unit does not bode well for American society, apart from cultural rejuvenation. Americans find themselves confronted with rights claims that are ultimate in their character, and pernicious as well. In our day, advocates of abortion, homosexuality, transexuality, and euthanasia all employ the grammar of "rights." This invasion of rights rhetoric into the realm of the sacred and the natural calls for a discerning and thoughtful response.

A fusion of freedom *and* responsibility, with an accent on the latter, is the only "mix" that will permit a distinctly free society to remain genuinely "free"—and civil—while conducting its political life in a way that truly protects the common good. Humans are truly free when they choose to serve and build the capacities of others rather than using their "freedom" as a pretext to ignore or obliterate moral obligations and restrains. If freedom *from* restrains becomes the dominant mode by which a culture interprets its liberties, the basic social institutions of that culture, in the end, will no longer be tolerated. Gone is *any* understanding of the common good.

But the notion of "human rights," properly construed, transcends the aforementioned individualism and moral relativism that becloud our wider duties. "Human rights" accord with human nature and design, and thus what *universally* needs affirming and protecting. Human life is not a mere instrumental or social-cultural good; it is an intrinsic good, and thus needs protecting *always and everywhere.* Upholding human dignity and honoring basic moral obligations or duties require that both elements be anchored in a transcendent view of human nature. And they apply to both the community in which we live and the community of nations of which we are a part.

Among the community of nations, those obligations take on a serious and sobering cast. For to whom much has been given, much is required. We might recall the words of the former chief prosecutor of the International Criminal Tribunals for the former Yugoslavia and Rwanda, who stated,

> where there have been egregious human rights violations that have been unaccounted for, where there has been no justice, where the victims have not received any acknowledgment, where they have been forgotten, where there's been a national amnesia, the effect is a cancer in the society."[6]

At bottom, for human beings individually and nations collectively to fail to affirm and protect that which is "inalienable" is to invite evil in manifold ways.

22

Is there a natural law tradition in Judaism?

In several previous Questions we have noted the tension between Pharisaical Judaism of the first century and Jesus's teaching. That tension, based on the New Testament Gospel narratives that have come to us, usually had to do with a proper interpretation of "the Law." Law was integral to Israel's life as recorded in the Old Testament, and it continued to be so following the roughly four centuries of exile and return. Scribes and Pharisees, as mirrored in the Gospel accounts, tended to focus on the "letter of the law" in this "post-exilic" period of the Christian advent. This interpretation is not infrequently challenged by Jesus. These aforementioned preliminary thoughts are necessary, if only to point out the differences between the "Judaism" of the Old Testament covenant people of Israel, the Judaism of Jewish exile and transition, and the Judaism of the last two millennia. The answer to the above question—"Is there a natural law tradition in Judaism?"—is, broadly speaking, yes, if we mean thereby the overall historical sweep of the Judeo-Christian tradition. This is true even when there exists some debate as to whether natural law thinking is compatible with Jewish faith, and even when some Jewish scholars would argue that Judaism contains no natural law tradition *per se*.

Jewish natural law theorist David Novak argues that two basic assumptions about natural law that have prevented many from seeing how Judaism affirms it need to be set aside. These assumptions, he insists, must be rejected at the outset in order for a discussion of "Judaism and natural law" to have the seriousness any discussion of either Judaism or natural law requires.[1] The first assumption to be rejected is that the true matrix of the idea of natural law is lodged in classical Greek philosophy. Where this is thought, any subsequent attempts to "graft" natural law thinking into another mode of thinking—particularly in the case of a "theology of revelation"—are ultimately incoherent. The second assumption to be rejected is that natural law is a solely Roman Catholic construct, inasmuch as the idea of natural law seems to a large extent far more embraced by the Catholic tradition than others.

In order to address these misguided assumptions responsibly, Novak suggests several principles to assist us in guiding our ethical thinking. One is the fact that the idea of natural law lies at the junction of theology *and* philosophy. This is, of course, how it was understood by Thomas Aquinas. Theologically, natural law is central to an understanding of Judaism, given the role that the Torah—the revealed law of God—played in the Old Testament. To deny the law would be to deny what Maimonides considered "the foundation of all foundations."[2] In any event, if it is in fact the case that natural law lies at the intersection of theology and philosophy, then both theologians as well as philosophers will need to rise to the challenge of arguing its reality, since representatives of both realms tend to doubt or reject it. Its normative substance and its logical evidence surrounding human patterns of behavior must be emphasized (and explained). In addition, its detractors should be confronted with the fact that absent the natural law, there is no basis for *any* framework of morality other than personal whim, changing circumstance, or the politics of power.

Another aid is to view natural law as the practical outworking of the doctrine of creation. The "doctrine of creation," however, is not solely—or even primarily—concerned to answer questions such as "When did the world begin?" or "How did the world begin?" Rather, it focuses human attention on the question "*Why* does the world even exist?", and this is an eminently practical question—one which occupies every human being to one extent or another. After all, the great apes do not wrestle with this question; nor does inanimate nature. "Why do we exist?" is *the* human question. This question, of course, is both moral and political in its ramifications.

A further aid to our understanding of natural law is to view it as a moral norm by which interhuman relationships are governed. Hence, in Jewish thought, commandments are central to Jewish identity and daily living. Commandments come from the Creator, their source and ultimate end. These commandments, moreover, are known or intuited by all human beings, not merely Jews; hence, the importance of philosophical reflection. And because natural law norms govern human relations, they have legal as well as social-political significance.

From the standpoint of Judaism, then, natural law can be viewed as "the necessary and perpetual critique needed by all culture and all positive law."[3] As described by Novak, natural law is

> the essential limit on the pretensions of human action for the sake of human existence and its transcendent intention. It operates best when its rightful role is understood, when neither too much nor too little is expected of it. Whatever it has been called at various points in Jewish history, it has been functioning from the beginning of Judaism. But when natural law has been ignored, Judaism has often become distorted in the process, either by understating or overstating its own worldly dimension.[4]

At bottom, the notion of the natural law is consistent with Jewish theology and with the assumptions of Judaism: namely, it represents a sphere of morality mirroring divine providential care and guidance and is accessible through human reasoning, reflective of human nature, and universally binding.[5]

The well-known Jewish convert, Paul the Apostle, identified in the introduction of his letter to the Christians in Rome three groups of people—Jews, Gentiles, and Christians. The natural law, he insists, furnishes basic awareness of moral reality not just for the Christian and Jew but for the Gentile as well, even when the Gentile has not received the Law as have the Jews or the revelation of Christ. In addition to the universe, which witnesses to the Creator, the Gentile, as well, has an implanted awareness of the moral law and, in the end, cannot be viewed as innocent or excused (Rom. 1:18–2:29). Both Jew and Gentile, then, stand accountable to a holy and perfect Creator. Paul's argument is that the natural law exists and is valid universally, wherever human beings are found.

23

Is there a natural law tradition in Islam?

As this volume has argued thus far, natural law reasoning recognizes the existence of common ground in which and from which different people-groups—whether religious and non-religious people in character—can approach moral issues in a pluralistic cultural environment. Perhaps, one might well assume, this provides hope and promise as it pertains to Islamic faith. Might not only secular types but also non-Christian religious people such as Muslims, who do not confess a triune God and who reject the unique claims of Jesus Christ, nevertheless affirm an objective moral law? In the previous question we observed that the theological and philosophical assumptions of Judaism permit the embrace of natural law realities. We in the Western cultural context typically speak of Judeo-Christian faith to express this wider shared framework, even when Jewish religion rejects the trinitarian faith of Christianity and the deity of Jesus Christ. Both the Old Testament and the traditions of Judaism presuppose the foundations of moral law—for example, as expressed in the Ten Commandments or reiterated by the Hebrew prophets—that are intuited and known by all people. Both Jewish and Christian religion, moreover, acknowledge the symbiotic role of reason and faith. While reason does not replace faith, it is understood to work in concert with faith. Hence, in the wider Judeo-Christian tradition, people cannot be coerced into belief; their confession of faith must always and everywhere be *voluntary*, which is why religious freedom historically has been a defining characteristic of Western societies.[1] Such, it needs reiterating, is in accordance with natural law reasoning; since all people have some knowledge of moral and spiritual truth, they cannot be coerced into a place of belief, confession, and submission.

This is precisely where difficulties arise when we examine the Islamic tradition. Things get muddled when we raise the question of whether there is a "natural law" tradition in Islam. Our answer hinges on several critical factors—among these: (1) a precise definition of the "natural law" tradition, (2) the wider sweep of history from Islam's inception in the seventh century to the present day, and (3) the theological assumptions of *shari'a* law, which has been normative for Islamic societies. On the one hand, evidence of some diversity historically can be found in Muslim thought. For example, a revival of Aristotelian thought can be observed in the high middle ages—something that would be utterly unthinkable today. Why this would be unthinkable both today and in the early centuries of Islam's growth is telling and should give us pause. In addition, Muslims regard their faith as a "religion of nature" (*din al-fitrah*) to the extent that everything in the cosmos is submitted to its creator. In the Qur'an one reads that everything in the heavens and on earth, inclusive of human life, is subject to Allah.[2] From this basic belief one can infer that all of nature is but a mirror of its laws, behind which stands the creator and subjugator.

At the same time, human nature in Islam is depicted in ways that differ significantly from the Judeo-Christian tradition. One difference is Islam's rejection of the doctrine of original sin and human fallenness and the consequent understanding of human nature. Qur'an 7:172 teaches that human nature was determined covenantally by Allah even before the birth of the first humans. Thus, it is Islam's understanding—and teaching—that human beings are subjugated—which is to say, "slaves"—to Allah. They are born in a state of subjugation and submission and live out their lives in such a state. As one perceptive commentator has noted, it therefore makes sense that Islam is fundamentally characterized by the need for "struggle" (*jihad)*, both at the personal level but also at the social-cultural level.[3] In this light we may understand the commands that are thought to proceed from Allah to *fight for the advance* of Islam (Qur'an 2:216). This rationale, it needs emphasizing, has been with Islamic religion since its inception; as a theological underpinning it is lodged at the very heart of Muslim faith. While there *is* to be found the "moderate" (which is to say, non-radical) Muslim voice in our world today, all too often that voice is persecuted or silenced by a more radicalized version of the faith—one that is best described as "Islamic" rather than "Muslim" and whose modus operandi is compulsion rather than reason, subjugation rather than respect for the sacred rights of conscience.[4]

In the end, our opening question must unfortunately yield a "no" response, given several confluent factors: (a) the beginnings of Islam as mirrored in the priorities and practice of Muhammad, (b) the teachings of the Quran as well as the *hadith* (the "sayings") that inform Islamic law, (c) the particular theological underpinnings of Islam which inform the Muslim understanding of human nature and human existence ("subjection" and "submission" as opposed to moral reflection and voluntarism), and (d) the application of *jihad* ("struggle") not merely to the inner struggle but to *the wider cultural context*, which requires *coercive advancement* of the faith where it is perceived as being resisted.[5] All of these factors, to a greater or lesser extent, combine to deny, both in theory and in practice, the natural law concept, which is grounded in a respect for "right reason," moral reflection, and voluntarism and which acknowledges "common ground" with all (non-Muslim) humanity—characteristics that, not insignificantly, undergird the Judeo-Christian moral tradition.[6] Human beings, based on Islamic thought, are "subjects" of Allah. There is no theological room for questioning or rejecting Islamic claims; hence, "apostasy," historically, depending on the interpretive historical tradition, may even call for a death sentence in response.[7] While there indeed are "moderate" Muslims, as noted previously, these tend to be found in the Western cultural context, where religious freedom is taken for granted and where dialogue or debate is even possible.[8] But even they very often are subject to persecution, given the increasing radicalization of Islam in Western nations.[9]

The question of reason and faith in Islam is well illustrated by events that occurred in 2006 and 2007 as the result of a 2006 lecture at the University of Regensburg (Germany) by Pope Benedict XVI.[10] This address, which was designed to emphasis the importance of reason working with faith, resulted in unprecedented offense to Muslims worldwide. Benedict, who had previously taught in the university, was reflecting on the need for reason and faith to intersect—a dialogue in partnership, as it were. Wishing to illustrate the symbiotic relationship between the two, the Pope compared the "structures of faith" as taught in Christianity with those taught in the Qur'an. Acknowledging, by way of historical example, the differing attitudes toward faith in the two religions, he stressed that compulsion "is incompatible with the nature of God and the nature of the soul."

And for this comparison he was not to be forgiven, for a nerve had been struck. Immediately following his address, not a few Muslim leaders demanded of Benedict an apology. One month after the address, a group of 38 Muslim leaders wrote an open letter attempting to correct perceived errors in Benedict's address. Then, one year after Regensburg, in October of 2007 at the end of Ramadan, an open letter signed by 138 Muslims representing diverse traditions and titled "A Common Word between Us and You" was addressed and hand-delivered to 27 "Leaders of Christian Churches," including the Pope, Bartholomew I, the Orthodox Church's Patriarch of Constantinople, and the Archbishop of Canterbury, Rowan Williams. Produced at the initiative of the Aal al-Bayt Institute for Islamic Thought, which seeks to represent Islamic interests to governments and international bodies, the document called for dialogue on the basis of "common theological ground" between the two faiths.[11]

"A Common Word" created a firestorm of reaction among church bodies and Christian institutions. Most significant was the publication by the Yale Center for Faith and Culture of "Loving God and Neighbor Together: A Christian Response to *A Common Word between Us and You.*" This document, in the end, was accompanied by over 300 signatories—all prominent Christian leaders, clergymen, and scholars—and published in *The New York Times.* Significantly, the document offered no theological assessment of the claims of "A Common Word," nor of Christianity's own unique claims—specifically, as it concerns the doctrine of God, the ethics of authentic "neighbor-love," and the insistence on religious freedom and priority of human rights. As it is, on each of these critically important theological commitments, Christianity and Islam differ radically. Neither "A Common Word" nor the vapid response published by the Yale Center did justice to the significant theological and philosophical issues that exist between the two religions.[12]

While dialogue between Christians and Muslims is to be encouraged, unlike the unwitting attempts of the Yale Center for Faith and Culture, the reality is that the two faiths share very little theological "common ground"—a reality that is borne out not only by the vehement Muslim reaction to Benedict's speech noted above[13] but the fact that converts from Islam to Christianity in our day are routinely subject to surveillance, arrest, interrogation, imprisonment, destruction of property, displacement, and death.[14] In the end, at bottom one cannot make the argument that there is a natural-law tradition in Islam.[15]

24

How does the natural law bear upon the killing of other human beings?

We have noted in several Questions thus far the manner in which the precepts of the Decalogue mirror the basic contours of natural law thinking. None of these precepts would appear as clear and self-evident as the immutability of the commandment "Thou shalt not kill." Recall again the moral baseline toward which natural law points: good or justice is to be done, and evil or injustice is to be avoided. At the same time, when we recall the classic definition of justice—render to each what is due—we encounter potential problems. The precept "Thou shalt not kill" would appear not to be valid everywhere and at all times. For one, the state historically has been understood in most cultures to be authorized to put to death certain categories of criminal. And until fairly recently, many states in the U.S. had laws in the books that sent convicted murderers to their deaths.[1] In addition, based on just war moral reasoning, the ethics of warfare is predicated on a distinction between the relatively innocent and the guilty. The classic definition of a just war has been that of Thomas Aquinas, with most subsequent theorists following suit: in order for a war to be just, at minimum it must be waged for a just cause, by a legitimate political authority, and with right intention.[2] Thus, the above-mentioned distinction between innocence and guilt informs the precise meaning of "Thou shalt not kill." The Hebrew verb usually translated "kill" (*rātsach*), moreover, helps clarify the nature of killing. The precise meaning of the commandment is "Thou shalt not kill an innocent person," or, "Thou shalt not murder." This precept in the Decalogue represents an *absolute* prohibition; it is always and everywhere forbidden, applicable in foreign affairs (for example, in war) as well as in domestic affairs (for example, as it applies to criminal justice, abortion, infanticide, or euthanasia/mercy-killing).

In assorted Questions thus far we have ascribed human dignity to having been created in the image of God. This permits us to reflect with sobriety on ethical dilemmas such as war and coercive intervention, capital punishment, and abortion, to name but several. Such controversies cut to the heart of natural law moral reasoning—do good and avoid doing evil—and hence require sober reflection on our part. Humans must discern not only *what* is morally permissible but *why*. While two of these three matters are discussed in Questions later on in this volume, the latter issue is the focus of some commentary here.

Rather than rehearse the recent history of abortion politics in the U.S., we may simply state that the moral injunction "Thou shalt not murder" extends to all human beings. It is irrelevant to argue on the basis of fetal development at what point abortion is morally justified. With very few exceptions, every fetus develops *in utero* and will be born; conversely, every human person was a fetus and an embryo. Hence, we may legitimately argue, based on natural law moral reasoning, human nature, and the wonder of human creation, that it is our duty to protect the lives of the most vulnerable human beings—children in the womb.

To feign uncertainty about "when life actually begins" might be seen as politically expedient, but it is intellectually and morally indefensible. One social philosopher has stated the matter with utmost clarity:

> The facts of human embryogenesis and early development make the conclusion inescapable: from a purely biological perspective, *scientists can identify the point at which a human life begins*. The relevant studies are legion. The biological facts are uncontested. The method of analysis applied to the data is universally accepted... Your life began, as did the life of every other human being, when the fusion of egg and sperm produced a new, complete, living organism—an embryonic human being. You were never an ovum or a sperm cell...But you *were* once an embryo, just as you were an adolescent, a child, an infant, and a fetus...You are the same being—the same human being—who once was an embryo.[3]

In this regard it needs emphasizing that the debate over human life and fetal development is not really—and has never really been—about biology. When we debate issues related to assisted reproductive technologies, stem-cell research, human cloning or abortion, that debate is really not narrowly about biological facts or whether or when human embryos are human beings. Rather, it is a question of "whether we ought to respect and defend human beings in the earliest stages of their lives"; that is, it is about "the nature of human dignity and the equality of human beings"—a dignity and equality that exist *by virtue of their shared humanity*.[4]

This reality is not merely a "religious" conviction. It is biological and reproductive fact, issuing out of the natural law's moral boundaries: do good and avoid doing evil. In the end, despite the controversy that surrounds abortion politics, there exists *no moral argument* that can justify killing the unborn *in utero*—at any stage in their development.[5]

25

How does natural law thinking affect "crimes against humanity" and humanitarian intervention?

WHAT ARE THE PREROGATIVES OF the sovereign state? This is a question with which international law has wrestled in recent generations. Generally, international law assumes that a nation's sovereignty is limited. Sovereignty cannot outweigh impunity; that is to say, where state sovereignty is absolute, international law is impossible. The more pressing question, particularly since World War II, is whether nations are morally obligated to defend basic human rights in scenarios in which there is egregious, outrageous socio-political evil such as genocide, mass murder, and widespread human rights violations. This question is no less urgent in the third decade of the 21st century.

Human beings living in a moral universe cannot prosecute moral atrocity and socio-political evils if nations, or coalitions of nations, do not take this task seriously. As several Questions in this volume have argued, the very purpose of governing authority is to reward the good and prohibit and punish the evil. International law, if it has teeth, must do more than simply honor the victims of socio-political evil (important as that honoring is). The challenge today, given the mix of moral erosion in the West and the extent of totalitarianism globally, is whether the international community has the ability to prosecute what are typically called "crimes against humanity." This term, issuing out of post-World War II criminal tribunals, calls for constant reflection and reiteration. At the Nuremberg trials following on the heels of the end of World War II, three categories of international crime were identified: (1) "crimes against peace" (that is, aggression), (2) "war crimes," and (3) "crimes against humanity." Today we encounter all three of these challenges, not infrequently in the form of mass murder, ethnic cleansing, rape, and torture.

The natural law binds nations in the form of a *ius gentium* toward mutual obligations and duties.[1] This law and these obligations are perpetual in validity, for all times and culture. While natural law reasoning acknowledges the realm of state sovereignty, that sovereignty is not absolute. The presumption of sovereignty is negated when and where the intolerable occurs, when and where a state permits egregious human rights violations either among its own people or among other people. International law does not need a "world government" for its enactment; what it does need is a federation or coalition of nations that are committed to holding accountable any violators of the most basic of human rights. The prosecution of the abovementioned three violations of human rights is philosophically and politically justified. The great challenge to international law is to find agreement among the nations and the will toward holding violators accountable through punishment according to international criminal law. Justice, after all, requires an accounting, and therefore, punishment where gross injustice occurs. Can, for example, the International Criminal Court get the job done?

It needs emphasizing that natural law reasoning does not equate to some form of colonialism or imperialism. It translates into responsible policy in the same way that it provides moral wisdom to nations through "just war" moral conditions that assist them in discerning whether or not to undertake coercive intervention. Hence, it operates on the basis of moral principles such as just cause, identifying sufficient harm, proportionality, public condemnation, and the restoration of basic rights that have been violated. "War crimes" are precisely that—crimes—because they are unchosen expressions of evil that are forced upon the innocent. War itself need not be evil or an act of cruelty. Nor is it the case that war is uncontrollable. *Ius in bello* (justice in executing war) moral conditions, noted in the following Question, guide military leaders and soldiers in terms of what *may and may not* be done.

We react to catastrophic geopolitical events in the world because of natural law reasoning—do good and avoid doing evil—and we treat others as we would wish to be treated ourselves because of its practical application in the form of a "Golden Rule" ethic.[2] This confronts relatively free nations with the difficult issue of both humanitarian and military intervention. The former is the focus here in the present context, while the latter is treated later in this volume.[3] Thirty years ago many were inclined to view the Cold War as the result of defects in the international order. However, the tragic reality is that (a) the Cold War never really ended but rather simply went underground while the West pursued appeasement, and (b) geopolitical catastrophe after geopolitical disaster has visited the international community in the decades since. How, then, might those who are responsible for policy in relatively free nations propose to deal with the scale of humanitarian need in our day that is massive—situations that usually fall short of war *per se* but which require some measure of interventionary force for humanitarian purposes?

Here perplexing issues confront us. When, if ever, should a nation engage in coercive intervention for the primary purpose of saving lives or protecting innocent lives where vital national interests are not directly at stake? Should governments respond and intervene to prevent—or retard the effects of—genocide, mass murder, enslavement of peoples or people-groups, and egregious human rights violations? Why or why not? If so, by what rationale?

Writing on the ethics of humanitarianism five decades ago, Princeton ethicist Paul Ramsey set forth the argument that military intervention for the sake of justice remains both a right and a duty. According to Ramsey, the failure of free nations to intervene, based on a stewardship of responsibilities in the world, would be "tragically to fail to undertake responsibilities that ...are not likely to be accomplished by other political actors."[4] Responding to the common objection that intervention can be unjust, Ramsey acknowledged both possibilities—unjust as well as just causes. But the mere possibility that intervention can be unjust, he insisted, did not release political actors from their *moral responsibility*. "Anyone who is impressed only by the immorality and probable ineffectiveness of interventionary action," he noted, "should sensitize his conscience to the immorality and probable ineffectiveness of nonintervention."[5] Nor, in Ramsey's view, did the presence of the United Nations change this moral reality, since the UN does not supplant individual states' sovereignty or reorder their respective societies. In addition, the UN has become increasingly powerless to prevent or retard socio-political evil around the globe.

Ramsey's views were not popular then, just as they would be unpopular today. Nevertheless, Ramsey's wrestling with the international obligations that attend "neighbor-love" placed him squarely within the mainstream of classic just war thinking and the Christian moral tradition. All people, based on their shared humanity, possess an intrinsic dignity and hence are to be sheltered from arbitrary and inhumane acts of oppression. To wrestle with our response to egregious and massive human rights violations around the globe is to be caught between two accusations, namely, that of "imperialism" (or Western bias) and cultural particularity (or state sovereignty). Political responses in relatively free nations to atrocity tend generally to be predictable and weak, without any moral-philosophical basis upon which to construct responsible policy as it applies to humanitarian disaster. And if we look to Christian thinkers and moral philosophers we find a paucity of substantive contributions to public debate that might bear on responsible policy.

While a detailed discussion of humanitarian debate among political, legal, and social theorists remains well beyond the scope of this Question and the present volume, a general rule of thumb regarding intervention may be stated: intervention must always be proportionate to the degree of human suffering where it is found and oriented toward a greater good in a reasonably comprehensive manner. This is self-evident moral truth assumed by natural law reasoning and embodied in a "Golden Rule" ethic, even when wisdom and political prudence are needed to discern the particular strategies—what, where, and how—that should be applied in responding to a specific catastrophic scenario in order to implement justice.

Human goods need protecting. For this reason, just war moral reasoning, with its severe qualification of intervention, represents a necessary mediating character—between ideological pacifism and *Realpolitik*—in the face of geopolitical evil. One political historian frames the matter in this way:

> there are [certain moral] goods worth the risk [of intervening]... and "peace at any price" is unacceptable...The pacifist misses this complex reality of the possibility and political conditions for human flourishing...The realist approach, by which the conduct [of intervening] is bound by no moral limit, undermines the very moral and political legitimacy of the regime.[6]

The fact that certain human goods need protecting and force can be morally guided finds confirmation both in domestic policy and in foreign affairs, particularly in the context of possible humanitarian or military intervention. Both natural law reasoning and the Christian moral tradition contribute what is perhaps the most important element to the moral equation by which humanitarian intervention in some cases is justified. Because of its view that human beings are a representation of the image of God, one significant ramification is that human beings *qua* human beings possess an intrinsic dignity and thus deserve equal regard. This dignity cannot be revoked by governments or political actors. It follows, then, that

> the spectacle of people being harried, deported, slaughtered, tortured, or starved en masse constitutes a *prima facie* justice claim. Depending on the circumstances on the ground as well as the relative scales of power, an equal regard claim may trigger a [needed] movement toward armed intervention on behalf of the hounded, tortured, murdered, and aggrieved.[7]

Remarkably, humanitarian scholars have identified no less than twenty-one international humanitarian and human rights accords between 1946 and 1990 to illustrate the extent of codification and institutionalization of the humanitarian ideal.[8] These conventions cover a wide range of scenarios in which basic human rights are denied; they include political asylum, international refugee status, prevention and punishment of genocide, political rights of women and children, war crimes, hostage-taking, and torture. In addition, a 2005 United Nations World Summit which brought together various heads of state affirmed the responsibility to protect (R2P) populations from genocide, ethnic cleansing, war crimes, and crimes against humanity. At the heart of R2P is the principle that states must act to prevent mass atrocity and protect population-groups from such risks. Accordingly, when states lack the capacity to take such measures, the international community has a responsibility to provide assistance in doing so. Should peaceful means be inadequate and a state be either unable or unwilling to protect its population, then military intervention is justifiable.

However, at least three phenomena in our day challenge the efficacy of R2P thinking. On the one hand, the increasingly aggressive nature of rogue and totalitarian states such as North Korea, China, Iran, and Russia would currently indicate that the international community lacks either the will or the authority (or both) to apply interventionary assistance. Secondly, failed states and unstable states present a challenge to the free world, not infrequently in our day due to a third factor, namely, a resurgent radicalized Islam that is resistant—and violently so—to any form of Western intervention. Making matters worse, as political philosopher Jean Elshtain has noted,

> all too often UN "peacekeepers" are obliged by their rules of engagement (rules of "disengagement" would be more like it) to stand by as people are being slaughtered. International bodies have tended to avoid using coercive force in order to protect innocent victims of political chaos. As a result, in many cases it will be other political institutions that must respond to the grievances and horrors at hand, provided they can do so in a manner that avoids—to the extent that this is humanly possible—either deepening the injustice at hand or creating new instances of injustice, doubly difficult to sort out.[9]

To intervene or not to intervene? This should always be a difficult question. The use of force in other nations should always induce hesitation and anxiety. At the same time, the mood of Western nations currently is decidedly non-interventionist. The aim of much humanitarian assistance, where it is found, is only to ameliorate symptoms of the catastrophe—for example, bringing food and medical supplies to population groups that are under siege or oppression—rather than to interfere with the siege and oppression at the causal level, that is, at the level of power structures. Nevertheless, non-intervention is not an absolute moral principle. In fact, it is becoming increasingly apparent in the third decade of the 21st century that a regime can do things to people either within its own borders or beyond that are so evil and so thoroughly wrong that another nation or coalition of nations would be justified in intervening. Stated differently, the right of a people or people group to escape evil being inflicted upon them cannot necessarily hinge on whether they themselves possess the strength and resources to defend their own interests.

"Peace," in the end, must be highly qualified, for it is not a social-political good unless it is justly ordered, as the Mafia, pirates, terrorists, and any cartel of organized crime well illustrate. The principles of justice are primordial and pre-political in nature. They existed before states were formed and particular laws were enacted. Justice demands that duty—i.e., moral obligation—comes first (i.e., serving others). This commitment, doing good and avoiding evil, is anchored in natural law moral reasoning, yielding a wedding of justice and charity. In accordance with a "Golden Rule" ethic (on which see below), we treat others as we ourselves wish to be treated. This is the foundation of any morally just interventionary theory and policy.

It has been said that people will not cherish their own freedom if they are unwilling to intervene on behalf of others. Ancient proverbial wisdom beckons people of principle, irrespective of their location in life and history, to intervene on behalf of the traumatized. Such a call bears repeating in our post-consensus, non-interventionist cultural climate:

> If you faint in the day of adversity,
> How small is your strength.
> Rescue those who are being led away toward death,
> Hold back those stumbling toward the slaughter.
> If you say, "But we knew nothing about this,"
> Does not He who weighs the heart consider it?
> Does not He who guards your life
> Not know it?
> And will He not repay each person
> According to what that person has done?[10]

26

How does natural law thinking inform issues of war and peace?

STANDARD VIEWS OF WAR AND peace—for example, that peace is *the absence of war*—place the two in utter opposition. Natural law moral reasoning, which underpins the just war tradition, produces a far more accurate understanding of the relationship between war and peace. Thereby it is understood that a nation goes to war for the purposes of *establishing peace*. War and peace are not two incommensurable worlds that have nothing to do with one another. The just war idea is birthed in the conviction that peace must be justly ordered. After all, the Mafia, pirates, and terrorists all maintain an orbit of illicit "peace"; they do this in order to carry out their business. But such is only the appearance of peace and not authentic. Peace, therefore, is properly understood to be the *tranquillitas ordinis* ("the tranquility of order") described by Augustine in *The City of God*.[1] Justice seeks to guard concord within the context of human community.

Classically speaking, the just war tradition has always had a moral-theoretical foundation, by which the "cardinal" virtue of justice and the "theological" virtue of charity—i.e., neighbor-love—operate in symbiosis.[2] Within natural law moral reasoning, wars are justifiable if they are directed by morally good intentions and actions. Moral reflection—*How might good be done and evil avoided?*—lies at the heart of natural law thinking. This gives rise to a moral norm that admits of no exceptions in the just war ethic: evil may not be done for the sake of good, which translates automatically into the just war axiom that forbids the killing of innocent human beings. The norms of justice determine and guide human beings in terms of the harms that may be inflicted on other people. Reflection on moral norms underpins the entire just war idea, requiring of us that we severely qualify whether or not to undertake war and coercive intervention. Undertaking coercive intervention should only be for the purposes of establishing—or restoring—justice and a *justly-ordered peace*. Hence, a "just war"—or more accurately, a *justified war*—cannot intend anything other than fostering a just peace, the common good, and human flourishing.

Most discussions of just war are anchored in Thomas Aquinas's concise summary in *Summa Theologica*. Aquinas asks "Whether it is always sinful to wage war?"[3] Three principal moral criteria are identified in wrestling with whether or not to prosecute war: legitimate political authority, just cause, and right intention. All other secondary criteria—for example, last resort and reasonable chance of success—may be understood as grounded in and issuing from these primary, organically-linked elements. Moreover, in its application natural law moral reasoning knows no division or separation between the just war categories of *ad bellum* (going to war), *in bello* (conducting war), and *post bellum* (post-war) considerations. All three phases of just war deliberation are organically unified.[4] Historically, just war moral reasoning identifies and unifies the conditions for a war to be just; thereby *all* conditions need to be satisfied. The unity of these conditions, as well as the incorporation of secondary conditions, might rightly be described as implications of a "Golden Rule" ethic.[5] Grounds for going to war by a legitimate political authority must agree with motive or intention in going to war. That is to say, without a proper intention, there exists the very real possibility that "just cause" might merely serve as a pretext for unjust intervention. The need to re-state this basic assumption—namely, that moral criteria of the just war concept are unified—is considerable, given how often in contemporary "just war" debate and discussion the categories of moral criteria are viewed as independent of one another. Against many modern voices on the subject, classic just war thinking assumes an organic unity; natural law moral reasoning requires such.

In bello conditions, thus, are grounded in *ad bellum* considerations and not independent of or in isolation from them. *Jus in bello*, rather, arises from satisfying *ad bellum* conditions in general and the criterion of right intention in particular. A fundamental error of those who advance the "independent" thesis, as Anthony Coates has succinctly and accurately argued, is that it views permission and restraint as opposites rather than as a unity: "The just conduct of war *is* the restrained conduct of war."[6] The means, we might say with Hugo Grotius, are *the end in the making*.[7] We may thus define military necessity in terms of both *permission* and *limitation*. It proceeds in accordance with morally legitimate and just ends and operates within the *in bello* parameters of discrimination and proportionality.[8] By standard utilitarian or consequentialist judgments, proportion or disproportion are impossible to gauge, only reducible to numbers. What natural law reasoning yields in the just war ethic is the justice of doing good and avoiding evil, a determination that is anchored in right intention (discussed below), and as a result refracted through proportionality and discrimination.

To divorce *ad bellum* and *in bello* considerations is to forsake moral judgment and to succumb to a utilitarian scheme that is ungrounded, if not incoherent. Thus, for example, it would be wrong to go to war in the first place if policy exists that violates *ius in bello* from the outset.[9] We are justified, then, in arguing that the unity and integrity of the just war ethic are realized—and concretized—through the criterion of right intention. Right intention unifies *ad bellum* and *in bello* considerations; that is, coercive intervention must serve a morally *good* purpose. It reminds us that ends and means must agree. Morally calibrated means have the effect of "verifying" the justness of an interventionary cause.

In the classical just war tradition, right intention is a primary moral qualification. It can be traced from Augustinian thinking through Aquinas to early-modern just war theorists such as Vitoria, Suárez, and Grotius, resurfacing again, in modified ways, in post-World War II thinking. Augustinian reflection on war is anchored in a full-orbed understanding of charity. Charity is not a mere emotion; rather, it expresses human volition and intention. All people possess and mirror this faculty. Charity is central to Augustinian thinking about coercive force, for charity is the *summum bonum;*[10] it must inform *all* that we do, even going to war. For this reason, in his letter to Boniface, Augustine writes: "Be, then, a peacemaker even while you make war, that by your victory you may lead those whom you defeat to know the desirability of peace."[11]

Relatedly, as noted in Question 13, it is significant that Aquinas's treatment of war in the *Summa* is contextualized not under the rubric of justice but *caritas*. Similarly, Suárez addresses the subject of war as a duty of charity. This, along with his belief that the laws of war are binding on all nations, forms the main argument of his treatise on war found in *De Triplici Virtute Theologica, Fide, Spe, and Charitate* (*On the Three Theological Virtues, Faith, Hope, and Charity*). Charity is best observed in human action, and by its active nature it might rebuke, punish, even permit going to war (though with strict demands). In the conduct of war, neighbor-love prevents us from pressing upon the adversary unrestrained violence. While severity is compatible with justice and charity, cruelty and barbarism are not. Authentic justice entails retribution, but it is guided by human dignity and charity, not driven by retributivism and the spirit of retaliation.

Right intention wrestles not only with what is deemed unjust behavior but what particular reasons inform that injustice. Hence, based on natural law reasoning, just and unjust wars are not two alternative species of the same genus; they are in fact worlds removed, arising from wholly different (and unjust) motivations. Aquinas enunciates quite clearly the character of intention: "The way a moral act is to be classified depends on what is intended, not what goes beyond such an intention, since this is merely incidental."[12] Human beings can intend either good or evil. This natural law assumption manifests itself in the just war idea in the doctrine of double effect, which presupposes that human actions are morally guided and intended. Accordingly, the side effects of intended action—for example, the death of innocents who were not intended to be killed in war—have moral significance. Intellectual honesty requires us to acknowledge that this doctrine and its implications are scarcely intelligible—much less acknowledged—apart from natural law thinking.

Given the moral character of this criterion, right intention concerns the inner quality of an agent's action. (That "agent," it should be specified, includes people at three levels: the politician, the military leader, as well as the combatant.) While we may grant that measuring the "inner quality" of various acts can be difficult, it is nevertheless not impossible. Several characteristics define the essence of right intention: (1) it limits the agent to pursuit of the avowed cause, (2) it requires the agent always to have in mind the ultimate objective of a just and lasting peace, and (3) it necessitates charity, which views people as fellow human beings.[13] Classic just war thinking refuses to divorce justice and charity; the two are not at odds, as they typically are in modern and contemporary thought.[14] To divorce these two virtues is to do irreparable damage to the character of both as well as to alter the very moral foundation upon which just war thinking rests. Justice will always seek to render "what is due" (the classical definition) to human beings and properly order human community,[15] while charity will always seek the means by which to respect human dignity and uphold justice.[16] Justice and charity meld in the just war tradition, and this union can be observed at three distinct levels. At one level, it is both just and charitable to *the criminal element* to prevent them from doing evil. At another level, that hindering is both just and charitable to *those in society or the community of nations* who are watching. Finally, that hindering is just and charitable to *potential offenders* who might be tempted in the future to do evil and undermine the common good.

Relatedly, justice and charity together distinguish between the criminal and the retributive act. Retribution, understood properly, has upper and lower limits. Negatively, it acknowledges the moral repugnance of draconian punishment for petty crimes as well as light punishment for heinous crimes. Positively, it has as its goal a greater social good and takes no pleasure in employing coercive force to guard the common good. Retributive justice thus serves a civilized culture, whether in the domestic or international context. In the end, charity and justice are not at odds; rather, they are two sides of the same ethical coin.[17]

In the Judeo-Christian tradition, charity—which is anchored in love of God and expresses itself as love of neighbor—compels human beings to seek justice for their neighbors. The just war tradition provides the moral means and qualifications to determine how justice, motivated by right intention (charity), is to be sought in the community of nations. This way of thinking is underpinned by the natural law requirement of doing good and avoiding evil.

A final word concerning pacifism is in order. As will be intuited by the reader, the just war and natural law traditions, by virtue of their (a) definition of justice, (b) definition of charity, and (c) understanding of the application of both justice and charity, thus exclude ideological pacifism, the view that coercive or lethal force can *never* serve just and moral purposes. Without question, it is true that most wars are conducted with inadequate grounds for just cause and/or wrong intention. In this sense, pacifists might be correct that such conflicts are "unjust" and immoral. And indeed, as we have argued, evil may not be done in order that "good" might emerge. But the very fact that wars have been wrongly intended or waged historically does not eliminate the need, when and where it occurs, to defend the helpless, prevent genocide or mass murder, protect basic human rights, and help establish (or re-establish) a justly-ordered peace. Such is the goal of *both* justice *and* charity. Such mirrors the

"Golden Rule" ethic; and, one might argue, it manifests the "Good Samaritan" ethic. Pacifists, if they are ethically consistent, deny that such a scenario would *ever* require interventionary efforts by fellow human beings.

Just war moral principles find their grounding in the natural law, with its metaphysical foundation of transcendent good, human design, and human moral responsibility.

27

How did natural law thinking inform early-modern just war thinkers, and why was it important in "new world" discoveries?

THREE EARLY-MODERN THEORISTS WHO PROVIDE important adaptations of just war principles on the basis of an appeal to natural law are Francisco de Vitoria (1480–1546), Francisco Suárez (1548–1617), and Hugo Grotius (1583–1645). By the year 1510, disquieting reports had reached Spain that Native Americans were being denied basic liberty and property. The immediate challenge confronting Vitoria was the Spanish vision to colonize the new peoples of the Americas. Spain was prepared to justify war with Native Americans to possess their land and seek their "conversion" to Christianity. Vitoria's task was to challenge the Spanish king on the basis of the unjust treatment of the American Indians. Against conventional thinking his argument was nothing short of scandalous: neither the king, nor the Pope for that matter, could authorize war against the Indians. Neither religious nor economic nor political reasons alone could make coercion and warfare just, Vitoria argues in *Reflections on the Indians and the Law of War*; Indians and Spaniards have equal rights. The only cause for war that is just is a wrong that is intuited through natural moral law, a wrong that is discernible to all people everywhere through reason and evidence. Going to war based on religious differences or "the spirit of discovery" is not justifiable. No war is just that inflicts upon a population unprovoked injustice. And even were the Indians to attack the Spanish, a just response would be only a defensive response that sought to minimize loss.

In Vitoria are to be found the beginnings of international law, that is, principles governing all nations that are anchored in natural moral law. Vitoria's argument is significant because it acknowledges an international community of independent states or people-groups that have rights, territorial sovereignty, and reciprocal duties as to conduct. Unlike just war thinkers before him, Vitoria grounds the notion of just war not in Christian theology *per se*, but in moral obligation that is known through natural law reasoning. What natural reason has established among the nations is that certain rights and privileges, rooted in justice, are inviolable. Nature establishes a bond between all men; man is not a wolf to his fellow man but another man. If, from the Spanish perspective, principles of just war are applicable to non-Christian peoples, then the rationale, the very basis, for justice and peace could not be narrowly "Christian." Human rights violations and justification for going to war are the same for all people everywhere; they are anchored in moral realities that are unchanging and universally applicable.

The work of Suárez is significant given the degree to which natural law reasoning is applied to political issues such as just war, unjust authority, and how states are to conduct themselves. Whereas civil law is alterable, based on customs and usage, the law of nature is universal and unchanging, governing how human beings as well as nations deal with one another. All aspects of justice flow from this reality. Under the rubric of charity, Suárez scrutinizes the role of the state in both defensive and offensive modes: "A required mode and uniformity as to it [warfare] must be observed at its beginning, during its prosecution and after victory."[1] This mode of moral conformity, Suárez was careful to maintain, is founded upon the natural law and is common to religious and non-religious alike.[2]

Considered the father of modern international law, Grotius confronts the dilemma of just limits to war in much the same way as Vitoria and Suárez. The results of his work would be foundational for just war thinking in the modern era. In his important work *On the Law of War and Peace* (1625), Grotius argues that how nations relate to one another is governed by universally binding moral principles. These are "binding on all kings" and "known through reason."[3] This argument has important implications for both the church and the state, for it places limitations on both. It also places limitations on whether nations may go to war justly and how warfare is to be conducted. Given the reality of the natural law, such rules of military engagement are valid for all people. All in all, among the enduring contributions of Grotius's work, three stand out: (1) "the laws of humanity" that ground international relations and international law, (2) advocacy of universal, natural laws that impose moral and legal restrictions on nations, and (3) clearly articulated rules of international law for the conduct of war that specify *ius ad bellum* (justice in going to war) and *ius in bello* (justice in the conduct of war) requirements.[4]

Vitoria, Suárez, and Grotius understand justice to have deeper roots than mere religious confession. Justice is known through nature and is intuited universally as binding upon all people everywhere. Thus, the "law of nature" becomes a "law to the nations" (*ius gentium*), holding people-groups accountable to the unchanging demands of justice, which orders right relations. As an extension of antecedent Christian moral thinking, just war principles find confirmation in the natural law and are not solely an appeal to religious faith.[5]

28

What is the relationship between religious freedom and the natural law?

EARLIER IT WAS ARGUED THAT there exists a symbiotic relationship between reason and faith. While reason does not replace faith (and in fact *all people* place faith in certain unseen ultimate realities), it is understood to work in concert with faith. Hence, it follows in the wider Judeo-Christian tradition that people cannot be coerced into belief; their convictions must always and everywhere be *voluntary*. Historically, this foundational principle is why religious freedom has been a defining characteristic of not only Western societies but any relatively free society. The reason for this is anchored in the natural law. Because all people have *some* knowledge of moral and spiritual truth, they cannot be coerced into affirming and submitting to particular beliefs. It is only from the natural law that human beings have an awareness of "rights" which we call inalienable and inviolable. Human rights have no foundation apart from natural law, that is, apart from our intrinsic nature.

On what basis, we might ask, could the founders of the American experiment—indeed could anyone—speak of "self-evident truths"? We can grant that such language two centuries removed strikes us as antiquated, when not downright offensive in light of the contemporary *Zeitgeist*. Today it would appear that the presupposition

There are no "self-evident truths" is self-evidently true. But based on moral reality, this assertion is self-contradictory. Moreover, because society must be ordered, indeed justly ordered, every successive generation of citizens must wrestle with the complicated task of working out how certain moral realities bear upon the ordering of society (politics) and civic life (the common good). What's more, every successive generation must decide *if* "civil society" as we have known it is to remain "civil," and on what basis.

Although the United States was not simply the *outcome* of religious belief, it is undeniable that religious belief was important at its founding. As one historian has observed, the distinctive—and normative—feature of the American beginning was neither its religious underpinnings nor its emancipation from them, but rather the intersection and blending of religious conviction and "secular" common sense that manifested itself in moral principle and self-government.[1] The acknowledgement of—and reliance upon—religiously grounded morality, it needs emphasizing in our day, is *not* a violation of the so-called establishment clause, constitutionally speaking. As the founders well knew and believed, religion is a necessary source of moral impulse and thus should be welcomed.[2]

Religious freedom has been called the "first freedom," and this for important reasons. Those belonging to the generation of the American founders spoke and wrote of the "sacred rights of conscience." Their conviction was rooted in their reflection on the European experience and their attempt to avoid both religious coercion on the one hand and social anarchy or the totalitarian temptation on the other. The "first freedom," in its essence, is moral in nature. In a totalitarian scheme, whether ancient or modern, secular or religious in justification, the options are twofold: (1) live according to the dictates of the state (and live a meager life) or (2) live according to the dictates of conscience (and live in prison or die). On occasion in human history there is an in-breaking of human wisdom and a non-totalitarian alternative. This alternative is anchored in religious freedom.

Religious freedom, then, means a freedom to obey one's conscience—a freedom that is neither coercive nor exclusionary. Authentic freedom suggests that in society a healthy dialogue between civil and religious institutions is both possible and desirable, even when this dialogue is at times messy and difficult. The Frenchman Alexis de Tocqueville was given a vivid (and enduring) impression upon visiting the United States two generations after its founding, causing him to write, "From the beginning, politics and religion were in accord, and they have not ceased to be so since."[3] It is noteworthy that only thirty years after Thomas Jefferson had served as foreign minister in France, Tocqueville describes the relationship between religion and the state not as a "wall"—that is, something "high" and "impregnable" as 20th-century Supreme Court rulings have understood it—but, we might say, as a sort of "fence," by which interaction and protection are facilitated while acknowledging built-in distinctions between the two realms. Religious freedom supports rather than undermines republican democracy. While we may grant that the U.S. Constitution is "secular" to the extent that it does not make direct or formal reference to God, the founders, in representative charter documents elsewhere, utilize language of "self-evident truths," the "law of nature," and "nature's God." They believed that "all men are created equal" and that "all men are endowed with certain inalienable rights." This language was contemporary parlance for the natural moral law, and it drew from a broadly theistic framework that was assumed to anchor responsible citizenship.

Religious freedom, it needs emphasizing, is not merely the immunity from coercion (which it is). Most fundamentally, it is an ability to order one's own choices in accordance with truth.[4] At bottom, religious freedom is *the condition for the pursuit of truth*. At bottom, threats to religious freedom guarantee potential threats to other civil liberties as well. For this reason, religious freedom is accurately—and properly—called the "first freedom," the *fons et origo* of all other freedoms and rights. It is the *most basic* of human goods, for it gives meaning to all others. Coercion, by contrast, dishonors a person's dignity as a free and rational moral agent. Moreover, coercion can operate in two directions: it can force conformity to religious belief on the one hand and it can force the exclusion and/or denial of religious belief on the other.

Chief among the foundational principles of a decent society is the natural-law requisite to do good—wherever and however possible—and to avoid doing evil or harm. At the base of any decent society, thus, is its commitment to respect the human person and to protect basic human goods. Where there is no presumed human dignity, as several Questions in this volume have enunciated, there can be no environment in which justice, the "common good," or human flourishing can exist. This natural law presumption is on display, for example, in the language of Article 1 of the United Nations Declarations on Human Rights, adopted in December of 1948 by the General Assembly of the United Nations, which states: "All human beings are born free and equal in dignity and rights. They are endowed with reason and conscience and should act towards one another in a spirit of brotherhood." In its preamble, the UDHR refers to "the inherent dignity" of "all members of the human family," the implications of which are spelled out in Article 18:

> Everyone has the right to freedom of thought, conscience and religion; this right includes freedom to change his religion or belief, and freedom, either alone or in community with others and in public or private, to manifest his religion or belief in teaching, practice, worship and observance.[5]

Most of the American founders were part of this tradition, which acknowledged "self-evident truths" and drank from its resources.

Religious freedom, it needs emphasizing, is not the exclusive reserve of religious believers. It should be the concern of all people, since, as a foundational element of a constitutional state, its denial has the effect of encroaching on all fundamental freedoms and rights. These freedoms and rights are "pre-political"; for this reason, governments have a moral obligation to respect and protect those freedoms and rights. And because they are pre-political, anchored in an awareness of the natural law, they are not created or constructed, but rather *discovered.*

29

How does the parable of the "Good Samaritan" mirror the natural law?

The parable of the "Good Samaritan" (Luke 10:25–37) retains its familiarity even among people who espouse no particular religious faith. The story lines are well known and found in the Gospel according to Luke, which is the only Gospel narrative in the New Testament to record Jesus's use of this parable.[1] This may well be the case because Luke generally includes a significant amount of material having to do with Jesus's interaction with Gentiles (i.e., non-Jews).

The context of the parable helps clarify for the reader its relationship to the natural law and moral "first principles." A certain lawyer wishes to test Jesus by raising the question of life's basic obligations: "What shall I do…?" Jesus's answer, in the form of a question, is instructive: "What is written in the law, and what is your reading of it?" The lawyer responds, correctly, according to the double command: "You shall love God and love your neighbor as yourself." Jesus commends him for his response both to love God and love his neighbor. However, the text indicates that the lawyer "wanted to justify himself," and this expresses itself in a second qualifying question: "And who is my neighbor, after all?" In order to answer the lawyer's second question, Jesus proceeds with the parable.

A certain man was traveling between Jerusalem and Jericho, a distance of roughly eighteen miles. As it happens, this particular route, though descending through conditions that were desert-like, was nevertheless used by many people—military personnel, those visiting Jerusalem on pilgrimages, merchants, and various travelers. The nature of the terrain, however, resulted both in its travelers being open prey for thieves and bandits and in those criminals finding readily accessible escape alternatives. Surely Jesus's introductory words to the parable—"A man was going down from Jerusalem to Jericho, when he fell into the hands of robbers"—resonated with his hearers; they knew all too well that this route was susceptible to misfortune.

But there is more to the story, for it is infused with racial tensions and prejudices that would have been normative in this part of the first-century world. Two Jews—a priest and a Levite—happened to come upon the victim who was left for dead. Priests and Levites, we need reminding, would have constituted the leadership of the Jewish people in the first century and thus would have been accorded respect by all. Alas, both men, after discovering the victim, "passed by [him] on the other side" of the road. A third passer-by, however, in discovering the victim "took pity on him." This traveler, as it happens, was a Samaritan.

While Luke's Gospel adds no relevant ethnic commentary, the animosity between Jews and Samaritans was legendary, and this animosity has its roots in Israel's history, part of which has to do with racial intermarrying (cf. Deut. 7:3–5) and the years of Israel's exile.[2] One episode during these years records that Samaritans were part of a combined resistance to the rebuilding of Jerusalem following the nation's Babylonian captivity (Nehemiah 4). By Jesus's day, Samaritans would have been regarded by Jews as a mixed race devoted to semi-pagan religious practices.

If this history between the two peoples were not enough, Jesus adds vivid detail to the parable in a manner that probably stunned his listeners. Consider the specifics of the Samaritan's aid: he took pity on the victim; he disinfected and bandaged his wounds; he loaded the man on his own donkey and took him to an inn, caring for him; he paid the innkeeper to look after him; he left instructions for the man's care and promised, upon return, to reimburse the innkeeper for any additional expenses.

The parable ends with Jesus questioning the lawyer: "Which of these three [the priest, the Levite, or the Samaritan] do you think was a neighbor to the man who fell into the hands of robbers?" The lawyer, with scarcely any wiggle-room, answers, "The one who had mercy on him." And to this, Jesus responds, "Go and do likewise."

The parable of the "Good Samaritan" teaches that authentic neighbor-love must transcend the typical human boundaries of race and ethnicity, religion, and social standing.[3] In its context, the parable is intended to illustrate charity. With other words, it represents the application of Jesus's "Golden Rule" ethic: *do to others as you would have them do to you.* This is none other than the natural law: *do good and avoid doing evil.* Such is the basis for all human action. The "Golden Rule" simply concretizes the natural law, and the parable of the "Good Samaritan" concretizes the implications of the "Golden Rule."

In a fitting way, ethicist Paul Ramsey has this to say about the character of neighbor-love: "No authority on earth can withdraw from 'social charity' and 'social justice' their intrinsic and justifiable tendencies to rescue from dereliction."[4] Ramsey, however, wishes to probe the nature of "Good Samaritan" ethics further. It was a work of charity—or, "social charity"—for the "Good Samaritan" to offer help to the man who fell among thieves and was left to die. This Ramsey acknowledges. But he does not leave the implications of the parable there where the Gospel of Luke does; he extends its ramifications:

> But one step more, it may have been a work of charity for the innkeeper to hold himself ready to receive beaten and wounded men, and for him to have conducted his business so that he was solvent

> enough to extend credit to the Good Samaritan. By another step it would have been a work of charity, and not of justice alone, to maintain and serve in a police patrol on the Jericho road to prevent such things from happening. By yet another step, it might well be a work of charity to resist, by force of arms, any external aggression against the social order that maintains the police patrol along the road to Jericho.[5]

Acknowledging that he has taken the ramifications of the parable beyond what is recorded in Luke's Gospel narrative, Ramsey concludes with a riveting question: *What do you think Jesus would have required of the Samaritan if he had come upon the scene while the robbers were actually attacking and plundering the victim?* Ramsey concludes with the following point about charity and the "Golden Rule":

> While Jesus taught that a disciple in his own case should turn the other cheek, he did not enjoin that his disciples should lift up the face of another oppressed man for *him* to be struck again on *his* other cheek. It is no part of the work of charity to allow this to continue to happen.[6]

When even people of faith encounter choices that need to be made between the perpetrator(s) of injustice and the many victims thereof, the latter are always to be preferred and protected, even when and where coercive or armed force is necessary. All too often, whether domestically in the legal/criminal justice system or in foreign affairs, the forgotten or neglected people are the real victims of crime. To defend them, as Ramsey insisted, is a work of charity. In its application, this is what the natural law requires.

30

How does "Golden Rule" ethics mirror the natural law?

In the previous Question we considered the wonderfully illuminating example of the "Good Samaritan" ethic. It is an ethic that is universal, free of socio-cultural prejudice, and attendant to basic human need. This is the essence of the natural law—doing good and avoiding doing evil or harm. In Jesus's teaching we find a similar expression of natural law thinking, one which exposes the internal roots of human behavior in terms of motivation. The "Golden Rule" ethic, taught by people as diverse as Plato and Jesus and on display in other world- and life-views, perfectly captures the inner dimension of virtue. In truth, the very fact that various world-views affirm the notion of a "Golden Rule" attests to the wider argument that it is an expression of the natural law.

The natural lawyer is less taken by the differences in moral codes and customs found among diverse peoples around the world than by what is shared in common among these diverse people-groups. *Why* is it that murder and thievery and fraud and incest and disrespect toward elders are unacceptable, and *universally* so? Why can the moral principle we call the "Golden Rule" not only be intelligible but accepted everywhere at all times by all people? Different people and cultures, of course, have used different means to describe what we call "the natural moral law," as the very first Question in this volume observed.

The basic positive statement of the "Golden Rule," known to all, is "Do unto others as you would have them do to you." Its negative corollary expresses the same moral principle: "Do not do unto others what you would not want done to you." There is yet a third corollary of the "Golden Rule," one that has meaningful application in the context of both criminal justice and humanitarian intervention. That is, "Do not allow to be done to others what you would not want done to you." Consider, for a moment the implications of this principle for foreign affairs. Where a nation—or coalition of nations—has the wherewithal to prevent, retard, or stop outrageous socio-political evil from happening, a "Golden Rule" approach to policy—one in which defense, protection, or preservation is motivated by "neighbor-love"—is the moral and political responsibility of that nation or group of nations. Where relatively free nations are able to inhibit evil, based on our common humanity and the natural law they have the moral obligation to inhibit it.

This priority of "neighbor-love" can be measured by our commitment to human rights. We wish for others the very same freedoms attending natural rights that we ourselves enjoy. As has been argued frequently throughout this volume justice and neighbor-love underpin a basic commitment to guard and protect fellow human beings in a global context. This moral duty to protect others begins with the sacred rights of conscience—what we call religious freedom.

The viewpoint being espoused here is that humanitarian intervention is justified in *some*, even when not all, cases. The reason for this is that the purpose of government is to protect and secure basic human rights of all people by virtue of their personhood, worth, and dignity. Those regimes that violate these basic rights in the end forfeit their own right to be protected by international law. State sovereignty is not an intrinsic value, as is human personhood. Sovereignty must serve human ends and human needs. A commitment to respect basic human rights results in the duty to assist and rescue others at reasonable cost to ourselves, and, where possible, assist in the social-political reconstruction of those victims' lives. This is none other than the "Golden Rule" ethic: we do for others what we wish that they would do for us, if we stood in the same need.

In this regard, the just war ethic allows us to conceptualize the assistance of a "neighbor" in need. It does so through its moral qualifying and justifying the use of limited coercive force. Our duties to the "neighbor" in need, moreover, are not limited to family, ethnicity, or politics; they extend to any who stand in gross need. These duties, as many Questions in this volume have argued, are "pre-political," anchored in an awareness of a higher law, the natural law, from which any form of civil or positive law must derive.[1]

31

Why is moral law "pre-political"?

In the previous Question it was argued that, based on natural law moral reasoning and our common humanity, human beings have moral duties and responsibilities to the "neighbor," particularly that neighbor (or neighbors) standing in need. Those needs, moreover, are not limited to family, ethnicity, or politics but extend to *whoever stands in gross need* in the community. Such duties, as this volume has consistently argued, can be described as "pre-political" inasmuch as they are anchored in an awareness of a higher law, the natural law.[1] And if we extend this way of thinking beyond our local communities to the community of nations, we are then able to posit a legitimate grounding for "universal human rights." Human rights—and foremost the sacred rights of conscience—are pre-political. They do not originate in the state. The notion of rights originates in the nature of man, not the state or legality or political authority.

Family, likewise, is pre-political in its essence; it is prior to the state. For this reason, the state may never legitimately determine the ends and functions of the family, even when it has the duty to protect the family where the family is threatened either by outside factors or its own delinquency. Because the very nature of the family is anchored in nature and thus is pre-political, it possesses a relative autonomy in terms of rights and privileges. These rights are not conferred upon the family by the law or by the state; they are, rather, *recognized*. The sacred nature of the marriage covenant between husband and wife exists independent of positive law. In the same way a breach of marital rights and privileges through unfaithfulness and adultery stands as unjust—an injustice that exists independent of positive law. The very meaning and fulfillment of marriage and family exist wholly apart from political authority and the state; their rights and duties are grounded in the natural law and thus are pre-political in nature.

It is here that we observe once more the manner in which the natural law is given summary expression by the Decalogue. The precepts of the Decalogue simply outline the basic contours of our social relations and obligations—relations and obligations that are grounded not in the state, not in positive law, and not in culture, but in the natural law. Thus, they are antecedent to law, the state, and culture.

In Question 10, we noted the remarkable dialogue between the renowned philosopher Jürgen Habermas and Joseph Cardinal Ratzinger one year prior to the latter becoming Pope Benedict XVI. The two were asked to address the following question: "What are the pre-political foundations of a democratic state?" Habermas, as previously noted, answered in surprising ways, acknowledging that in our "post-secular" cultural moment the "sacred" and the secular" cannot—and should not—be partitioned or separated. Dual respect demands that citizens acknowledge the "rational" character of public disagreement. In the public and political arena, then, this means that a naturalistic or secularistic worldview does not trump religious views of ultimate reality. In practical terms, according to Habermas, this means that "neutrality" of the state should not be interpreted as excluding the religious viewpoint but rather that every citizen has the same ethical freedom—a freedom that is incompatible with militant secularism. In fact, Habermas conceded, "a liberal political culture can expect that the secularized citizens play their part in the endeavors to translate relevant contributions from the religious language into a language that is accessible to the public as a whole."[2]

Part of Ratzinger's response to Habermas was to accentuate the fact that neither science and technology nor politics and the state can address our most pressing moral questions. The matter of doing good or doing evil—i.e., making moral decisions—is pre-political and pre-cultural. Only philosophy and religion can address these basic questions. The task of politics, by contrast, Ratzinger insisted, is to structure the use of power in a moral and meaningful way. Law must be rooted in its antecedent, the moral law. Freedom without morally-grounded law is nothing less than anarchy, which ends up destroying authentic freedom. Moreover, Ratzinger noted, there will always arise suspicion of the law and rebellion against it when and where "law itself appears to be no longer the expression of a justice that is at the service of all, but rather the product of arbitrariness and legislative arrogance on the part of those who have the power for it."[3]

This, for Ratzinger, presses upon society an antecedent question: What is the *genesis* of law? The answer cannot be majoritarian opinion, for the simple reason that "majorities" themselves can be wrong; they can be "blind or unjust, as history teaches us very plainly."[4] Rather, there must be "self-subsistent" values, pre-political beliefs, and universal moral principles that are rationally discerned and inviolable—values that inform basic "human rights," upon which no one can infringe.[5] Ratzinger is led to conclude that there is a law that is *discovered*, not created. It is a law that transcends legal systems and cultures, a law binding on human beings in their mutual relationships and informing them of their moral obligations.[6] This law—the natural law—"transcends the confessional borders of faith by establishing reason as the instrument whereby law can be posited in common."[7] And because it seeks a rational basis for developing a moral consensus in a pluralistic cultural context, the natural law remains central to dialogue and debate between religious and secular interlocutors and communities. Without the natural law, there are no "human rights," Ratzinger insists. Without human moral obligations, human rights, in truth, cannot exist. Whence, then, come these basic moral obligations?

32

What was the role of religion and natural law thinking among America's founders?

Religious expression and religious freedom, it is accurate to say, flourished in the early American republic. The reason for this is not hard to grasp: from the start, religion and democracy were not co-belligerents; they were, rather, close friends. Significantly, late in his career James Madison testified on multiple occasions not only that religion had been thriving since the revolution ("with an increase in religious instruction") but also that religious freedom had proven itself to be the fruit of non-establishment and non-coercive tendencies of the state.[1] Moreover, Tocqueville, cited in a previous Question, concluded from his visit to the U.S., "Religion, which among Americans never mixes directly in the government of society, should therefore be considered as *the first of their political institutions.*"[2] Careful to note those social-cultural "mores" as well as mental habits that distinguished the Americans, Tocqueville writes, "From the beginning politics and religion were in accord, and they have not ceased to be so since."[3] One might conclude from a reading of Tocqueville's *Democracy in America*, which offers ample critique of the possibility of a "majoritarian tyranny," that human beings—and we Americans—will either be "governed" or "self-governed." Tyranny, at bottom, manifests itself where and when a society must be "governed," which is always oppressive in character.

In Question 6 above we observed how Locke's writings undergirded the American "experiment in ordered liberty." His definition of natural law was presumed by America's founders in their attempts to ground the new nation's establishment; thus it is worth repeating:

> By the foundation of natural law we understand that which supports and upon which are erected, as upon a foundation, all other precepts of this law, even the less obvious, and that from which [these precepts] can be deduced in some manner. As a consequence, these derive their entire force and their binding power from this [foundation] because they are in agreement with primary and, as it were, fundamental law, which is the rule and measure of all other laws which depend upon it.[4]

Locke helps the founders in fusing the two elements of religion and natural law reasoning. As noted in several previous Questions, the founders' and framers' appeals to "Laws of Nature and Nature's God" are mirrored in those "self-evident truths" spelled out in the Declaration of Independence. Moreover, the fact that the framers of America's charter documents speak of human beings possessing certain inalienable rights mirrors their debt to Lockean thinking.[5]

Political philosopher Hadley Arkes has argued, with considerable persuasion, that the American founders' understanding of the matter of "self-evident truths" was grasped and confirmed by few as it was with the clarity and eloquence of Alexander Hamilton in *The Federalist*, No. 31. It is worth citing Hamilton in this regard at length:

> In disquisitions of every kind there are certain primary truths, or first principles, upon which all subsequent reasonings must depend. These contain an internal evidence which, antecedent

> to all reflection or combination, command the assent of the mind... Of this nature are the maxims in geometry that the whole is greater than its parts; that things equal to the same are equal to one another; that two straight lines cannot enclose a space; and that all right angles are equal to each other. Of the same nature are these other maxims in ethics and politics, that there cannot be an effect without a cause; that the means ought to be proportioned to the end; that every power ought to be commensurate with its object; that there ought to be no limitation of a power destined to effect a purpose which is itself incapable of limitation.[6]

That the founders grasped the "first principles" or "primary truths" of natural law, as Hamilton does, is further confirmed by their belief that "All men are created equal." This awareness of equality and dignity does not arise from mere human experience, experimentation, or induction.[7] It is a moral truth that transcends the human experience, human customs, and social location. It is anchored in the awareness of the Creator, whose moral character is on display in human beings by virtue of their having been created in his image.[8]

One curiosity—indeed, a lacunae in traditional scholarship—needs accounting. In standard accounts of the founders' political thinking, there seems to exist a reticence to acknowledge one of the most conspicuous features of the founders' understanding of human nature. It concerns their *overwhelming* conviction that political power must be constrained and limited, and this due to the fact that human beings, in theological language, are "fallen" and "sinful." Two illustrations serve to make this point. One is a series of reflections offered by George Washington to John Jay—the latter being a neglected if not forgotten founder—in August of 1786 ("Deficiencies of the Confederation") in which Washington expresses concerns about the need to balance coercive power and human freedom. He notes:

> We have probably had too good an opinion of human nature in forming our confederation. Experience has taught us, that men will not adopt and carry into execution, measures the best calculated for their own good without the intervention of a coercive power.[9]

Commenting on human nature, Washington concludes, "Perfection falls not to the share of mortals."[10] The combined experience of leading American troops in the Revolutionary War and an American presidency would surely inculcate this moral realism in America's first leader.

Yet another example of the founders' view of human nature lies with James Madison. A curious fact often overlooked in scholarly treatments of Madison is that his mentor was John Witherspoon, the only clergyman among the signers of the Declaration of Independence.[11] Madison appears to have shared Witherspoon's thinking regarding both the disestablishment of religion and the perils of unrestrained authority based on human nature. A serious reading of Madison suggests that his anti-establishment sentiments were rooted in the virtue of religious freedom and the "sacred rights" of conscience. Indeed, Madison appears to have been as much an heir to the Christian tradition, with deep sensitivities to religious tolerance, as he was a "son of the Enlightenment." Unquestionably, the area of shared understanding between Madison and Witherspoon—a belief in human fallenness, owing to natural law and Christian moral reasoning—has received far less scholarly attention than their shared anti-establishment sentiments. Yet it is fundamental to understanding Madison.

Take, for example, Madison's oft-cited observation, recorded in *The Federalist* No.51, that "if men were angels, no government would be necessary." As the context indicates, Madison was a moral realist:

> If angels were to govern men, neither external nor internal controls on government would be necessary. In framing a government

> which is to be administered by men over men, the great difficulty lies in this: you must first enable the government to control the governed; and in the next place oblige it to control itself. A dependence on the people is, no doubt, the primary control on the government; but experience has taught mankind the necessity of auxiliary precautions.[12]

Here we may justifiably ask, *whence comes this understanding of human nature*? What is the source of this moral "realism"? Such is by no means the product of "Enlightenment rationalism," the assumption of which undergirds most scholarly treatments of this era. Such anthropological wisdom, coupled with the founders' and framers' reflection on (and reaction to) European excesses, caused the founding generation to think and act with a moral realism anchored in natural law thinking and religious conviction that commends itself to every generation, including our own.

In his important volume *The Religious Roots of the First Amendment*, Nicholas P. Miller argues that the Protestant theological commitment to the right of personal conscience in religious matters in fact propelled the ideas of both religious liberty and disestablishment in the early modern era. The burden of Miller's argument is to show religion's ideological contribution to the political culture of the day and to insist that the notion of religious freedom is owing to religion and not the Enlightenment, even when the two are overlapping in their influence and defects.

The typical story line, as summarized by Miller, is that in the 18th century reason triumphed over faith. But this is mistaken, he insists. Rather, a more accurate telling of the American founding is that faith and reason worked in symbiosis, not mutual exclusion. In early America, the disestablishment impulse was decidedly *religious* in nature, not secularist—or even narrowly political, for that matter. Noted presidential scholar and historian William Lee Miller (a "Miller" unrelated to the former) stands in agreement, framing the matter helpfully: "America's tradition of religious liberty is not the work of Jefferson…and the Enlightenment alone, nor simply the result of expediency and necessity." While "[t]he stream of liberty does not run straight from the Protestant Reformation, or from the main body of the Puritan movement in England, or from the largest group of Puritan settlers in America," Miller insists that it "does, however, run crookedly, as it were, from those sources, a tributary that grows."[13]

The historical record shows that the "second wing" of the American founding—a wing that accurately understands human nature and is underpinned by religious conviction—is owing to biblical religion.[14] Consequently, as one thoughtful observer of American history has written,

> One can see in the American founding…the workings of a God who wishes to be worshiped in spirit and truth, in the honesty of conscience within, and in uncoerced exercise in the public square of daily life, among men and women who are free, independent, self-reliant, cooperative with one another in civil society, and responsible for their own destiny.[15]

This posture, doubtless, was the consequence of the founders' understanding of the role of religion in a free society and their being grounded in natural law thinking, which presumes that human beings are capable of doing good or doing evil.

33

How does natural law reasoning interact with various worldview assumptions and one's view of ultimate reality?

THE VERY ATTEMPT OF THE present volume to address issues of "ultimate reality," moral law and moral reasoning, faith and reason, religious conviction and the public square, or commonalities among diverse cultures requires that we speak to the wider question of worldview. Here we enter the world of ideas, bumping into the philosophical roots of our most cherished beliefs. Here we are also entering the little-examined realm of baseline assumptions, which inform and undergird every world- and life-view. It is these underlying assumptions—often unspoken or unidentified—which give rise to the public positions that people take on most political and ethical issues.

A "worldview"—and here I shall assume the interchangeability of the terms "worldview," "world- and life- view," "ultimate philosophy," and "philosophy of life"—can be described simply as a structure of thinking that attempts to make sense of the surrounding world. An awareness of this structure is important for the simple fact that in a pluralist society one must be able to offer justification both for his or her view of ultimate reality and for those positions held regarding deeply significant moral issues. To avoid the need for such justification is either to be intellectually dishonest or to descend into the realm of the irrational. Moreover, we live in a world in which we encounter many world- and life-views. This confronts us with the need to understand the nature of pluralism.[1]

A worldview can be identified and understood by a basic structure. Constituent elements of any world- or life-view include, at minimum, (1) an understanding of the nature of the physical cosmos and its origins, (2) a theory of human nature and its constitution, and (3) the nature of ethical values and human behavior. Every worldview, we may argue, is an expression of *faith*; that is to say, every world- and life-view is religious in nature. Accordingly, people base their beliefs, their assumptions, and their actions on that which cannot be demonstrated with absolute, one-hundred-percent degree of certainty. Because all people have ultimate beliefs, all people are exercising *faith* in one way or another. Whether these beliefs or assumptions are *rational* (and thus *worthy* of faith and trust) is, of course, a different question. Our disputes over whether particular worldviews are rational or irrational must, in the end, be measured by an appeal to reason, evidence, logic, and objectivity.

For the sake of illustration, one may argue that there are two primary competing world- or life-views views regnant in Western culture at present.[2] One is religious and broadly Christian, though receding; the other is secularist and ascendant, what we may call secularism, materialism, naturalism, or metaphysical naturalism. The former is theistic, with corresponding views of design and purpose standing behind cosmic and human creation and with a corresponding understanding of ethical norms anchored in the natural law. The latter is built on the assumption that all of reality is material in nature. Because of its influence in the public sphere, notably as it concerns significant moral issues, it deserves our focus.

The metaphysical assumption of secularism/naturalism is that all of reality—whether cosmic or human—is physical and mirroring the interplay of energy and matter. Both the wider universe and human life exist as random phenomena as the result of evolutionary processes. Because any notion of a creator is ruled out, there is technically no design or purpose. Consequently, religious beliefs are rigidly excluded from the public sphere, under the assumptions that (a) religion is "unreasonable" and dangerous to democracy (and thus should be kept private) and (b) church and state require complete separation. Secularist approaches to law and social policy tend to be utilitarian and rights-oriented (as opposed to duty-obligated) in nature.

In light of the aforementioned understanding of a "worldview," it is accurate to maintain that secularism is "religious" in nature, given its metaphysical assumptions about the universe, human nature, ethics, law, and public life.[3] These assumptions, it needs emphasizing, are based on *faith*; that is, people are firmly committed to these beliefs which cannot be *proved* but which nevertheless guide and inform their actions and behavior. While secularism as a world- and life-view is not new, its influence has increased substantially over the last two centuries as a result of concerted efforts by influential people in the culture. One sociologist of note chronicles the "secular revolution" in the U.S. as it has spread to encompass every major "gate-keeping" element in American society—for example, in science, in all levels of education, in law and political theory, in social and public policy, in spirituality and therapeutic culture, and in various media forms.[4] Secularism/metaphysical naturalism has not occurred, then, by accident; rather, it has been promoted by people who have been committed to various moral, social, and political objectives. At bottom, those committed to the secular/materialist vision share one thing in common: namely, a rejection of the natural law assumptions of a shared human nature and universal moral norms.

34

Why is teleology important to natural law reasoning?

AQUINAS DESCRIBES HUMAN INCLINATIONS AS ordered toward proper ends—toward the proper *telos*—by means of human reasoning and the exercise of the will.[1] Reason and conscience in human beings give evidence of the natural law as humans live their daily lives and respond to various circumstances. Aquinas is simply advancing what Aristotle had taught: ends subsist in human "nature" and are guided by right intention. The virtuous life is the goal of the human person.

At the same time, without the observance of rules or "laws" in human life to properly guide us, argued Matthew Hale, no one can attain any desired ends. Hale's rationale is this: in virtually all natural realms of existence, rules are requisite. Thus, for example, for the grammarian, rules of words and composition must govern. For the rhetorician, the rules of expression, persuasion, and gesture are paramount. For the logician, rules for argumentation must guide. And for the physician, rules for prescribing certain medicinal and health-related measures are normative. Regarding the "laws" of health, no one is required to obey or follow these prescriptions; they can be ignored. And indeed the physician has no authority to inflict any sort of penalty when and where the patient refuses such prescription, other than to allow his patient to undergo the fruits of his or her unwillingness.[2]

Again we are reminded of how important the matter of design is to natural law thinking. Everything within us and everything we do has a purpose. For this reason, when the natural law theorist speaks of "natural inclinations," some clarity is needed. A natural inclination, in the present context, is not merely what I or what we collectively desire. Rather, in accordance with Thomas Aquinas, we may distinguish between two understandings of "natural inclinations": between those inclinations that, based on our design, are properly oriented toward human flourishing and "the good," and those that have been "oriented" in an improper way.[3] Desires themselves are a neutral entity; that is to say, they can be pursued or used for either proper or improper ends. Most of us, to illustrate, can acknowledge that an addiction—*any* addiction—is wrong; hence, our desires need qualifying and filtering as it were. Human desires or inclinations are only meaningful when they are rightly ordered, when they express our design, which indicates the very reason for which we exist.[4] In the words of one natural lawyer, "what matters is not how we 'incline'—[for] that may need correction. What matters is how we 'naturally' incline—[which is to say] by the blueprint, by the layout, by the plan."[5]

Human desires and inclinations, thus, must be ordered, and this ordering is according to the good, i.e., that for which human beings exist.[6] Natural law reasoning points us in the direction of that for which we were designed.[7]

35

How does natural law reasoning view materialism?

The term "materialism" as it is being used in this Question can be understood in the sense of naturalism, or metaphysical naturalism, as was argued in a previous Question.[1] Because we have referred regularly in this volume to "nature," certain qualifications are in order. Most natural lawyers are theists and thus use the term to refer to human *design* and the way that we are created. But to the non-theist or the metaphysical naturalist, "nature" means something very different. Absent a "designer" in the universe, naturalists reject any line of reasoning that would posit first cause, "intelligent design," purpose and meaning, and, at bottom, a transcendent source of "the good." Thus, the Darwinian explanation: "the first foundation or origin of the moral sense lies in the social instincts... and these instincts no doubt were primarily gained, as in the case of the lower animals, through natural selection."[2]

The difference between the two understandings of "nature" yields unbridgeable differences in terms of how we might approach ethics. And for good reason. Morality becomes adaptation, since no intrinsic moral principles or laws exist in the universe. Ethics becomes, in the famous words of two renowned evolutionary thinkers, "an illusion fobbed off on us by our genes to get us to cooperate" just as "our biology enforces its ends...by making us think that there is an objective higher code," which alas does not exist.[3] How "getting us to cooperate," "enforcing" particular ends, and "making us think" actually occurs we are not told. At the very least, for the metaphysical naturalist to use this sort of language strikes the average person as freeloading, requiring that will, purposes, ends, and meaning originate at the material, rather than the non-material, level. If metaphysical materialism is true, then it seems that there is no way of actually *knowing* that it is true. And remaining unanswered is why *any* sort of moral duties or obligations even exist among human beings.[4] Largely missing from contemporary scientific discussions and materialist accounts of human behavior is what biology, genetics, and neuroscience are *incapable* of telling us about ourselves—for example, why the beauty of diverse life forms exists, why human beings behave as they do, why human beings are given to moral reflection, and why they agonize over "good" and "evil."[5] In the end, a biologically-explained ethics on the part of the metaphysical naturalist cannot offer a satisfactory account of the "Good Samaritan," since "Good Samaritans" are maladaptive and would tend to be eliminated due the fact that natural selection works against them.

The natural lawyer, by contrast, recognizes that materialism/naturalism is a metaphysic itself; that is, it posits answers to the ultimate issues of life and hence is comprehensive as a world- and life-view. At the same time, the natural lawyer recognizes—and defends—the moral significance of "nature." This, of course, acknowledges the importance of a philosophy and theology of nature (which is one of the reasons Aquinas remains a guiding light in discussions of natural law).[6] The natural lawyer insists on the intelligibility of nature, which is to say that nature can be comprehended by human reason. Reason is not divorced from how and why we function as we do. Reflection, contemplation, discernment, and judgment are all rational processes, even when the proper use of reason—toward moral ends—does not reduce merely to the intellect.[7]

In contrast to the metaphysical naturalist, natural law reasoning presupposes a teleological conception of human nature, as was argued in the previous Question. This is to say that human inclinations and actions are ordered toward proper ends—toward the proper *telos*—by means of human reasoning and the exercise of the will. Reason and conscience combine in the human experience to give evidence of the natural law as humans live their daily lives and respond to various circumstances. Again, it is worth observing that thinkers as diverse as Aristotle and Aquinas agree in this regard: ends subsist in human "nature" and are guided by right intention. The virtuous life is the goal of the human person, irrespective of where that person is located in the sweep of human history and human culture.

The metaphysical naturalist, then, rejects at its root any teleological notion of the natural law, for the "god" of the evolutionary process is strictly material in conception, and therefore immanent. While an examination of recent dialogue and interaction between evolutionary theorists and theists or "creationists" takes us well beyond the scope of the present question, it is accurate to say that most natural lawyers have presupposed some argument from design, whether of the entire cosmos or human creatures. Aquinas's understanding of design and ends as it concerns non-human creation is instructive:

> Nothing however that lacks awareness tends to a goal, except under the direction of someone with awareness and with understanding; the arrow, for example, requires an archer. Everything in nature, therefore, is directed to its goal by someone with understanding, and this we call "God."[8]

Just as "the arrow requires an archer," not only human nature but physical nature as a whole is directed toward particular ends. Even when evolutionary theorists and biologists may insist that design indeed *does* exist around us, that "design" is not understood as *externally* generated. After all, naturalism is a metaphysical view; therefore, we are confronted by those questions anchored in "first principles." Whose purposes? Toward what end? What functions? And why those particular functions? Such queries find their home in natural law thinking.

If materialists are correct that moral impulses—be they virtuous or vicious—have a foremost biological and genetic explanation, we thereby invite the end to "civility," "criminal justice," and "Good Samaritan" or "Golden Rule" ethics as traditionally understood and practiced. The reason for this is simply that the concepts of natural law, moral agency, innocence over against guilt, and human culpability disappear (see the following Question). If people cannot be held responsible for their actions based on moral principle, moral norms, and some awareness of those norms, then cultivating virtue is an impossibility and it is only a matter of time before society as a whole collapses, at which point a new form of tyranny surfaces.

36

What are factors contributing to natural law's eclipse?

THE PRESENT VOLUME UNDERSTANDS—AND HAS sought to present—natural law reasoning as a tradition, that is, a kind of heritage or endowment of moral first principles that, based on *human design* and our *common humanity*, undergirds the entirety of human civilization. It is not a "tradition" in the sense of being culturally contained or culturally specific—for example, a Western or Oriental or even a medieval cultural tradition. Rather, it is a tradition uniting *human* culture. Much like a river, which is characterized by various lakes, eddies, inlets, and tributaries yet is *one and unified* at any point along the way, so too we might characterize the natural law tradition.

At the same time, the reader of this volume will get the strong impression that to discuss the natural law idea is to become reacquainted with a neglected world—in the words of one social philosopher, a "lost world" of "common truths."[1] They evidence themselves as "common truths" insofar as all people mirror the weight and effects of the moral law, even when they might deny its existence.[2] What, then, is responsible for the "neglect" of this "tradition"? What factors might be seen as preventing an acknowledgement of basic moral truths? Natural law proponent J. Budsizewski speaks of an "eclipse" of natural law moral reasoning in our day and identifies numerous cultural components to help explain this phenomenon.[3] Several of these surely are worthy of some comment.

At the most basic level, we may speak of the atrophy of tradition and moral education. We live in a cultural climate (at least, those of us in Western societies) in which history and the value of what is "passed on" (*traditio*) are undervalued, if not forgotten. Much of the West suffers from amnesia; we have forgotten or neglected what previous generations have passed along and have replaced these elements with "traditions" or tendencies that are unwise or unhealthy. One might compare, for example, what parents today pass on to their children (or, what they do *not* pass on) with what prior generations passed along. Where are moral education, training in the virtues, and a concern for the common good and serving our "neighbor" to be found? A "transient" or rootless culture might not merely indicate mobility; it might be a sign of the *absence* of moral values.

In an intriguing volume titled *Intellectuals and Society*, social theorist Thomas Sowell observes the unparalleled role that "intellectuals" play in the modern era.[4] By "intellectuals" Sowell is referring to those whose ideas are influential in shaping public attitudes and beliefs. Sowell is concerned not only to examine the vision of such people but also to ponder the motivations and constraints behind those whose ideas are considered influential. But as numerous Questions in this volume have attempted to make clear, the idea of common moral truths, of moral first principles, does not need great minds or the accumulation of brilliant people to confirm their reality. Rather, this is the realm of common sense and wisdom. While the influence of "experts" in some highly specialized fields is understandable, in moral matters the necessary—indeed, irreplaceable—component is wisdom. And wisdom, as the next-to-last Question in this volume seeks to demonstrate, is accessible to all. All human beings possess moral knowledge and intuit the natural law. Whether and how human beings respond to this knowledge, of course, is an entirely different matter.

In Question 6 we observed that the idea of universal moral truths dates several generations prior even to Socrates and Aristotle. Heraclitus had argued that wisdom points to a wider "law" in the universe, a transcending *logos* or reason, to which human nature and human ethical striving are ordered. Wisdom, therefore, he insisted, was "the foremost virtue." His understanding of wisdom needs reiteration: "wisdom consists in speaking the truth, and in lending an ear to nature and acting according to her."[5] Heraclitus' attempt, however dim or beclouded, to perceive some sense of an unchanging "natural moral law" stood in notable contrast both to a capricious general population and to the demagoguery of the Sophists. The Sophists of his day, like the sophists of any era, refused to venerate the "natural moral law," since they viewed laws as artificial constructs that merely serve the interests of those in power. Our own day, perhaps in some ways mirroring that of the Sophists, is characterized not by a pursuit of the truth (with a capital "T") but with its construction or "deconstruction." To acknowledge moral absolutes and moral principle in the public sphere, as we have emphasized throughout this volume, is often to incur the wrath of our contemporaries, and especially that of the "experts" and "intellectuals."

When and where there is an atrophy of moral sensibilities, there is a commensurate inability to react to what is morally repugnant. The human being, both mentally and physically, grows accustomed to both pain and profligacy. Consider alone the types of media that vie for our attention, whether in the form of news or entertainment, whether individually or collectively. The human capacity for desensitization is mind-boggling, knowing no seeming limits. "Tolerance" in our day is based not on moral principle—that is, we tolerate what is unpleasant or different for a *greater good*—but what might be called a "lowest-common-denominator"—that is, what a prior generation rejected as undermining the common social good.

One of the defining features of our "therapeutic culture" is its tendency to undermine the rational and the intellectual. This can be measured, for example, by its accent on the self, on the place of feelings and emotions, on one's sense of worth and "self-esteem," and on popular versions of "victimhood." As evidenced by countless self-help books and magazines, internet blogs and resources, and television and radio shows, ideas and techniques issuing out of popular psychology have aggressively inserted themselves throughout mainstream culture. Not what one thinks or what is good or what is right but *how one feels* determines a person's meaning and worth. Not personal values but personal feelings dictate to a large degree how people act in a therapeutic cultural climate. Without question, a proper view of personhood does not ignore or rule out desires and emotions; these are part of our design, our God-given constitution. However, they must be directed in the right way for the right purposes. Moral values allow us to order—and make sense of—our often conflicting feelings and desires. If we permit the moral meaning of our lives to be dictated by the whims and fancies of our emotions and desires, we consign ourselves as human beings in the end to moral confusion, not to mention moral pollution.

37

How does natural law thinking inform criminal justice?

A PERENNIAL QUESTION FOR HUMAN civilization, and not merely the post-Christian West, is to define and then implement—in our laws, our institutions, and our social relations—the essence of justice. This challenge, however, has become increasingly difficult among Western societies, wherein competing understandings of law, sociology, and criminal justice are on display. At the most basic level, we have difficulty deciding not only *if* wrongdoers should be held accountable for their actions but *why* and then *how* they should be punished (*if* in fact they should). Widely—when not universally—assumed among contemporary social theorists is that human beings are not morally responsible for their actions. Crime, alas, has become broadly understood in accordance with "root causes" which are chiefly sociological, therapeutic, or biological—and not *moral*—in nature. This development, of course, did not begin yesterday; it has been cultivated for decades. In any case, the result is an incoherent criminal justice system that, in the words of one social critic, "tries to deter yet forgive, punish yet reform, incapacitate yet rehabilitate."[1] And as most people intuit, this is a system that is in vast need of reform. As virtually all people realize, at least in the U.S., crime does pay.

For two generations the dominant philosophy of approaching law and criminal justice has been broadly utilitarian. As classically defined, utilitarian thought aims at "the greatest good for the greatest number of people." Hence, utilitarian approaches to criminal justice and crime control are based not on justice as it concerns both offender and victim, or even the punishment of the offender in proportionate (i.e., just) ways, but to suppress criminal behavior in a broad or general sort of way, in accordance with the utilitarian notion of social "utility." What are typical utilitarian strategies that, at least in the U.S., find common expression? Prevention, rehabilitation, and a qualified approach to incapacitation through incarceration are the most prominent. Because deterrence is debated endlessly among theorists, deterrence cannot be said to be a characteristically utilitarian strategy. To illustrate: social scientists tend to favor models that assume that crime cannot be deterred through punishment. Most economists, by contrast, are inclined toward the conclusion that punishment will indeed deter criminal behavior. And the reason for this is not difficult to perceive. If we increase the cost of something, it will be less frequent in our midst; the same applies to committing crime: the greater the cost, the fewer the crimes. The argument against deterrence is really no argument because *we can never know* how many people have refrained from crime because of the fear of punishment.

Let us take note of the potential outworking of the aforementioned utilitarian strategies. "Prevention" has as its focus environmental factors—i.e., social conditions encouraging or inhibiting criminal behavior. "Rehabilitation" assumes the importance of the offender's psychology and his or her future decisions through working with psychiatrists, psychologists, social workers, and other trained professionals. And the notion of "incapacitation" through limited incarceration is predicated not on the harm done to the victim (proportionality) but also the psychological effect of a longer or shorter period of incarceration—a measurement that does not necessarily take into account the nature of the crime committed. What might we conclude from the combined effect of these factors? The principal lesson to be gleaned is that punishment bears little to no formal or practical relationship to the crime committed; it is chiefly a predictive measurement of future criminality. But this sort of measurement violates the very nature of justice, for justice requires *proportionality*. That is, society's response to criminal behavior must be proportionate to the nature of the offense. Any parent knows this, and most children—based on natural-law intuitions, even if they don't have "parents"—sense this as well.

Broader utilitarian approaches to crime and criminal justice have been popular since the 1960s and 70s. What do we know to be the results of these strategies, based on the wider availability of data? In general terms, utilitarian approaches to crime and criminal justice have tended to exclude the moral component. They do injustice *both* to the offender and to the victimized party. Why is it the case that victims of crime routinely express outrage and disgust at the criminal justice system? Philosophically, the answer is not difficult to find. By standard utilitarian calculations, "there is no place for the anguished human face of an individual crime victim. He or she is homogenized and obliterated in faceless statistical tables—reduced to just one more digit amid the annual household victimization rates, parolee recidivism rates, and prison furlough failure rates."[2]

Despite—or perhaps more accurately, because of—the dominant approaches to "criminal justice" over the last two generations, particular patterns regarding crime and society's response are readily on display. Most of these are commonsensical and readily observable—for example:

1. most serious crime is committed by a violent minority of recidivists;
2. the rehabilitative model has lacked demonstrable results among persistent criminal offenders;
3. a remarkably low percentage of arrests, even for serious crime, actually leads to actual prison sentences (stated

otherwise, by the time a criminal is initially imprisoned he or she has normally committed multitudes of crimes);

4. many troubled youths have multiple encounters with the criminal justice system before bearing significant consequences for their crimes;
5. punishment is effective in suppressing crime, but where punishment is irregular future arrests tend to multiply in frequency;
6. features such as the plea bargain[3] and parole do immeasurable harm to the criminal justice system inasmuch as they negate the notions of desert and basic justice, thereby teaching criminals and future offenders that crime, in many ways, does pay while at the same time demoralizing the true victims of crime as well as law-enforcement officers; in most jurisdictions, eligibility for parole is offered after the offender has served only a fraction of the term handed down by a judge;
7. despite all of the criticism of prisons, incarceration works, serving the immediate need of preventing crime and protecting the common good; and
8. perhaps most importantly, healthy families serve as the "first line of defense" against crime, whereas unstable or less-than-intact families represent "cradles of crime."[4]

Traditional approaches to criminal behavior, when compared to utilitarian strategies, have much to commend them because of the moral component, which not infrequently in our day is absent. Basic to traditional moral theory is the element of desert. Accordingly, an offender should be punished proportionately according to what he or she deserves, that is, in proportion to the crime committed. Such agrees with the traditional definition of "justice"—what is "owed."

After all, everyone would acknowledge that to assign draconian punishment (say, the death penalty) for a minor offense, while at the same time assigning a slap-on-the wrist for murder or rape, would be gross injustice. Whether punishment according to the traditional (natural law) model actually results in a change or reform of the offender's motivation and future behavior is entirely secondary. Does punishment deter? As noted above, economists—over against social-scientists—are wholly convinced of its efficacy: *increase the costs and watch the behavior change.*

What a *just* measure and motivation for punishment aims for is a moral standard that in non-fluid ways protects the common social good by shedding light on acceptable and unacceptable social behavior. This measurement, as the following Question concerning moral retribution argues, can be distinguished from revenge and the retaliatory spirit. *Why* do we as human beings punish? We do this because the moral order, underpinned by the natural law, *requires* it. Human dignity requires it.

At bottom, a proper view of retribution, as we have suggested, has to do with the notion of *just desert* and causality. To speak of "desert" is to reaffirm the authentic sense of justice that human beings so desperately, and intuitively, desire. It is to acknowledge natural law moral categories—"good" and "evil," and hence praise and punishment—to define and demarcate humans' behavior as they live in community as "social animals." We may therefore demand that the criminal justice system be capable of defining "crime" and "criminal behavior," not in therapeutic or biological terms, but according to what people—*all* people—intuit based on *human nature*. Here we may concede that *not all* criminals will be deterred by punishment, any more than all children will develop according to the wishes of their parents. The argument for deterrence is not dependent on whether *all* will respond. In the realm of criminal justice, we can acknowledge the reality of the "psychopath" or hardened "career criminal" who quite simply will *not* be deterred from doing evil. But this does *not* mean that most people, according to human "nature," will not be deterred from doing evil in the interest of doing good. In any event, the fact that some will *not* be deterred from doing wrong does not impinge on what all economists know, namely, that increasing the costs will indeed lessen the presence of a commodity. And as noted above, we can never know how many people have refrained from crime because of the fear of consequences.

In the end, a criminal must accept full responsibility for his or her actions, a key element of which is punishment (discussed in the following Question). Moreover, not even penal excesses, which are *far less* frequent than penal restraint, can repudiate the need for "criminal justice." The ordering of a "free" society and the common social good are at stake.

38

How does natural law reasoning understand retributive justice and punishment?

The purpose of law—and specifically, criminal law—is to regulate social conduct, to protect the common good, and to "educate" both wider society and those whose behavior is being sanctioned. Historically, criminal justice in relatively free societies has been predicated on standards of justice as known through the light of reason and the natural law (rewarding good and punishing evil). Where those standards are fluid, then they are unjust. Few people, even in a truth-denying culture, would deny or reject the standard of *just measures*—i.e., receiving what is in fact *due* or deserved. Historically, it needs emphasizing that crime control is indebted in large part to the role of religious thinking in furnishing an ethical ground for "civil society," despite our deeply secular tendencies to the contrary.

For several generations in Western culture, the notion of punishment as traditionally understood has been called into question.[1] Already in his day, the writer C. S. Lewis waxed critical of attempts to remove—or at best moderate—retribution in the criminal justice system and replace it with what he called the "Humanitarian" theory of punishment.[2] According to those espousing a "Humanitarian" approach, to punish a person because he or she deserves it, and to the degree that he or she deserves it, is merely a pretext for revenge, and thus, barbaric and immoral. Correlatively, the chief goal for "punishing" a person is to cure or mend that individual and to deter others by example. If one assumes, as is frequently the case today, that crime is biological or pathological in explanation, the goal of crime control and reform becomes largely therapeutic—the healing or curing of the criminal. With a focus on the therapeutic, it would thus appear that as a society we have passed from the "cruel" and self-righteous notion of "just deserts" to a more charitable and enlightened notion of behavioral change.[3] The dominance of the therapeutic model can be seen in the fact that we now call prisons not *penitentiaries*—i.e., places where penitence and sorrow are exacted for public crimes—but "correctional facilities."

Lewis's contention, however, is that although this approach gives the appearance of being more humane, it actually deprives individuals of "rights" that are lodged in human nature. This is done by removing from "punishment" the very concept of desert, which, at bottom, is "the only connecting link between punishment and justice." That is, it is only as *deserved or undeserved* that a sentence can be *just or unjust*. We can, of course, ask whether punishment is likely to reform the criminal and deter others. And debates over deterrence have been waging for decades, as the previous Question noted, with sociologists almost in virtual agreement that punishment does not deter, while economists tend to argue quite the opposite, based on costs. However, neither the matter of deterrence nor the matter of potential reform is itself a question about justice *per se*, Lewis insists; there is no sense in talking about a "just deterrent" or a "just cure." When, then, we cease to ask what the criminal deserves and ask what will cure him or what might deter, we have removed him from the sphere of justice altogether and made him, in essence, a patient or a "case." And if according to the rehabilitative or therapeutic model curing is the goal, then no judges or juries are needed. If to cure the criminal is our aim, then only a medical professional or psychotherapist can determine "justice."

Theoretically, we have hereby relegated criminality to a *disease*. In the past, society was guided by the light of reason and natural law (as well as Scripture) and thus treated the criminal as a rational being, a "social animal" who nevertheless possessed the natural light of reason—at least, *some* light of reason. But now, in negating the concept of desert, what we have traditionally understood as "criminal justice" has changed. More and more we look to the psychotherapist rather than to the penologist or criminal lawyer, since punishment is broadly viewed as archaic and vindictive. Whether the "root cause" of criminal behavior is viewed as society itself and one's environment, economics and poverty, psychology, biology and genetics, or brain structure, a growing intellectual consensus over the decades has been that the criminal is not responsible for his behavior; forces outside his control "cause" him to behave the way he does.[4] Thus, cultivating virtue becomes an impossibility. After all, what are "the virtues"? And if people are not responsible for their behavior, then it is incumbent upon us to renounce what renowned psychiatrist Karl Menninger in the 1960s famously called "the crime of punishment."[5]

In practical terms, the initial effect of "Humanitarian" thinking is to substitute for a *definite* sentence—which in the past was predicated on proportionality and thus desert—an *indefinite* sentence that is subject to predictive and less "vindictive" elements. In consequence, the measurements of so-called "criminal justice" are now no longer moral (or even strictly legal) in nature. To reiterate: in removing the classic element of just desert, we are declaring that punishment has nothing to do with guilt or innocence; it has nothing to do with what a criminal through his or her actions in fact deserves. What's more, even where the "career criminal" has been convicted of multiple felonies, he is very likely to receive "concurrent sentences," which are served then simultaneously rather than consecutively. And, in most jurisdictions, eligibility for parole will arrive after having served only a fraction of the prison sentence handed down by the judge.[6] Fully aside from the dashed hopes of millions of citizens who hope for justice, the effects of these sorts of injustices greatly undermine the confidence and motivation of those working in law and law enforcement.

Already in 1992, in a remarkable speech titled "Defining Deviancy Down," Senator Daniel Patrick Moynihan addressed the American Sociological Association and described what had been transpiring over the previous generation.[7] Moynihan observed that the amount of deviant behavior had increased beyond levels which American society could afford to recognize. As a result, he noted, we have been redefining deviancy in order to exempt ourselves from behavior that previously had been stigmatized, and condemned. As it was, Moynihan happened to be a sociologist by training. The reaction by many fellow sociologists who heard Moynihan's speech is telling; not a few believed that he was simply "blaming the victim."[8] And precisely this is the next step: once we have removed guilt or innocence from criminal behavior, it is then assumed that the criminal is a "victim"—a "victim" of the "criminal justice" system, a "victim" of economics and poverty, a "victim" of racism, a "victim" of society's wider imperfections. And when a "victim" is needed by society's gate-keepers, "punishment" on the basis of guilt and desert is no longer justifiable as it had been previously according to traditional understandings of justice.

But clinical psychologist Stanton Samenow, a pioneer in the study of criminal psychology and co-author, with the late Samuel Yochelson, of the path-breaking three-volume study *The Criminal Personality*, is critical of the assumption that the criminal has become the "victim." Samenow writes:

> By taking the position that the criminal is a victim, society has provided him with excuses for crime and thereby supported his contention that he is not to blame. Partly to atone for its alleged injustices to the criminal, society has offered him countless opportunities to "rehabilitate" himself and enter the mainstream. Surprise has given way to despair as the criminal rejects

> the very opportunities that he rejected before (work, school, counseling) or else shamelessly exploits them while continuing to commit crimes.[9]

At bottom, the logic of determinism—whether psychological, sociological, or biological—combines with the criminal's victimization to produce a *reversal* of justice.

A moral realism that is underpinned by natural law assumptions will refuse to make the criminal a "victim," even when sociological, psychological, and biological factors all contribute to human development. In the end, C. S. Lewis is compelled to reaffirm the traditional or retributive approach to punishment, not solely—and not even primarily—in the interests of society but also in the interests of the criminal. Lewis's reasoning is anchored in the simple fact that it is precisely *because* human beings are fashioned in the divine image, not in spite of it, that we hold them accountable for their actions. To hold our fellow human beings accountable is, in truth, to affirm their intrinsic dignity as humans, and to fail to hold them accountable is to disavow their dignity altogether. Lewis's reasoning, despite generations removed, serves us well in a "post-consensus" cultural climate.

The rationality and accessibility of Lewis's argument is grounded in his reliance on natural law reasoning. Viewed from the Judeo-Christian standpoint, which Lewis shared, law as the contextualized expression of divine character was integral to the life of humanity from the beginning, as Israel of old well demonstrates. Disregard for the law, the *torah*, inevitably resulted in a rotting of Israelite social character. But what applied to Israel of old is universal in its application. When the unity of divine revelation containing moral truth and human cooperation is severed, chaos and calamity follow. All of history attests to this basic pattern.

Frequently overlooked in studies of the biblical and theological framework for criminal justice is the central importance of "purification." As it concerns the relationship between temporal punishment and purification/cleansing from sin, in 1976 Karol Wojtyla, at that time Archbishop of Cracow, delivered a series of homilies at the invitation of Pope Paul VI on the occasion of the annual Vatican Lenten retreat. In this remarkable series, collected and published under the title *Sign of Contradiction*, sustained reflection was given to the question of man's purification from sin in the present life, with the future pontiff demonstrating keen insight into the divinely-ordained virtues of punishment. Guilt incurred by sin constitutes a debt in the present life that must be paid. Punitive dealings, he maintained, provide the necessary atonement and restore the balance of justice and moral order that has been disturbed; they prepare man for a destiny in eternity. The "law of purification," noted the Archbishop, "reveals both the temporal and the eternal perspectives of mankind." Purification comes by way of suffering; it prepares the individual to meet his Maker.[10] The "law of purification," in very practical ways, mirrors the outworking of natural law realities.[11] Punishment, hence, is neither scapegoating nor the imposition of power, contrary to many of our own contemporaries. Rather, punishment is pedagogical in its effect—for the offender, for society, and for future offenders.

Not many religious believers, however, or even professional theologians, hold to this view of punishment. Playing on the Old Testament principle of retributive justice, someone has famously quipped that "an eye for an eye keeps the whole world blind." There is not a little subterfuge lodged in this sort of comment. At the most basic level, it fails to acknowledge the context in which the moral principle of the *lex talionis* is delineated. Early on in Israel's history, following the reiteration of the "Ten Commandments," we read instructions given on how to handle personal injury. It is stated that "if there is serious injury you are to take life for life" (Exo. 21:23).[12] The context of such "serious injury" has already been previously identified: "Anyone who strikes a person with a fatal blow is to be put to death. However, if it is not done intentionally, but God lets it happen, they are to flee to a place I will designate. But if anyone schemes and kills someone deliberately, that person is to be taken from my altar and put to death" (Exo. 21:12–14, NIV). Notice the qualifier here: the intent of murder. And notice here as well the effect of deterrence in the "eye for eye" measure. Elsewhere in the Pentateuch, that effect is stated in no uncertain terms: "The rest of the people will hear of this [the convicted murderer] and be afraid, and never again will such an evil thing be done among you. Show no pity; life for life, eye for eye, tooth for tooth, hand for hand, foot for foot" (Deut. 19:20–21).

The fact that punishment, Scripturally viewed, has a deterrent effect in terms of "criminal justice" finds confirmation in the context of war as well, based on natural law reasoning: "Without the fear of punishment to deter them from wrongdoing, the enemy would simply grow more bold about invading a second time."[13] The point of the aforementioned Old Testament instruction is clear: (1) deterrence is to be used against willful, malicious crime, and (2) as a moral principle, the punishment should fit the crime. The principle, then, bespeaks proportionality, which is not "harsh," even when it offends our modern/postmodern sensibilities; rather, it mirrors justice, properly understood. Nor is this mere "revenge," inasmuch as judges would have adjudicated, as Lev. 19:18 and narratives such as Numbers 35 make very clear.

If we move forward to Jesus's day and consider the context in which Jesus was citing the "eye for an eye" measure (Matt. 5:38–42), the purpose of the citation is to correct misinterpretations and misappropriations of "legal recourse."[14] Here, following Jesus's formula "You have heard it said…but I tell you…," four examples of *personal* insult or injury are cited: being slapped on the cheek, losing one's tunic, going a second mile, and giving to the person wanting to borrow. These are *personal* matters, not issues of *public policy*. What is the point of Jesus's teaching? To oppose personal revenge or retaliatory responses. The context here mirrors that of Romans 12, where Paul gives similar advice. But in matters of policy and guarding the common good, Paul's advice shifts then in Romans

13, where "criminal justice" is acknowledged as the proper domain of governing authorities.

Can the measure of proportionality, which is lodged at the heart of just punishment and finds expression in the classic formulation "An eye for an eye," be abused? Can retribution shade into retaliation or vengeance? Without question. Punishment can be wrongly motivated and unjustly applied, and we find evidence of this universally. But because something is abused or has the potential for abuse does not render it illicit or unjust in principle. In the last fifty years multiple regression studies have demonstrated the common-sense principle that increasing the severity (or frequency) of punishment in fact reduces the likelihood of crime. Scientific studies, however, are not the only—or even the main—source of our knowledge; most parents know this intuitively. As noted above, the concepts of deterrence and desert in our day tend not to be favored by those who are working in the social sciences. Nor are they acceptable to many "progressive" activists who operate on the fringes of the criminal justice system. And if we as a society prefer the rehabilitative approach to "criminal justice," then we are in part relieved of the burden of having to perceive ourselves as "injuring" or "inflicting harm" on others.[15]

But for civil society to deal honestly—and justly—with crime, the choice between more agreeable or "pleasant" models and disagreeable methods is a false choice. Criminal justice is by nature necessarily unpleasant. Either we punish and seek to deter criminal behavior—a method that *typically*, when not always, works—or we continue to endure higher crime rates and breed a lawless society.

The best defense of punishment as a principle is not merely that it upholds the social order (which it does), but that it affirms important moral and cultural values. We might say, in this regard, that just punishment is both backward- and forward-looking. That is, it assesses (and rewards) according to the severity of the crime committed while serving as a deterrent to future or potential criminals. Hereby we are constrained to reject the false dichotomy between punishment and "humanitarian" values. In our day, according to two authorities who have devoted their lives to the study of our criminal justice system, one of the "biggest myths of all" is that "punishment itself is inherently wrong."[16] But what rationale undergirds this "biggest myth of all"? Those predisposed against punishment in general and against imprisonment in particular believe that "we must address the root causes of crime, that our criminal justice system discriminates, that we are overly punitive and haven't considered alternatives, that prisons are too costly and overcrowded, and that we must look to the courts for reform."[17]

Note here the basic assumption at work: punishment is *inherently wrong*, having no intrinsic value and being only a "necessary evil" to the extent that it can be shown in a utilitarian or pragmatic fashion that it has some (unmeasurable) utility. But against this vaguely "humanitarian" and "rehabilitative" view, we are required to ask, as any parent is required to do, whether punishing those we love is in fact an "evil." Against contemporary "wisdom" that has been advanced for decades in the social sciences and more recently in the hard sciences, we must insist that it is precisely *within the context of punishment* that humanistic concepts—properly understood—are most relevant. Moreover, punishment is administered by the political community and its representative judges, not individuals; it is therefore the domain of public law and not narrowly "retaliatory," as the following Question attempts to make clear.[18] Principled and just punishment for wrongdoing "treats individuals as persons and as human beings, rather than as objects. Punishment is an affirmation of the autonomy, responsibility, and dignity of the individual."[19] We dignify fellow human beings by holding them accountable for the wrong that they commit. Punishment, thus, has positive moral value; it is *not* a necessary evil. Time-tested wisdom, then, accords with human nature, dignifies human beings by holding them accountable for their actions, and hence rewards doing good and punishes doing evil. Such is the moral baseline of the natural law.

By its nature as a cardinal virtue, justice is a mirror of—and dependent on—the very value of human life. At bottom, punishment is "just" only to the extent that it fits the crime, and hence, is proportionate to that criminal act. Any other measurement of criminal behavior renders justice impossible. The chief aim of punishment, as any parent knows, is to assert—and enforce—a moral standard for social behavior that does not undermine the common good.

39

How does natural law reasoning distinguish between retribution and revenge?

Because of confusion at both the academic and the more popular level, clarifying the terms "retribution" and "revenge" is our first order of business. At the academic level, there exists some confusion in the literature as to what "retribution" means. Some theorists virtually equate the concept with revenge or retaliation, making little or no contrast between (a) differing motivations or aims of punishment as well as (b) moral-philosophical distinctions regarding the essence of justice that would qualify "retribution." Making these distinctions is absolutely critical.

At the more popular level, there exists much talk in contemporary culture about "social justice." As a result, the concept of justice (properly understood) has largely lost its meaning, as the previous Question suggested. Justice—that cardinal virtue and moral tissue by which and in which a decent and relatively free society coheres—requires *inter alia* that crimes in society be punished and that criminals suffer temporal consequences that are proportionate in their magnitude to the crimes they commit. In its essential character, justice protects the common social good. This means that evil incurs a public debt that is only addressed and satisfied adequately by retributive justice. For this reason, classical writers in the natural law tradition use the term *vindicatio* to refer to the justice of moral retribution.[1] This is an important distinction: *vindication* over against being *vindictive*. And not only in its intention but its effects, retribution contrasts with both the utilitarian and the rehabilitative view of punishment.[2]

The moral indignation that is expressed through retributive justice is first and foremost rooted in moral principle, not mere emotional outrage or hatred. Its outrage is the expression of abiding moral markers, grounded in the baseline principles of doing good and avoiding evil—principles such as "Thou shalt not murder" or "Thou shalt not steal" or "Thou shalt not defraud others." The nature and extent of retributive justice are lodged in two unbending ethical realities: (1) the degree of wrongness of the criminal act and (2) the degree of the party's criminal responsibility in committing such acts. Retributive justice, then, requires that wrongdoers get no more but no less than what is proportionate—that is, what is their *due*. Apart from the concept of desert, punishment becomes immeasurable, and therefore unjust.[3]

The average person is likely to object that retribution is often a pretext for vengeance and the retaliatory impulse. Isn't retribution a mirror of human bloodthirst, in the final analysis only an excuse to exact vengeance? Many—perhaps most—people are inclined to argue that *in practice* it is impossible to distinguish between vengeance and retribution. However, retribution is not revenge; neither is it domesticated hatred, nor the imposition of power, nor the attempt to inflict suffering, all of which are commonly assumed. The retributive act distinguishes itself from revenge or vengeance in four important and unmistakable ways that require our attention.

Whereas revenge strikes out at real or perceived injury, retribution speaks to an objective wrong. Whereas revenge is wild and "insatiable," not subject to limitations, retribution has both upper and lower limits, acknowledging the moral repugnance of assigning draconian punishment to petty crime, as well as assigning light punishment to violent, heinous crime.

In addition, whereas vengeance has a thirst for injury and delights in bringing evil upon the offending party—the avenger will not only kill but rape, torture, plunder, and burn what is left, deriving satisfaction from its victim's suffering—retribution has as its goal a greater social good and takes no pleasure in punishment. And finally, whereas revenge will operate out of a retaliatory mode due to something done to the avenger or those associated, retribution is impersonal and therefore demands impartiality, not subject to personal bias. For this reason, Lady Justice is depicted as blindfolded with equal weights in hand.

The fundamental aim of moral retribution is to reflect back on the criminal the undeserved negative consequences—i.e., harm and injury—that were imposed upon the innocent victim. Retributive justice, when properly understood, serves a civilized culture in several important ways. It isolates individuals who endanger the community; it expresses social outrage at morally perverse acts; it controls the extent to which the citizenry is victimized by criminal acts; it rewards the perpetrator proportionately with consequences befitting the crime; and it "rehabilitates" the offender by forcing him to reflect on the grievous nature of the crime.[4] Each of these elements is critical in preserving the social order.

When we express social outrage at morally heinous acts, we are responding with moral intuitions in accordance with our fundamental nature. It is virtuous, not vicious, to feel anger at moral evil. In truth, if we do *not* express anger and moral outrage at evil, something is very wrong with us; all human beings sense the need for and justice of punishment. To affirm retribution, which is consonant with moral thinking throughout human history, integral to the history of Judeo-Christian moral thinking, and foundational to any self-governing society, is *not* to abandon one's belief in mercy or forgiveness. Rather, it is to acknowledge the difference between private and public spheres and to recognize that mercy does not release the public demands that justice imposes. Even where "forgiveness" has been granted, the consequences of criminal acts—and these are always very *public* consequences—are *not* set aside. Justice always requires that a public debt be paid.

It is critically important that democratic societies not drive a wedge between "justice" and "retribution," in the end reducing "justice" itself to incoherence. In this regard, two opposite reactions are to be avoided. On the one hand it is necessary to distinguish between retribution and "retributivism," that is, between the reciprocal element of justice and retaliation. On the other hand, it is important, given the moral underpinnings of retributive justice, to discern the widespread and mistaken notion of "forgiveness" that often exists among both religious and non-religious pacifist types. In the name of "forgiveness," such people conflate the demands of justice with the release of criminals from the consequences and public debt of their crimes.

In Judeo-Christian ethics, forgiveness is predicated on the offender's contrition and repentance. Moreover, the biblical teaching on forgiveness occurs in the context of personal relationships, not duties of the state or magistrate. Where social evil occurs, a public debt is incurred, and judgment—which is to say, the execution of justice—ensues, regardless of whether it applies in the domestic or the international context. Theologian Oliver O'Donovan describes the necessary tension between justice and mercy that must be preserved and not loosened:

> In Christian thought retribution is one pole of a dialectic with forgiveness. One reason, indeed, that Christians have insisted on retributive justice (when they have insisted on it), is that if one pole is lost, the opposite pole will be lost, too. The theological doctrines of forgiven sin, redemption from punishment, reconciliation of the offender with the offended God, those and nothing else are what have held the philosophical notions of desert and retribution firmly in place.[5]

What we have labeled "retributive justice" O'Donovan calls "corrective justice" or "adjudicative justice"—i.e., justice that expresses itself in the correcting of ruptures or imbalances in society or between nations.[6] And while individuals or groups can work for "social justice," only governments can practice "corrective justice," which is to say, justice as judgment for the purpose of protecting the common social good. It is the latter that undergirds just war moral reasoning, which just as retributive justice in the domestic context is also guided by upper and lower limits, just cause, right intention, proportionality, and is exercised by legitimate political authority.

The distinction between vengeance and retribution, between the spheres of personal relations and governing authority, is precisely the rationale behind St. Paul's argument in the New Testament epistle to the Romans. Whereas Romans 12 passionately proscribes private vengeance ("Do not repay anyone evil for evil"; "Do not take revenge, but leave room for the wrath of God"; "Vengeance is mine, says the Lord; I will repay"), Romans 13 clearly and unambiguously prescribes government's ordained role in executing justice on evildoers. Thus, we find the apostle condemning revenge in the private sphere, delegitimized by the absence of legitimate political-legal authority (Rom. 13:1–2, 5), while condoning and authorizing just retribution, symbolized by the sword (13:4). Contextually, the one follows on the heels of the other. Taken together, Romans 12 and Romans 13 illustrate the distinction we are making: intention, context, and legitimate authority distinguish retributive justice from revenge or retaliation.

Retributive justice, thus, is a necessity for a civilized society. At its heart, it accomplishes several things that are irreplaceable: it reaffirms and restores moral values that have been discarded; it anchors itself in the principle of proportionality, without which justice is non-existent; it encourages procedural justice through law and the courts; and it stresses compensation for those who have been victimized and traumatized by criminal acts. In short, it concerns itself with restoring moral and social imbalances that have injured civil society. In responding retributively to moral evil, we channel our energies in several directions. We respond to the victim(s) being wronged, to wider society being "scandalized" by the wrong done in its midst, to future offenders who might be tempted to do the same wrong, and, not least, to the actual offending party. Understood correctly, retributive justice performs a multifaceted good. It is true that there will always be the cry of retaliationists who, in the name of "justice," demand that torture be meted out to the torturer. But that outcry in itself does not cancel the fact that retributive justice performs a necessary social good.

Pacifist types will not infrequently argue that retribution constitutes an "uncivilized" or "barbaric" response by society to crime. It is common to hear complaints in our day of "harsh" sentencing.[7] But is this the case? The answer to this question depends fundamentally on how society perceives the moral difference between the criminal and the punitive act. Those who would contend that retribution is unsuited to "civilized" society, whether in criminal justice or in foreign affairs and military engagement, are mistaken on two fronts. They conflate the punitive and the criminal act on the basis of a seeming moral equivalence, and they fail to understand the rupture in society caused by moral evil that must be addressed in the temporal order. Both errors are catastrophic to any society that conceives of itself as "free" and "just." Rather, the fundamental aim of retributive justice—what we may properly designate as moral retribution—is to mirror those negative consequences of harm and injury committed by a criminal back onto him in a way that is proportionate to the criminal act itself. Recall once more that the natural law, based on human nature, bids us to do good and forbids us from doing harm. The consequences of such criminal justice policy are both moral and practical.

> Moral, because it upholds both the ultimate moral value, which is individual human life, and the just social framework upon which individual survival and well-being depend. Practical, because a

> policy of reflecting proportionate harm back upon the criminal frustrates and negates his goal, which is to profit at someone else's expense.[8]

To distinguish between the criminal and the punitive act is to be guided by—and held accountable to—the cardinal virtue of justice. If, as has been argued throughout this volume, the standard of justice is not abiding and universally held through deliberate action, then it is impossible to denounce moral evil—anywhere, in any form, at any time. Thus viewed, the Nuremberg trials were wrongheaded, since Nazi war crimes *by definition* cannot be denounced; much less can mass murderers be put on trial and sentenced, and the Nazis merely came out on the wrong end. In the end, one man's torture is another man's good time, and might, as the saying goes, makes right (with a little help from stealth). In such a moral vacuum, retribution is indistinguishable from revenge, and moral chaos follows.

40

How does natural law reasoning bear on capital punishment?

Few issues bear out the state of moral confusion in Western societies—and particularly the U.S.—as the matter of murder. Most cities in the U.S., as I write, are currently reeling from the sheer frequency of killings that have descended upon our streets, our neighborhoods, our families, and even our schools. In the four months of June, July, August, and September of 2022, there were respectively 73, 100, 71, and 70 mass shootings, with the number of injured or dead being 297, 439, 262, and 272 respectively.[1]

According to The Marshall Project, more mass shootings (i.e., four or more victims) have occurred in the last five years than in any other half-decade since 1966.[2] This should give us pause. We are surely justified in asking, even when it is not socially or politically expedient in our day, what murderers deserve. No civilized nation or people-group takes the matter of murder for granted; no civilized society is casual about its response to the need for protecting the wider common good in light of violent crime.

The increasingly barbaric face of crime in the U.S. as mirrored in murder rates would seem to guarantee that debates over capital punishment would intensify. This, however, has not been the case. In fact, what is striking is the relative absence of discussion and debate over the death penalty, whether in a secular or religious context. As with most controversies, the debate over capital punishment proceeds quite frequently along misguided emotional or mental-health lines rather than in the light of philosophical and theological grounding and what justice and the common weal require.

It is no exaggeration to say that contemporary Western culture is awash with arguments against capital punishment. In our post-enlightened, postmodern thinking we have grown increasingly intolerant of meting out punishment that is perceived as "cruel" or "barbaric." Quite strangely, however, our abhorrence of penal "barbarity" is displayed against the backdrop of increasingly barbaric criminal acts themselves. The reticence to apply just standards to cases of murder, however, was *not* the case in 1791 when both the Eighth and Fourteenth Amendments were enacted. Because the death penalty was viewed neither as "cruel" nor as "unusual" at that time, the Eighth Amendment cannot be said to apply to capital punishment. In summarizing contemporary attitudes toward criminal justice, we may conclude that *retributive justice in general* is called into question in our day, with capital punishment merely being understood as one—though highly visible—facet of our culture's aversion to punishment in general.[3]

The abolitionist argument regarding capital justice takes any number of forms and rationales. Such arguments, moreover, are employed equally among both secular and religious types. Among these, for example, are (1) the mental health of the murderer; (2) the possibility of prematurely ending a criminal's rehabilitation; (3) the claim that deterrence does not work (usually based on inconclusive data); (4) the misconstruing of retribution as revenge (i.e., retributivism); (5) fallibility of the criminal justice system (i.e., the possibility of sentencing an innocent person to death and mistaken convictions); (6) the costs associated with death penalty cases; (7) modern notions of "civility"; and (8) a supposed racial imbalance in sentencing.[4] Several additional arguments among religiously-motivated abolitionists include (9) the annulment of the

Mosaic code, (10) assumed ethical discontinuity between the Old and New Testaments; and (11) Christ's teaching on forgiveness.

Evidence indicates that in earliest recorded history capital punishment was practiced. Its prescription appears in the mid-eighteenth-century BCE Hammurabi Code, in sixteenth-century BCE Assyrian codes, in fifteenth-century BCE Hittite codes, in the thirteenth-century BCE Mosaic Code, as well as in ancient Greek and Roman law. Among the church fathers one finds varying perspectives on the death penalty, although there is a general recognition of the state's responsibility to implement capital justice. Tertullian (late second century) and Lactantius (late third century) affirmed that in the case of murder divine law consistently required a life for a life. Both Augustine (late fourth and early fifth century) and Theodosius II (mid-fifth century) acknowledged the state's role in mediating capital sanctions. In addition, various councils from the seventh century (the Eleventh Council of Toledo) to the thirteenth (the Fourth Lateran Council) followed the lead of Leo the Great (fifth century) in forbidding clerics from engagement in matters of capital justice. Aquinas would insist that the community had both the right and the duty to "cut away" an individual in order "to safeguard the common good." The common good, he reasoned, is "better than the good of the individual," notably because of "certain pestilent fellows" who serve as "a hindrance to the common good, that is, to the concord of human society." Such persons, he concluded, therefore "are to be withdrawn by death from the society of men."[5]

Late-medieval and Reformation-era theologians maintained continuity in this regard, affirming that the state has a rightful duty before God to impose capital sanctions upon murderers. Even the so-called "left wing" of the Protestant reform movement—from which much modern religious opposition to capital punishment is thought to derive—recognized the death penalty. The Schleitheim Confession of 1527, an exemplary document adopted by the Swiss Brethren (the progenitors of earliest Anabaptism), reads: "The sword is an ordinance of God… Princes and Rulers are ordained for the punishment of evildoers and putting them to death." This Anabaptist declaration concurs with the 1580 Lutheran Formula of Concord, which prescribes for "wild and intractable men" a commensurate "external punishment."

In summary, the patristic, medieval, and late-medieval periods generally mirror the church's tacit acknowledgement of capital punishment in cases of murder. Early-modern abolitionist responses to penal excesses, of course, will find voice in influential eighteenth- and nineteenth-century thinkers—among them, Voltaire, Montesquieu, Rousseau, David Hume, Ben Franklin, Thomas Paine, Jeremy Bentham, and Karl Marx.

While much ink has been spilled in recent decades as to the place that capital punishment might occupy in Catholic social thought and particularly in the thinking of recent popes, what often goes unstated is the truth specified by the *Catechism of the Catholic Church*. Such needs reiterating:

> Preserving the common good of society requires rendering the aggressor unable to inflict harm. For this reason the traditional teaching of the Church has acknowledged as well-founded *the right and duty* of legitimate public authority to punish malefactors by means of penalties *commensurate with the gravity of the crime*, not excluding, in cases of extreme gravity, the death penalty.[6]

Throughout its history, Christian teaching has affirmed the death penalty in the case of premeditated murder, a fact utterly ignored by not only pacifists but many sincere Christians, regardless of their theological orientation. Guilt incurred by sin constitutes a debt in the present order that must be paid. Punitive dealings, thus, provide necessary atonement and restore the balance of justice and moral order that has been disturbed. In theological terms, they prepare the human being for a destiny in eternity, thereby preparing us all to meet our Maker in a way that is ethically significant in the temporal order. Religious abolitionists tend to ground their bias against capital punishment in a particular (mis)reading of Jesus's teaching in the "Sermon on the Mount" and a purported "forgiveness" ethic. In addition, while ignoring ethical continuity in the broader sweep of biblical revelation, they prefer, based on the flaws of human government, to dismiss its divinely instituted commission to punish evil and reward good.[7]

Justification for capital punishment in the case of murder is found in the narrative of Genesis 9, a text that is often ignored even by religious abolitionists. Its teaching is quite clear: precisely *because* the human being is fashioned in the image of God, one who purposely sheds the blood of another must die. Genesis 9:5–6 is to be understood foremost as an institution that *protects* life. The rationale for this morale imperative is none other than the *safeguarding* of human life.[8] The accompanying retribution sanction has the effect of discouraging invasions on the sanctity of the human creature. What is explicit and emphatic in this narrative is the utterly heinous nature of premeditated murder: an assault on human life is comparable, as it were, to an assault on the very being of God. The fact that justice demands punishment befitting the crime—i.e., just retribution—reveals the essential difference in character between revenge and retribution. Having been created in the *imago Dei*, human life is declared to be a sacred trust. The implication is clear: murder—i.e., the deliberate extermination of a life by another human being—is tantamount to killing God in effigy. Moreover, as confirmed in Mosaic legislation, premeditated murder is the *one* crime for which there exists *no* restitution. In the litany of capital crimes delineated in the Pentateuch, only one precludes the possibility of ransom (Numbers 35); only one criminal act transcends the principles of restitution and restoration. Thus, as C. S. Lewis noted in his wonderfully prescient essay "The Humanitarian Theory of Punishment," to be punished however severely because we in fact *deserve* it is to be treated as a human being created in the very image of God.

When a murder occurs in our community, we are obliged, regardless of our comfort level, to clear our throat as it were and make a public, communal declaration. The deliberate extermination of another human being is an absolute evil and therefore absolutely intolerable. Such was the argument advanced by David Gelernter, a professor of computer science at Yale who was letter-bombed in June of 1993, almost losing his life.[9] The essence of Gelernter's argument was that we execute murderers in order to make a communal statement: deliberate murder embodies evil so terrible that it defiles the community, and as a result the community needs catharsis that occurs through criminal justice properly construed. Gelernter properly noted that in the face of murder contemporary society, however, is more prone to shrug it off than to exact just retribution and affirm binding moral standards. The problem, accordingly, is our moral evasiveness. After all, who in American society (or in the West, for that matter) believes that evil really does exist?

Justice has been classically defined as rendering to each person what is due. Desert, then, is foundational to ethics; it is a part of the human moral intuition. Parents know this, children know it, and indeed people from Kansas to Canada to Kenya to Kazakhstan know it as well. It needs restating in our day that it is virtuous, not vicious, to express anger and moral outrage at social evil and injustice. Retributive justice, then, where it is properly understood, is a social good, for it corrects social imbalances and perversions. Herein we find the wedding of justice and charity. When through social attitudes and the rule of law we affirm retributive justice, we are addressing several levels of "imbalance" and disturbance: we are attentive to (1) the victimized party who has been wronged, (2) society at large which has been offended and is watching, and (3) future offenders who might be tempted to do evil. This trifold application of justice, as both Augustine and Aquinas understood it, was in fact an application of charity. As an extreme example, both even saw going to war as an act that can express the wedding of charity and justice where properly motivated[10]: it is charitable to prevent the criminal from doing evil, it is charitable toward society which needs protecting, and it is charitable toward potential criminals who might be averted from doing evil.

Contrary to contemporary practice in most jurisdictions, punishment for a crime and restitution for the victim are interrelated concepts. In the case of premeditated murder, compensation is not available as an alternative. Hence, as much of human history attests and as the biblical witness affirms, it is the one crime that carries a mandatory death sentence. To suggest or argue that the ultimate human crime should not be met with the ultimate punishment being meted out by civil authorities, at least in a relatively free society, is not some "higher" ethic as some might contend; nor is it "Christian" by any stretch of the imagination. Rather, it is a moral travesty inasmuch as it fails to comprehend the nature and meaning of the *imago Dei* and stubbornly contradicts universally revealed canons of moral truth.

We do not need great minds to tell us that people such as Hitler, Stalin, Pol Pot, Idi Amin, or Vladimir Putin deserve to die, nor that those who murder in cold blood on our streets and in our neighborhoods deserve the same. The suffering of their victims and the families of those victims demand it, just as *human dignity* itself demands it[11]; such is a matter of simple justice. Civilized societies do not tolerate the murder of innocent human beings; uncivilized regimes do.[12]

In the final analysis, the argument from deterrence, regardless of the category of crime, is one of *probability*, not proof; it suggests what is *likely*, not leak-proof. The value of deterrence is intuited by virtually all parents; it is a common-sense intuition. The issue is *not* whether punishment will deter always and everywhere but whether it will deter more than other approaches in responding to criminal behavior; at bottom then, the issue is justice. The question is whether severity in fact works in motivating human behavior. If the death penalty has no deterrent value, then we may show the murderer mercy and attempt his rehabilitation. If, however, executions *do* have a deterrent value, then opposition becomes a moral perversion of "victimhood," resulting in far more deaths than the abolitionist argument will prevent. When we protect the lives of the guilty, we offer up innocent lives as a result. If as a society we affirm the morality of punishment, then we affirm the immorality of its abolition.

Reinforcing the moral order is critically important in a relatively free and self-governing society. For this reason, we emphasis the rule of law; hence, murder is always intolerable. To object to or reject capital punishment in cases of premeditated murder is to deny that punishment should fit the crime, that punishment should be proportionate to the crime committed. Alas, it is to place justice on a sliding scale and to confess that there are no ultimate and abiding moral values. Our contemporary problem is not that capital punishment is cruel but that it is unusual.[13]

41

How does natural law reasoning view the secularizing of law and the wider culture?

Several Questions thus far have suggested a natural law response to secularizing tendencies in broader Western culture. Such tendencies have undermined—if they have not resulted in rejection of—natural law arguments for the rule and application of law. The hallmark of our era, it scarcely needs mentioning, is its accent on rights. However, "rights" have moral meaning only when they issue out of a particular understanding of human nature. They have meaning, specifically, if we assume that dignity accords with a certain uniqueness about the human species. But we cannot conceptualize human "rights" properly unless we are willing to attach to it an equal commitment to *duties*.

In formal terms, a "right" confers an "advantageous position," as it were. Rights-based thinking, especially as mirrored in law, focuses on what is *due* a person; duty-based thinking, however, concerns itself with what is *required*. Properly construed, rights and duties are reciprocal in nature. Rights-based thinking in our present cultural context has transformed itself since our nation's founders and framers wrote of "inalienable rights." Today we have grown accustomed to understanding rights first and foremost in terms of personal freedoms and individual preferences. Thus, a measure of purification is in order.

Question 8 of this volume observed the inclination of an ideological secularism toward relativism and positivism, whether in its logical, moral, or legal form. Undergirding this outlook is both a rejection of revealed religion and a denial of the very possibility by human reason to know objective moral truth. Hence, law will assume a foremost utilitarian cast, given its rejection of transcendent authority. Whatever our assessment of this development, questions of enormous importance concerning the place of religion in society are raised—questions that challenge our understanding of public life and authentic pluralism. Accompanying these questions is the realization that secularism, as a world- and life-view, is not "neutral."

Robert George, McCormick Professor of Jurisprudence and Director of the James Madison Program in American Ideals and Institutions at Princeton University, has argued that any healthy, decent society will rest on three pillars—(1) respect for the human person, (2) the institution of the family, and (3) a fair and just system of law and government.[1] At the heart of the first is lodged human dignity and respect for the human person—beginning with the child in the womb and including the mentally and physically impaired. The second brings stability insofar as it transmits to each new generation virtue and character. The third is important because of its protective element. Those in society who intend to do wrong undermine the common social good. Thus, public authorities must administer justice and both create and interpret law in a manner that underpins rather than undermines human flourishing. Ideological secularism, as we observed, tends to spawn relativism, in both its moral and legal form, which over time expresses itself with a "rights"-based orientation that is supremely individualistic and detrimental to the common good. Where no just system is in place, where there is no sense of duty and obligation, all of society will suffer.

In assorted Questions thus far the present volume has been supremely critical of the world- and life-view of ideological secularism. In this vein, however, a little-reported but quite significant event which occurred two decades ago, is worthy of our attention, if for no other reason that it illustrates what might be called a "post-secular" moment in the West. I have already alluded to this event in QQ. 10 and 31, but it is worth reexamining because it illustrates so tellingly why the "sacred" and the "secular" simply may not be walled off in a pluralistic society. At the invitation of the Catholic Academy of Bavaria, in January of 2004 two intellectual "antipodes" agreed to dialogue on the political and moral foundations of secular Western societies. The meeting of Jürgen Habermas, one of the most influential contemporary philosophers and secular theorists alive, and Joseph Cardinal Ratzinger, the then Prefect of the Roman Catholic Congregation for the Doctrine of the Faith (to become Pope Benedict XVI one year later) was remarkable for several reasons. Not least was the high profile of both interlocutors—one as a preeminent secular theorist and the other as arguably the most visible Christian leader in the world. Consider as well the parallels between the two. Both were born in the 1920s—Habermas in 1929, Ratzinger in 1927. Both took their doctorate in the twelve-month span between 1953 and 1954. Both settled into their eventual influential positions in the early 1980s—Ratzinger as Prefect of the Congregation for the Doctrine of the Faith (1981) and Habermas assuming his final professorial position in Frankfurt (1983). Both, upon consideration, appear to be the ultimate embodiment of secular over against religious conviction.

The two interlocutors had agreed to address the topic of "pre-political foundations of a democratic state." Habermas asks at the outset, perhaps surprisingly to some, whether a free (i.e., "democratic") state presupposes as its basis what it cannot, at bottom, guarantee. Is it still possible to offer secular—which is to say, "post-metaphysical" and "non-religious"—justification for the state? And what precisely is it that unites the citizenry? Moreover, what happens if society degenerates and, in time, collapses? Habermas's own response to such questions is surprising. He suggests that society must understand "secularization" as a "double learning process that compels both the traditions of the Enlightenment and of religious doctrine to reflect on their own respective limits."[2] This he maintains, even when he rejects the overt assumptions that religion and natural law theory bring. To his credit, however, Habermas is able to ask *why* human rights are rooted in democracy from the very beginning. His response is that a democratic state is constituted, at its core, by the rule of law, even when he renounces antecedent moral principles of the natural law. Legality, not morality, governs Habermas's thinking. At the same time, Habermas is willing to acknowledge not only that a common language contributes to a society's heritage but also a common religious heritage. These, he readily admits, are "pre-political" in nature.

Where does this leave us? In the end, Habermas is willing to acknowledge that we in the West are in a "post-secular" cultural moment. This awareness concedes not only that religion is important to many people but also that it reflects "a normative insight that has consequences for the political dealings of unbelieving citizens with believing citizens." Habermas, at bottom, is willing to recognize the fact that the "secular" and the "sacred" cannot be partitioned or separated. This means, then, that reason and faith need to be in dialogue. It also means that contemporary secular and utilitarian approaches to law are inadequate. Law has an antecedent, and that antecedent—in its transcending of all cultural constructs—is the natural law.

42

How does natural law reasoning apply to basic "life" issues such as abortion, human sexuality, and euthanasia?

HUMAN FREEDOM AND NATURAL LAW go together much like love and marriage, writes one moral theologian.[1] This connection, of course, given the current cultural climate, is no longer self-evident, basic as it might be. Otherwise stated, freedom of choice needs natural law if human beings are to choose well and thus strive to be *good* persons. Natural law protects human beings insofar as it helps them in avoiding blind or arbitrary choices while enabling them to choose in accordance with their true nature and with the truth. This has particular relevance as applied to bioethics and broader "life" issues, wherein human beings are forbidden to destroy the lives of innocent human persons on the basis of their intrinsic good.

As it applies to abortion and euthanasia, natural law reasoning guides us in a direct manner because of its baseline directive to *harm no one* or do evil, a moral directive that has significant implications both for beginning-of-life and end-of-life issues. In such cases, law has a more proximate application of natural law principles. There exists no time, circumstance, or occasion in which this basic moral principle may be set aside; it is non-negotiable. In the logic of Aquinas, everything that is living has a "natural" *inclination* to preserve itself, and it is "natural" for the human species both to propagate and nurture as well as to preserve itself.[2] For this reason, based on natural law reasoning, government's responsibility—at the minimum—is to protect the lives of its citizens—*all* citizens.

Human life is inviolable; it is an intrinsic good in and of itself. And this, of course, is the rub. For proponents of abortion, the unborn—i.e., human life *in utero*—may not be declared as "persons." For to acknowledge the "personhood" of the fetus, at whatever point short of exit through the mother's womb, is to concede the fact of killing.[3] Even Peter Singer, the renowned professor of bioethics at Princeton University who has championed not only abortion but infanticide and euthanasia, concedes this much. He writes: "They [opponents of abortion] point out that abortion kills a unique, living human individual. *That claim is difficult to deny*, at least if by 'human' we mean 'member of the species *Homo sapiens*.'"[4]

Let us pause for a moment. Is the unborn child, at *any* stage of development, a "member of the human species"? And what does this say regarding the moral status of the unborn? At the very least, even if we grant that the newly created human in the womb is "potential" life, one might ask whether any protection against injury—"arbitrary injury"—is legally justified. In a similar vein, one might argue that the language of the "Equal Protection Clause" of the Fourteenth Amendment, conceived in the context of the racial situation in the South (the U.S.) based on newly freed slaves in the mid-19th century, might be applied to the matter of abortion. Even when states do not *prohibit* abortion, might they not in actuality be *denying equal protection* to a particular class of citizens—namely unborn humans?[5] Our response to these questions depends on whether we are willing to grant a natural law perspective on personhood, in which case (a) the unborn are considered human persons (i.e., "members of the human species") and (b) abortion, in this light, is the killing of innocent life.

As I write, there is widespread activism in the U.S. that calls for abortion to be a "human right." This is a far cry from attitudes a mere twenty-five years earlier, when abortion advocates (and, in fact, the U.S. president) declared abortion to be "safe, legal, and *rare*." Within a generation we have gone from "rarity" to a "right." Here the natural lawyer's position is that where the life of the mother is not at stake—and such cases are, relatively speaking, rare, despite popular rhetoric to the contrary—the matter of abortion constitutes, at bottom, "harm" done to the unborn. Even cases of rape, for example, do not *require* that an innocent human being dies, despite the unspeakable emotional and physical trauma associated therewith. Abortion almost always constitutes harm, and this, first, to the unborn—as an act of killing—and, second, to the mother who thereby suffers in a manner that is generally not acknowledged by abortion activists. Tragically, neither of these horrors finds the light of day in contemporary ethical discourse or public debate. From a moral standpoint (and natural law reasoning), the presumption of all laws affecting the issue of the unborn should be *on the side of protecting the unborn*. Period.

The same logic may be applied to euthanasia (physician-assisted suicide). Law's responsibility is to protect the life of all citizens. Whether through suicide, a self-determined decision, or the decision of family members or an administering doctor, government's responsibility is to *protect life*. There is simply no existing *moral-legal* basis on which governing authorities relinquish their responsibility to protect the citizenry by which they permit individual persons, their family members, or related doctors to enact euthanasia. A central issue is whether individuals should be granted control over their lives in matters of severe illness and dying. Natural law reasoning requires that we ask whether human beings, as members of a *human community*, are morally obligated to honor those responsibilities of "membership" based on *human nature*, irrespective of the *personal* challenges they face. Or, are they permitted to end human existence based on pain and suffering? At bottom, as in the context of beginning-of-life issues, we are justified in asking, *On what basis can humans contravene the moral principle to advance and protect human life?* Based on human nature, the principle of injury—which was applied in the case of abortion—may be applied here in terms of how we treat ourselves as well as others as it concerns end-of-life matters.

One argument that resists the current cultural trend is this: individuals who by reason of pain and suffering are driven toward the need to end their lives might indeed rush irrationally and prematurely toward ending their lives. Since human beings having *nothing* to do with *how or why* they enter the world (a matter that transcends them), they therefore have no decision in how they exit (again, a matter of transcendence). In addition, relatives of such individuals might bring pressure to bear on such suffering individuals to terminate their lives based on emotional-psychological, economic, or other reasons. And this is wholly aside from whether particular doctors, presiding over such cases, are available to assist in such ending-of-life matters.[6]

Is human bodily life an *instrumental* or an *intrinsic* good? How we answer this question will determine our view of end-of-life matters. In fact, it will inform our position on all bioethical issues. Because natural law reasoning is oriented toward the good, and because human nature is a composite of material and non-material, of the spiritual, mental-emotional, and physical, we may conclude that human bodily life is no mere instrumental good. Rather, it is an *intrinsic* good, and because of this reality, intrinsic human goods are not the possessions of human persons.[7] Personhood is not *possessing* something but *being* someone. There is a connection—a mysterious connection—of body and person, and this connection is absolutely crucial for respecting human dignity.[8] Therefore, moral norms anchored in the natural law forbid the destroying of innocent life. What establishes moral consistency in end-of-life matters is the criterion of intention. Do we *intend* to assist death? The distinction between what is *intended* over against what is *foreseen* is absolutely essential to Judeo-Christian ethics and natural law reasoning.[9] The reality of our responsibility to provide palliative measures and care for those who suffer does *not* justify killing them to relieve their suffering.

"Intolerable" suffering aside, many, of course, will argue in our day that because a person loses his or her conscious or meaningful awareness of other people or surroundings, or because some individuals lose some (or all) of their capacities and "social utility," there is no need to keep them alive. It is assumed, then, that no moral wrong is being done by terminating the lives of those persons who have become "burdensome" or "useless."[10] In an earlier Question we noted the position of one well-known bioethicist: namely, that some nonhuman animals have lives more valuable than the lives of some humans.[11] While this position may appear somewhat extreme and not represent the thinking of the average citizen, it expresses the inevitable result of utilitarian thinking that rejects natural law assumptions and views human personhood as possessing mere instrumental rather than intrinsic worth. While the German term for this—*lebensunwertes Leben* ("life unworthy of living"), referring to such individuals without "social utility"—initially appeared with force among German social theorists and became "mainstreamed" in the two decades leading up to the Second World War, the impulse toward euthanasia even in the U.S. during these years was surprisingly strong, given the influence both of economics trends and social Darwinism.[12] The good of life toward which we are directed by the first principles of natural law reasoning includes human bodily life. This truth, it needs re-emphasizing in our day, is the bedrock of all bioethical issues.[13] And let us be realistic: it is illusory in a relativistic age to assume that moral norms are in place to protect us—as individuals, as families, as communities—from the injustices and evils of private choices.

The matter of sexuality in our day, given the prominence of "same-sex" relationships as they become not only public but *legal* issues, begs several questions. The natural law perspective requires that we approach this matter from several, though related, angles. One is most basic, namely, how to distinguish between different kinds of relations or friendships. There exist various forms of friendship, including homosexual friendships. Until quite recently, *no* one and *no* legislative body or jurisdiction on the planet would have equated a homosexual friendship with marriage. Marriage, after all, has always—again, until recently—been identified with reproductive potential and family responsibilities, which no homosexual relationship can mirror or reproduce. Alas, this has changed. With cultural shifts on sexual attitudes we are once again confronted with what is "natural," what is normative, and thus what points to natural law realities.

The model of human design, and the witness of all of human civilization, has understood marriage as between the two created sexes, with reproductive potential and responsibility, which alas excludes homosexual relations. The reason for this cross-civilizational witness has to do with human *nature*. Human goods and the common good are ordered on the basis of moral judgment, not on the basis of desires that might (rightly or wrongly) motivate the human beings or human friendships. Human goods—that is to say, "natural goods"—are ordered toward particular ends and purposes, which are intrinsic elements of human well-being and flourishing. To say that homosexuality is "unnatural" is simply to argue for human sexuality based on our fundamental design. Sexual acts outside of marriage (as traditionally understood), a union that is an incomparable and indispensable "human good," are not unitive in an intrinsic way. That is, they do not unite partners in a wholistic and integral way biologically, morally, and spiritually; they merely instrumentalize the human body and thus constitute no *intrinsic* good.

While it is true that "the state should neither give special recognition to nor criminalize any form of friendship,"[14] the natural law advocate would oppose granting any sort of legal identification of gay/lesbian relationships with marriage. But why? The issue here is *not* the power of the state to prohibit homosexual friendships; nor is it religious opposition to homosexuality in principle. Rather, the issue is grounded in the natural law (and hence Christian) view that a pluralism of the marketplace and society can exist only so long as *the common good is upheld*. Any law that contradicts the natural law, which is bound to protecting the common social good, is counter to human nature and thus illicit. And here is precisely the rub in our day. Contemporary society wishes *not* to be reminded of the truth: namely, that to equate homosexual liasons with marriage, as traditionally and pan-civilizationally understood, undermines the common good—the *true* "good." It denies what, through *nature*, we know and seek to affirm as it concerns human flourishing.[15]

43

What is the role of the natural law in public discourse, political debate, and public persuasion?

This very question further illustrates the answer to Question 4 ("How broad or detailed is the content of the natural law?"), though deserving additional comment. While natural law reasoning serves as a general guide for moral matters (do good and avoid evil), it does not prescribe in specific social contexts *how or in what manner* that is to be done. For such, wisdom and discretion are needed, as well as genuine tolerance of differences of opinion and behavioral strategies. Nowhere is this more the case than in public discourse, political debate, and public persuasion. Not least among the reasons for this is the simple fact of social-cultural pluralism: the public consequences of the opinions and actions of millions of citizens—non-religious and religious people alike—require an ordering in society that is not easily achieved apart from certain transcending values and principles held in common. What values, then, truly unite a people? Moreover, even among religious folks, differences on socio-political issues and appropriate strategies for involvement vary greatly.

Let us illustrate through the contentious matter of mixing religion and politics, taken up as well in the following Question. Two opposite and extreme attitudes avail themselves as it concerns bringing religious convictions into the public arena. One of these has been identified already in the volume, namely, a secularist attempt to privatize religion so that it does not enter the sphere of public reasoning. This exclusionary assumption, as noted in a previous Question[1] and examined in the following Question, lies at the heart of John Rawls's (and the widely accepted) view of "public reason." Rawls's method is to bracket controversial moral, philosophical, or religious issues and to exclude them because of their grounding in "comprehensive doctrines." Because religion constitutes a "comprehensive doctrine," it is thought to be disqualified because it is not "neutral," thus needing exclusion from public discourse and political debate.[2] But in the words of the late Richard John Neuhaus, one of the most influential commentators on religion, politics, and culture of recent decades,

> What is relatively new [in American life] is the naked public square. The naked public square is the result of political doctrine and practice that would exclude religion and religiously grounded values from the conduct of public business. The doctrine is that America is a secular society. It finds dogmatic expression in the ideology of secularism.[3]

Neuhaus was convinced that "most liberal secularists are in deep denial about their articles of faith and acts of faith."[4] And indeed this seems to be the case. For even the aforementioned Rawlsian approach to "public reason," which is committed to excluding "comprehensive doctrines" (that is to say, religious beliefs) from public debate and which is assumed by many (if not most) of our contemporaries, is itself *comprehensive* in nature. In the end, a so-called "naked public square" is a vacuum begging to be filled, and the agent that will fill that vacuum will be the state. As Neuhaus rightly notes, a twisted notion of the disestablishment of religion invariably leads to the establishment of the state as "church." Having cast out one devil, committed secularists unavoidably invite the entrance of seven devils more perverse than the first.

By contrast, at the other end of the spectrum is the misguided attempt to wed or conflate religion and politics. In the U.S., this might take the form of "returning America to God" or, more recently, a "Christian nationalism."[5] The problem with this posture is its failure both to see the relative autonomy of both religion and government and to recognize the unique and limited theocratic character of Israel as represented in the Old Testament. This view fails, then, on both political as well as theological grounds.

A preferable, and more balanced, view is that of America's founders and framers, who saw the need for interaction between religion and the state—a view best described as a "fence" rather than a "wall"[6]—without coercion and without exclusion. After all, as George Washington insisted in his 1796 "Farewell" address ("To the People of the United States") at the conclusion of his second term, of "all the dispositions and habits which lead to political prosperity," religion and morality are "indispensable supports" for a self-governing nation. This is true, just as a politicized faith is a perversion of genuine faith.

From the standpoint of the Judeo-Christian moral tradition, which is underpinned by natural law thinking, *no realm* of human existence in the created order can be excluded from our care and consideration. This is surely the case for politics, since civil government itself was established by the Creator for the ordering of human behavior.[7] Jesus himself, when tested on the delicate matter of taxation in first-century Palestine, responded that we should "render to Caesar what is Caesar's" and "render to God what is God's."[8] This statement suggests both ambiguity and engagement. On the one hand, the state is not divine; the state has moral antecedents. On the other hand, we are to be politically involved since the citizen-state (the *polis*) has consequences for all of public life; it is able either to protect or pillage the common good. Thus, it should not surprise us that among religious believers historically, Jesus's "bipolar" assessment of political authority has led to very different, and at times diametrically opposed, interpretations.

What helps moderate both of the aforementioned extreme approaches to political discourse, as well as politics and governing, is the viewpoint espoused as early as Augustine (late fourth and early fifth century), and continuing through Protestant reformers such as Martin Luther and John Calvin, late-medieval and early-modern voices such as Francisco de Vitoria, Francisco Suárez, and Hugo Grotius, and modern voices to the present who have affirmed the natural law tradition. How should religious conviction and politics be viewed? Because of its baseline conviction that all human activity falls under the dominion of the Creator, and thus collapses any dichotomy between "sacred" and "secular," the Judeo-Christian moral tradition (and hence natural law reasoning) understands justice to be paramount, and therefore the very goal or aim of a self-governing society. The purpose of law and government is to encourage humans to do good and discourage them from doing evil. Law expresses moral convictions and hence judgments on the behavior of society's members. These judgments inform citizens on what is honorable and what is dishonorable, what is just and what is unjust—all for the common good. The power of a society's moral-legal judgments can be illustrated in the following way:

> Suppose that, next year, all fifty states decide to legalize marijuana and cocaine use, prostitution and same-sex marriage. Regardless of where you stand on the issues, do you doubt that, if such laws stayed in effect for fifty years, they wouldn't fundamentally alter our views, including our moral views, of these issues?[9]

Disagreements with fellow citizens, it needs acknowledging, are not always moral in nature—we can disagree over roadway speed limits, tax increases, utility rates, the zoning of public property, etc., etc. On our culture's more contentious issues which have to do with human *nature* and human *dignity*—for example, abortion, sexuality, end-of-life matters, or addressing crime—the character of our disagreements is profoundly moral. Here we must insist once more, against the reigning tenets of a militant secularism, that a person's "comprehensive doctrine" of life cannot be bracketed and removed from public discussion and debate. To argue such is blatantly discriminatory, at best, and intellectually dishonest, at worst.[10]

While our obligation to disagree with our opponents on contentious ethical issues does not exclude charity or proper public etiquette, the fact of our disagreement is by no means confined merely to etiquette.[11] As citizens we have a duty to disagree on ultimate matters, where in our view issues of injustice or moral evil are at play. "Public reason," therefore, cannot be defined only as representing positions that agree with secular or "liberal" thinking. We must make our case publicly, as concerned citizens, on the basis of an appeal to justice, the common good, and moral principle accessible through reason. This, of course, is what natural law reasoning seeks to accomplish in the public arena.[12] Public truths require that public decisions and public arguments be made that are publicly accessible.

The presence—and continual reemergence—of religion in our public life and political discourse will always result in charges that people are imposing their beliefs and moral judgments on others. But so it has always been. All are entitled to the "public square," and all make moral judgments—even militant secularists. And in the end, *someone's* moral judgments will be imposed through legislation. But as someone has wisely noted, this procedure, messy as it can be, is less about imposing than about proposing and persuading.[13]

44

Why is the natural law important to politics?

THE GOAL OF POLITICAL LIFE and the political community, from the natural law perspective, is to preserve the common good and a stable environment of peace, whereby citizens, irrespective of location or status, might flourish. This requires the presence of virtue, and especially the cardinal virtues—wisdom, justice, courage, and temperance—and not only among those who govern but citizens as well. Here, for our present purposes, the Question focuses on those who govern, for whom the responsibility is to strive for the *highest good* of the political community. Aristotle states it in this way: "For even if the good is the same for a city as for an individual, still the good of the city is apparently a greater and more complete good to acquire and preserve."[1]

Without the virtues, a society is consigned to disintegration, since what disturbs social life—hatred, divisions, lack of civility, or criminal behavior—is forbidden by the natural law. By design and right reason, human beings are oriented toward doing good and avoiding doing the evil. No one anywhere and in any social or cultural location would argue otherwise.

Justice, as defined in multiple Questions in this volume, is concerned with the ordering of right relations. Peace or tranquility in the social context cannot be realized if that peace is not justly ordered. This will entail the need for policy that rewards the good and punishes what is wrong or malicious. Wisdom (or prudence) has been called a "moderator" in political life.[2] Why? It assesses and discerns what edifies or harms the populace, being attentive to the environment which only justice can procure. It is, we might say, a "guardian" of the common good. In its essence, wisdom takes what is theoretical, even contingent, and applies it to the world of action. Courage is needed to the extent that those governing are under obligation to do what is best for the common good, opposing policies and laws that undermine the common good and are intrinsically harmful, regardless of the unpopularity of such actions. Temperance (or self-control) is required to the extent that the one governing must resist the temptation to endorse policy or law that encourages wrongful tendencies in the populace.

The crucial question raised by the need for virtues in social and political life—for example, justice, wisdom, temperance, and courage—is the matter of their source. Whence come human virtues? The American founders were quite convinced that the moral impulse is impossible apart from religion; for this reason, they struggled—and were successful—in establishing religious freedom. They knew that no society, no nation, and no people could be "self-governing" apart from the religious impulse. This, then, is why politics and the public arena need religion. Autocratic regimes can do without the religious impulse; "civil" society cannot.

Natural-law thinking is essential in helping to create and maintain a principled—and thus genuine—pluralism. It is surely a perverse mindset, and exceedingly undemocratic, to insist (or assume) that the relationship between politics and religion, between church and state, between contemporary liberalism and a "natural law liberalism" must always be one of conflict and confrontation.[3] Natural law principles of truth, human dignity, the common good, and family are essential in curbing the vices of freedom, individualism, and prosperity that typically attend contemporary liberalism. There was a time, of course, when democratic "liberalism" and natural law philosophy were not perceived as enemies.

Probing their conflicted relationship is especially needful, given the fact that in the "liberalism" as found in present-day Western societies the default position is to view religion as a private matter and hence to be excluded from the culture of democratic pluralism.[4] This is true regardless of the public issues at stake, whether they concern abortion, sexuality, health care, euthanasia, the homeless, or criminal justice. Today, in the third decade of the 21st century, one is tempted to conclude that there exists a widening gulf between "sectarianisms"—between the secular and the religious—particularly along the lines of broader "life" issues such as abortion and human sexuality. Perhaps the most widely held view of "public reason" has been a "political liberalism" that has marginalized the religious viewpoint for decades.[5] But this exclusion, alas, is exceedingly "undemocratic." The primary thrust of the present Question, therefore, concerns the need for the *moral* and not merely *legal* argument for religion in the public sphere. The order of these two must not be reversed, for the legal or constitutional question is dependent on the moral question. For this reason, in a previous Question the matter of world- and life-views was introduced.[6] A secularist world- and life-view, as we have argued, makes certain assumptions about ultimate reality, the human person, and the nature of morality. Thus, we can judge that *no* world-view can claim a "neutrality" as it concerns the public arena. This is as true for militant secularists as it is for people of religious faith. It is a fact that most contemporary philosophical and legal discussions of politics and the public arena assume that religious beliefs—something which all people possess (spoken or unspoken)—should somehow be bleached from the public square.[7] But such is neither true pluralism nor intellectual and moral honesty.

But what are standard arguments offered that tend to exclude the religious viewpoint from the political sphere? Among the most common are those contending that the religious viewpoint (1) is based on "religious sources"; (2) is not based on reason and evidence; (3) cannot create (as can secularism) any mediation or agreement among various world- or life-views in the public square; (4) consists of "higher order" beliefs (as opposed to "lower-order" convictions such as working out our social and political arrangements); (5) is divisive; (6) should not be imposed on others; and (7) does not address strictly "constitutional" and political issues.[8] The inconsistencies of most of the above arguments have been addressed in one form or fashion in previous Questions—for example, the rationality of religious faith, the contribution of religion to moral development, and the reality of world-view assumptions at work (spoken or unspoken).

The last claim above—the "constitutional" claim—requires only brief comment. In the words of the First Amendment to the Constitution, "Congress shall make no law respecting an establishment of religion, or prohibiting the free exercise thereof." The varied peoples inhabiting the American colonies represented diverse religious viewpoints. Given this reality, the founders and framers were, for the most part, united in their concern not to promote any one particular religious viewpoint; any sort of theocratic understanding of the state was to be avoided. The fact that the First Amendment addresses both sides of the religious issue—non-establishment yet free exercise—speaks for itself, despite the many legal cases in the last century that have beclouded the original intent of the framers: *non-establishment yet free exercise.*

Informing many of this volume's Questions thus far is the baseline, natural-law assumption that reason and religious belief are compatible, that they are *by nature* in dialogue with one another. Thus, any proper definition of "religion" must recognize that religious beliefs are rational in nature, that they comport with our fundamental nature, and that they are reasonably intuited. Even in the grammar of democratic liberty, we may insist that "human rights" and our duty to protect them issue out of fundamentally religious convictions. This is why, for much of recent human history, the Judeo-Christian religious tradition, with its unique, dignified view of human personhood, has undergirded a democratic political structure.[9] This linkage is by no means accidental; nor is it incidental. Human equality and freedom, rooted in the sacred rights of conscience and the natural law, ground civil law. In fact, one might argue that one of the classic doctrines associated with Judeo-Christian religion—namely, the doctrine of the Fall—alone explains, over against a secularist-materialist explanation, the reality of evil, dispelling any sort of belief that human beings are *good by nature and thus incapable of doing evil.*[10] The realm of politics requires a realist anthropology: we reward the good while punishing evil for the purposes of protecting the common social good.

Thus, the militant secularist viewpoint that religion represents a threat to democratic polity and the sphere of politics is not merely fiction; it is destructive in its own right. By way of example, we should try to imagine what American society might look like today if Martin Luther King, Jr., had decided not to bother promoting his religious views in public.[11] The truth is that religion has been a powerful force for good, and it might even be argued that more than any social force religion has contributed to the flourishing of human beings as well as to the alleviation of human suffering. If, as the ideological secularist believes, there exists no overall purpose either to human creation or to the wider universe, then logically it will be impossible to avoid relativism, even skepticism, and therefore, an inability to ground human dignity in anything other than material or pragmatic reasons. This is decisive for the arenas of ethics and politics, in which citizens wrestle with how society *should* be ordered. Here we might pause to note the "oughtness" of the language here—how a society *should* be ordered—wherein even the secularist resorts to the use of a *moral* grammar. Indeed, how *should* people live? And why? These are *moral* questions. In answering such questions, we may argue in all humility that religious people—Christians, for example—are far better equipped than their non-religious counterparts. Alone the subject of natural rights is indebted to religious thinking historically—a fact conveniently forgotten by many.[12] Contrary to the thinking of many in our day, religion cannot be successfully confined to the private realm.

In this context, however, we must also confront a social-political reality: legitimate governmental authority would be impossible if in fact that authority could not legitimately *impose* (even coercively) any policy on the broader populace, including on those who disagree with its political rationale. Governing authorities, by their very institution and necessity, act coercively. Were this not the case, then individual choices and actions would automatically produce a social anarchy that would destroy the very social fiber and essence of any people-group. This reality is the reason why Judeo-Christian religion allows for imperfect—and even at times unjust—authorities to carry out their office. Justice in the present life, alas, is not a zero-sum game; it is imperfectly constructed and orchestrated. Justice does not need perfection in order to be normative. And were this not the case, then we shall need to admit that *no attempts* at justice—*anywhere and in any context*—are worth pursuing. The question, therefore, remains *how*—humanly and humanely—we should go about working for justice. And *why?*

But the problem today, as Richard Neuhaus observed even decades ago, is not that the emperor has no clothes. It is that "the emperor's garments of moral authority have been stolen from the religion he has sent into exile from the public square."[13] For indeed there is no such thing as a "naked public square." For at its heart, Judeo-Christian religion is "incorrigibly interventionist," given its universalistic claims to truth as it relates to the totality of things.[14] If Americans care about a democratic future—and I write as a U.S. citizen—then we have "a deep stake in reconstructing a politics that was not begun by and cannot be sustained by the myth of secular America."[15] Such reconstruction will find clues in the past, even when we don't seek to recreate the past.

45

Is the natural law solely a "Christian" or "Roman Catholic" thing, and why do Protestants tend to be suspicious of the natural law idea?

DESPITE THE VERY PROTESTANT CAST of the American founding, with its debt to Lockean thinking, the concept of natural law has long been associated with Catholic social thought, and for good reason. Where a "renewal" of natural law thinking during the twentieth century has occurred, it has been chiefly due to the influence of Catholic thinkers.[1] This pattern has remained for the most part, with a few exceptions, up to the present. Contemporary Protestantism, by contrast, has "no comparable coherent framework for grounding its social thought." This was the conviction expressed twenty-five years ago by theologian and founding director of the Center for Catholic and Evangelical Theology Carl Braaten in his provocative essay "Protestants and Natural Law."[2]

Braaten, however, was not the first Protestant to make this observation. Precisely a century before a similar conviction was expressed by Dutch Reformed theologian (and former prime minister) Abraham Kuyper, whom Braaten cites.[3] In 1891, on the occasion of the publication of Pope Leo XIII's encyclical *Rerum Novarum*, Kuyper conceded:

> It must be admitted to our shame that the Roman Catholics are far ahead of us in their study of the social question. Indeed, very far ahead...The encyclical of Leo XIII gives the principles which are common to all Christians, and which we share with our Roman Catholic compatriots.[4]

Kuyper's appreciation of Roman Catholicism on matters moral and social would be reiterated seven years later in the 1898 Stone Lectures that Kuyper delivered at Princeton University. There Kuyper praised "the marvelous energy displayed in the latter half of this century by Rome" and "Rome's successful efforts in social life."[5] In both his 1891 and his 1898 remarks Kuyper was addressing two broader tendencies among his fellow Protestants. One was a sectarian spirit that failed to acknowledge Roman Catholics as fellow Christians who confess the same creedal realities in the face of a hostile cultural environment. The second was the Protestant inability to learn from Catholic social teaching. The "principles... common to all" used by Leo and noted by Kuyper relate *inter alia* to natural law—a concept that, in Braaten's words, "serves as a bridge category on ethical and social questions between church and world," between those with a commitment to Christian faith and those outside the community of faith.[6]

As the Reformation historian John T. McNeill wrote in the mid-20th century, there exists no discontinuity between the Protestant reformers and their predecessors with respect to natural law:

> Not one of the leaders of the Reformation assails the principle. Instead, with the possible exception of Zwingli, they all on occasion express a quite ungrudging respect for the moral law naturally implanted in the human heart and seek to inculcate this attitude in their readers. Natural law is not one of the issues on which they bring the Scholastics [or their contemporaries] under criticism...For the Reformers, as for the Fathers, canonists, and Scholastics, natural law stood affirmed on the pages of Scripture.[7]

As the next two Questions will attempt to make very clear, Protestant opposition to—or criticism of—natural law is a conspicuously modern phenomenon and cannot be found among any of the leaders of the Reformation. Some of that opposition has had to do with post-Enlightenment developments in philosophy that took the shape of utilitarianism and positivism. But because significant opposition, particularly over the last century, has been theological in nature and from within the Christian camp, it thus requires some commentary. That opposition or criticism takes several forms, each of which is anchored in some sort of theological justification. One form, for example, results from the view that natural law seems not to take serious enough the fact that all of creation has been wholly affected by the fall and sin. Correlatively, it is thought that natural law presupposes an autonomy of reason, whereby reason is elevated to a false level of moral awareness. For many who carry this conviction, it is thought that the image of God in humanity has been so damaged as to be virtually destroyed or eliminated. But while it is true that nature has been wounded, it has not been destroyed. Another reason for criticism is the view that natural law is not sufficiently Christocentric and that it undermines faith and grace. Yet another reason to be suspicious of natural law finds its roots in a skewed understanding of redemption and eschatology; hence, for some, reviving interest in natural law is akin to rearranging chairs on the Titanic, given the view that culture is "going to hell in a hand-basket." And yet a further criticism of natural law is that it appears to incorporate "pagan" or "worldly" philosophical elements into its framework—elements that are thought to be foreign to the Christian scriptures and to genuine faith.

At this point, the reason for our belaboring the fact of Protestant opposition to natural law should not be construed as purely academic or strictly theological. The consequence of such thinking, regardless of the theological rationale, is that it produces a *truncated social ethics*. As such, natural law critics fail to discern the role that our common humanity plays not only in moral theory but also in moral discourse.

This deficiency undermines any attempts to enter the public sphere and engage meaningfully in ethical discourse with non-likeminded people when and where critical social, political, and ethical issues are at stake. Alas, there remains for those who are so predisposed no language of ethical "transmission" which is intelligible to both religious believer and non-believer. In the end, apart from the natural law, we appear to lose any basis upon which to persuade and preserve "civil society." For this reason, the *Catechism of the Catholic Church* declares,

> In defending the ability of human reason to know God, the Church is expressing her confidence in the possibility of speaking about him to all men and with all men, and therefore of dialogue with other religions, with philosophy and science, as well as with unbelievers and atheists.[8]

If Carl Braaten's aforementioned challenge was timely in 1992, it is all the more relevant today, given (1) the vacuous and splintered nature (not to mention the theological bankruptcy) of American Protestantism in the 21st century as well as (2) the moral collapse of social, cultural, and political institutions around us. Braaten concluded his essay with the following challenge:

> Moral relativism joins political activism to sabotage the rules and standards needed to implement a societal system ordered by the principles of justice and truth. When the normlessness and the nihilistic effects of the deconstructionist mindset are no longer confined to academia but invade the wider public, the way is prepared for the moral collapse of social institutions or for the enthronement of the totalitarian state...Perhaps it is time to expose the current relativist and nihilist theories as the underside of totalitarian ideologies and political authoritarianism. A revival of natural law can be of use in that project.[9]

Braaten's words, in our present day, need rigorous reiteration.

46

How did the magisterial Protestant reformers view the natural law?

To THE SURPRISE OF SOME, natural law is resolutely affirmed in the writings of the magisterial Protestant reformers.[1] The conventional portrait of Luther, Calvin, and company is that in their concern to address matters of faith, Scripture, and the uniqueness and sufficiency of Christ, they cared little about—or were indifferent toward—the natural law emphasis of their Catholic counterparts. One noted Roman Catholic historian has even argued more recently, contrary to fact and the clear evidence, that the reformers rejected the natural law "as traditionally conceived."[2] To the contrary; nothing could be further from the truth. Without systematically treating the subject in their writings, the magisterial Protestant reformers presuppose the notion of the natural law and maintain continuity therein with Catholic theologians and philosophers.[3] This is the case even when they believed reason to have been effaced due to human fallenness.[4] And while it is decidedly true that they championed a particular understanding of grace and faith, this was not to the exclusion of other vehicles of revelation and divine agency.

Natural law thinking is firmly ensconced in the thought of Martin Luther. In his writings he describes the innate awareness of right and wrong behavior in two ways. He speaks both of

Naturrecht ("natural justice") and *natürliches Recht* ("natural law"), noting of the latter:

> Thus, "Thou shalt not kill, commit adultery, steal, etc." are not Mosaic laws only, but also the natural law [*natürliches Recht*] written on each man's heart, as St. Paul teaches (Rom. 2). Also Christ himself (Matt. 7) includes all of the law and the prophets in this natural law.[5]

Referring to the awareness of the so-called Golden Rule in all people, Luther writes, "By nature they judge that one should do to others what one wants done to oneself." Luther is well aware of the misperception among the religiously-minded that the natural law is the common fund of only Christian societies. To the contrary, he insists, it is demonstrated by human experience that all nations, cultures, and people-groups possess this rudimentary knowledge. The natural law "is written in the depth of the heart and cannot be erased."[6] It, therefore, exists as a moral standard among non-Christian people-groups: "Natural law is a practical first principle in the sphere of morality; it forbids evil and commands good...The basis of natural law is God, who has created this light, but the basis of positive law is civil authority."[7]

In his 1525 treatise *How Christians Should Regard Moses*, Luther distinguishes between the law of Moses, with its historically conditioned components, stipulations, and illustrations for theocratic Israel, and the natural law. "If the Ten Commandments are to be regarded as Moses' law, then Moses came too late," he can quip somewhat wryly, for "Moses agrees exactly with nature" and "what Moses commands is nothing new."[8] In addition, Moses

> also addressed himself to far too few people, because the Ten Commandments had spread over the whole world not only before Moses but even before Abraham and all the patriarchs. For even if a Moses had never appeared and Abraham had never

> been born, the Ten Commandments would have had to rule in all men from the very beginning, *as they indeed did and still do.*[9]

The law that stands behind the Ten Commandments, Luther notes emphatically, was in force prior to Moses, from the beginning of the world, and also among all the Gentiles. So far as the Ten Commandments are concerned, "there is no difference between Jews and Gentiles."[10]

Luther allows little room for misunderstanding: "We will regard Moses as a teacher, but we will not regard him as our lawgiver—unless he agrees with both the New Testament and the natural law."[11] "Where…the Mosaic law and the natural law are one, there the law remains and is not abrogated externally." By contrast, those aspects of the Mosaic code that were temporal and confined to theocratic Israel are "null and void" and "not supported by the natural law."[12]

In his treatise on temporal authority, Luther deliberates over particular situations that require Christians to participate intelligibly with non-Christians in the public sphere. Two such potential situations are the unlawful seizure of private property and resolving financial debts. Luther exhorts his readers to use both "the law of love" and "the natural law." However, when charity has no observable effect, the latter is to be our guide, since natural law is that "with which all reason is filled."[13] And where the two parties are not Christians, "then you may have them call in some other judge, and tell the obstinate one that they are acting contrary to God and natural law."[14]

It should be emphasized that Luther is perfectly content to allow faith or revelation and the natural law to stand side by side. The natural law was presumed to be at work in all people and thus to be lodged at the core of Christian social ethics. Were this not the case, "one would have to teach and practice the law for a long time before it became the concern of conscience. The heart must also find and feel the law in itself."[15]

Philip Melanchthon, Luther's colleague at the University of Wittenberg and in many ways the "quiet reformer,"[16] as well as John Calvin understand natural law in much the same way as Luther. Melanchthon, it needs emphasizing, devoted more attention to law and moral philosophy than any other Protestant reformer. There are several reasons for this. First, such was part of his integrated thinking as a true "Renaissance man" devoted to the liberal arts. Second, as "the ethicist of the Protestant Reformation,"[17] he saw the need to keep theology and philosophy wed. In addition, he constantly wrestled with finding a middle way between the poles of antinomianism (or law-denying, as found among the "radicals" and the Anabaptists, for example) on the one hand and works righteousness on the other. The events of the 1520s and 1530s—for example, the peasant uprisings and the radical Anabaptist experiment in the north-central German city of Münster to establish the "New Jerusalem" by force—well illustrated for Melanchthon the tragedy of a "lawless" view of Christian faith. Melanchthon worried much throughout his career about antinomian tendencies that often accompanied new outbreaks of religious enthusiasm. Melanchthon's response, similar to that of Luther, was that both law and gospel continually need to be preached. Law is not only a necessary preamble to the gospel of Christ; rather, it serves both to awaken within human beings the reality of human fallenness and to furnish the foundation for true piety and virtue.

Melanchthon joins Luther and Calvin in distinguishing between three types of law—ceremonial, judicial, and moral. Concerning moral law, all three reformers insist that the two former types have passed away while the latter, as the Decalogue illustrates, is abiding.[18] Melanchthon's defense of the natural law proceeds from his reading of Romans 2:15—awareness of the natural law has been "grafted into the nature of man," thereby mirroring the image of God.[19] But it also is shaped by two other theological premises. One is his understanding of human beings created in the image of God. Hence, humans possess "the natural knowledge of God and of the governance of our conduct"—an awareness that has been "grafted into the nature of man" as part of "the likeness of God." A second premise is that natural law has a pedagogical role. That is, moral law both serves as a restraint, thereby having a civil function, and it guides, protects, and assists us in cultivating virtue.[20] A feature unique to Melanchthon among the reformers is his development of the three purposes of natural law for civil use and criminal justice: it is retributive, deterrent, and rehabilitative in its character and function.[21]

Given the emphasis in Calvin's theological system on divine sovereignty and human depravity, one might assume that the reformer would have a dim view of natural law, yet he acknowledges the argument of St. Paul, that the Gentiles "show the work of the law written on their hearts" (Rom. 2:15). Calvin's description of natural law agrees with that of Melanchthon: "the very same things that are to be learned from the Two Tables [of the Ten Commandments]" are "written, even engraved, upon the hearts of all."[22] In Calvin's understanding, the activity and moral insights of conscience represent the mode and language by which the natural law is operative in the human person. An unchangeable "rule for the right conduct of life," the natural law for Calvin is the "apprehension of the conscience" and thus a common law among all people.[23]

Calvin shares the Thomistic assumption that the human person is "by nature a social animal," and because of this anthropological reality, human beings are disposed "through natural instinct to foster and preserve society." The consequence is that "every sort of human organization must be regulated by laws," without which there would be no civil order.[24] Since the "seeds" of just laws "have been implanted in all men," they are unchanging despite the vicissitudes of life. Neither war nor catastrophe nor theft nor human disagreement can alter these moral intuitions since nothing can "nullify the original conception of equity" that is implanted within.[25]

Above we noted the theme of human depravity for which Calvin is well known. How corrupt is the human heart? Thoroughly.

Is there any realm that has gone untouched by human fallenness? Emphatically not. But to acknowledge the pervasiveness of our fallen nature is not to obliterate the rudimentary moral sense in each person:

> When men grasp the conception of things with the mind and the understanding they are said "to know," from which the word "knowledge" is derived. In like manner, when men have an awareness of divine judgment adjoined to them as a witness which does not let them hide their sins but arraigns them as guilty before the judgment seat—this awareness is called "conscience."[26]

This inner awareness, notes Calvin, "pursues" the person to the point of "making him acknowledge his guilt." This, he writes, agrees with St. Paul's teaching in Romans 2, namely that "their thoughts accuse or excuse them in God's judgment."[27]

Both the restraining as well as the directing functions of natural law are presupposed by the Swiss reformers. Additionally, the threefold use of the law—ceremonial, judicial, and moral—for which the Protestant reformers are well known finds a supplemental use in the Swiss Reformational emphasis on covenant, belonging to the judicial realm. Covenant not only provides a theological basis for understanding divine work in history, but conjoined to natural law it furnishes the basis for communal and civil obligations that are thought to be binding on all people and societies.

In the thought of Huldrich Zwingli (1484–1531), the natural law serves as a bulwark and primary vehicle by which to resist injustice and political oppression. Zwingli is in agreement with other reformers that all human laws should conform to the natural law, which has been implanted in the hearts of all people, although he goes beyond Luther in asserting that the natural law is the equivalent of "true religion, to wit the knowledge, worship, and fear of the supreme deity."[28] In contrast to the Lutheran position but mirroring the Swiss Reformational distinctive, Zwingli believes that due to the imperfection of reason, only those rulers and magistrates who are God-fearers properly know natural law.

Heinrich Bullinger (1504–1575), perhaps best known for his role in drafting the Second Helvetic Confession of 1566, in even more pronounced ways affirmed the "law of nature" as "an instruction of the conscience, and as it were, a certain direction placed by God himself in the minds and hearts of men, to teach them what they have to do and what to eschew."[29] Have moral norms—and thus the requirements of human societies—changed at all in the period of the New Covenant? Bullinger answers emphatically in the negative. We are still to regard basic moral truth, respect parents, live out the Golden Rule, and keep the Ten Commandments, for the natural law reminds us that there exists an objective moral order in which human laws are said to inhere. The moral law is that which teaches men right conduct and sets down the nature of virtue.

In conclusion, the contention of one notable Roman Catholic theologian that "the sixteenth-century Protestant Reform championed grace and faith to the practical *exclusion* of all others instruments of divine agency" is shown to be utterly false.[30] The magisterial reformers *uniformly* affirmed the role of general revelation and the natural law, even when the accent of their teaching was faith and grace. They were one with their Catholic counterparts in the conviction that Christian social ethics presupposes—and stands—on the bedrock of the natural law.

47

What are standard objections to the natural law?

WHILE OBJECTIONS TO NATURAL LAW thinking can be grounded in both secular as well as religious thinking, those of a religious nature are worth scrutinizing, and this for two reasons.[1] First, the character of this opposition is chiefly Protestant in nature and has been on display notably during the last one hundred years. Second, those who have rejected natural law—or at least have been deeply suspicious—have exercised considerable influence among Protestants down to the present. One significant example is the Swiss theologian Karl Barth (1886–1968).

To his great credit, Barth would play a key role in drafting the "Barmen Declaration" following Hitler's accession to power. The Declaration consisted of six points that became the theological foundation for resistance by the "confessing church" to Nazi hegemony.[2] But Barth's examination of the eighteenth and nineteenth centuries convinced him that a romanticized view of "nature," coupled with Europe's increasing secularism, had tarnished German thinking. Any theological or philosophical concept rooted in "nature," he insisted, was not merely deficient but heretical, inasmuch as it undermines "Christ-centered" faith. For Barth, "natural theology" functions as a sort of Trojan horse inside the walls of Christendom. The God of "natural law" cannot be the God of the Bible. Natural law theory, he worried, creates a realm of autonomy separated from God's revelation in Jesus Christ. Any claim to another authority other than that of Christ and the word of God are to be rejected. Barth is unwilling to acknowledge that the natural law was affirmed by the fathers of the Church, and he is taken to task by fellow Swiss theologian Emil Brunner, who insists that God has also provided a general revelation discernible in *nature*. That is to say, something about the Creator can be known in and through his order of creation. Revelation in nature, per Brunner, was necessary in order to provide God with a means of assessing humanity's culpability.[3]

The Frenchman Jacques Ellul (1912–1994) is not particularly known for his theological writings, but his writings on technology, sociology, and political philosophy and his social critique are noteworthy. Ellul nonetheless warrants mention, given his adamant rejection of natural law on expressly theological grounds. In a brief but significant volume appearing in 1946 and subsequently translated into English (*The Theological Foundations of Law*), he argues that natural law thinking cannot address the state of modern culture with the social challenges that it poses. At the basic level, Ellul shares Barth's suspicion of any attempt to find common ground between Christians and non-Christians, since it ignores the difference, as he understands it, between "nature" and "grace." To posit a universal "law" is in effect to undermine grace. Ellul's bias against the natural law is not merely the fear of rationalist autonomy; it is undergirded by two other factors: a particular understanding of redemption through the cross of Christ and a particular reading of Genesis and understanding of the image of God. For Ellul, the *imago Dei* has not been preserved so that it can furnish the foundation of the natural law. Alas, natural knowledge of God by human beings is an impossibility. In the end, Ellul is forced to reject the notion of the natural law as a mistaken "medieval presupposition."[4] Like Barth, Ellul is unwilling to acknowledge patristic affirmation of the natural law.

Although not known as widely as Barth or Ellul, the German Lutheran theologian Helmut Thielicke (1908–1986) is perhaps best remembered for his impressive 1966 work *Theological Ethics*.[5] Therein Thielicke argues that through the New Covenant God "relativizes" law as expressed in the Old Covenant. This "relativizing" is grounded chiefly in two pieces of evidence: the so-called Sermon on the Mount teaching of Jesus and Paul's relating the law to human transgressions. It would be "quite erroneous," Thielicke argues, to ascribe to "law" a kind of "timeless validity," for "the moment we do this the Decalogue becomes 'natural law,'" and hence "abstract" and "ahistorical." Law as divinely given has significance *only* "for a particular historical epoch within salvation history"; it cannot stretch as a moral-legal norm from "creation across this [present] interim to the eschaton." Divine law only corresponds to humans in a fallen world and thus is *not part of the created order*.

Thielicke worries that Roman Catholic moral theology, because it affirms an objective component of our nature as human beings, skews our understanding of grace and justification. Given sin's pervasiveness, the natural law is a "doubtful concept," not part of the order of creation. In fact, Thielicke is convinced that Luther himself was "inconsistent" with his own doctrine of justification; there can be no cooperation of human reasoning in furnishing moral knowledge. Correlatively, Aquinas's view of "nature" is "invalidated" for the same reason, namely, "the structural form of fallen [human] existence."[6]

Closer to our time, two further "Protestant" (and thus protesting) names warrant inclusion, given the vehemence with which they have rejected natural law thinking. These two voices represent a different species of opposition to natural law, an opposition grounded in a supposed "radical obedience" to the biblical witness of Jesus. Unquestionably the most persuasive representative of this view is Anabaptist theologian John Howard Yoder, whose well-known work *The Politics of Jesus* sets forth the argument that the authentic Christian social ethic is rooted in a radical—and "nonviolent"—understanding of Jesus's teaching. In seeking to understand the political order theologically, Yoder laments two dominant interpretations that he believes to have clouded our thinking. One rests on the "catholic" concept of natural law, which is questionable because it presumes an "optimistic" view of human nature. A second is equally regrettable—namely, the "Augustinian-reformed" version, with its "order of preservation." Both of these interpretations, Yoder insists, are "unacceptable."

In all of his writings there is a baseline assumption that pervades Yoder's thought. It is the belief that the early Church, in time, wrongly absorbed pagan philosophical influence—for example, the Stoic emphasis on reason and the law of nature—which played a significant role in permitting it, by Ambrose's and Augustine's day, to be "compromised" by the political powers. Christian social ethics, according to Yoder, evolved in such a way as to justify presence and participation in Roman imperium; hence, Yoder's unrelenting "radical critique of Constantinianism." In the end, as an Anabaptist, Yoder is unwilling to submit his understanding of moral formation to the collective wisdom of the historic Christian tradition. His reading of Christian history is remarkably selective, guided chiefly by the assumption that only in the first three centuries of Christian history and only again twelve centuries later (in the form of the "radical reformation" of the 16th century) did authentic Christian social ethics display itself. Whether Yoder's rejection of the natural law is a by-product or a cause of his pacifism is difficult to say.

In assorted writings, the Methodist theologian Stanley Hauerwas confesses his debt to Yoderian Anabaptism, wishing to advance Yoder's vision of Christian social ethics. That one news magazine in 2001, rightly or wrongly, described Hauerwas as "the most influential" theologian in America is some indication not only of his celebrity but his influence on contemporary Protestant ethical thought. A prolific writer, Hauerwas has been explicit in his rejection of natural law thinking—notably in *The Peaceable Kingdom* and in *Truthfulness and Tragedy*. As with Yoder, a deep-seated distrust of natural law thinking in ethics is, for Hauerwas, related to the Church's purported compromise with "Constantinianism."

Thus, "the alleged transparency of the natural law norms reflects more the consensus within the Church than the universality of the natural law itself." The power of the natural law idea, Hauerwas believes, "was developed in and for the Roman imperium and then for 'Christendom.'" Thus, instead of being universally intuited by all and "the same for all, both as to rectitude and as to knowledge" (Aquinas), the natural law tradition is a "culturally assimilationist" attempt at Christian ethics that mirrors the Church's "cultural captivity" rather than the practice of Christian virtue.

Ultimately, for Hauerwas, "Christian ethics theologically does not have a stake in 'natural law.'" Several reasons are adduced: natural law's supposed "confusing" of nature and grace, the lack of an existing universal morality, and the failure of natural law to exhibit a "Christocentrism."

Mainstream Christian moral thinking through the ages stands in stark contrast not only to the Yoderian-Hauerwasian approach to social ethics—an approach that is exceedingly popular in our day—but to those objections observed in Barth, Ellul, and Thielicke above. The historic Christian tradition, along with the wider Judeo-Christian moral tradition, confesses that public morality must rest on publicly accessible principles—principles that are recognizable (Rom. 2:14–15) and anchored in human design. For this reason, natural law thinking has been lodged at the heart of the Christian moral tradition from the beginning. The general tone of Protestant resistance to natural law thinking would strike the Church fathers *of any era* as remarkable, wrong-headed, and theologically untenable. Individuals from the patristic era to Aquinas to Luther to C. S. Lewis to John Paul II and more recently Benedict XVI have argued in unison for the application of natural law reasoning to the realm of public discourse. To do so in a pluralistic cultural environment is *not* to capitulate to the culture or to "independent" or "autonomous" reasoning, as opponents of natural law ethics would have us believe.

As noted at the outset, objections to natural law thinking arise from both secular as well as religious reasoning. Standard non-religious objections have generally arisen among more contemporary forms of liberalism, in contrast to more classical approaches to liberalism in which natural law reasoning was assumed.[7] In *Written on the Heart: The Case for Natural Law*, J. Budziszewski has identified thirteen standard objections to the idea of natural law. Several of the more common among these are worth noting:

1. Natural law advocates articulate moral principles that are accepted by—or accessible to—everyone and everywhere. However, moral codes vary from culture to culture, and different principles are affirmed in different places.

   Response: There exists no society or people-group, for example, which views murder as a virtue and gratitude as a vice. Moreover, the natural law governs the "first principles" of morality and does not specify in detail how principles are applied in particular contexts. In addition, as we have argued in several Questions thus far, human beings do not always practice what they know to be true.

2. Even natural law advocates themselves disagree about what natural law entails.

   Response: In general, two types of difference may be found. One arises from those theorists who are secular in orientation—a minority among natural law advocates—over against those who are theist. The other stems either from a lack of familiarity with natural lawyers in the wider historical tradition or from a deficient reading of the works of those exponents.

3. In the name of natural law, false and horrible behaviors have been justified—for example, Aristotle's justification of slavery.

Response: While undercurrents of natural law thinking can be found among the ancients, their understanding of the natural law was incomplete. Furthermore, as already noted, given the fallenness of the human condition, there is a difference between what humans know and what they practice. All of the natural law proponents of the last two millennia would have rejected as evil the ancient tolerance of slavery, based on natural law's foundational assumptions about human nature and intrinsic dignity.

4. Apart from revelation there can be no autonomous moral knowledge.

   Response: Based on an awareness of two kinds of "revelation" (special versus general), the natural lawyer understands that no moral knowledge is autonomous or independent from human "nature"; reason and revelation work together and are in "dialogue." The theist acknowledges that both general and special revelation are true, even when one is authoritative.

5. Natural law advocates downplay the fact of human fallenness and the matter of sin, which obscures the "law written on the heart." Sin has erased the natural law.

   Response: None of the natural law proponents in the Christian moral tradition—past or present, whether among the early church fathers or Thomas Aquinas, among the magisterial Protestant reformers or among modern and contemporary natural lawyers—have understood human "nature" to be destroyed or eliminated by human fallenness and sin. Tainted? By all means. But not wholly altered so that human beings do not intuit the "law written on the heart."

6. Christianity maintains that we are reconciled to God by grace alone and through faith alone. Natural law, by contrast, assumes that salvation can by earned by human effort.

   Response: Salvation through works and human effort has never been believed or advanced by any natural law proponent in the Christian moral tradition. In fact, one could make the argument, based on Hebrews 11, that in the entire Judeo-Christian tradition people *always* experienced salvation by means of faith.[8]

7. The gospel of Christ liberates us from the bondage of law, whether the law of Moses, Levitical law, or the natural law.

   Response: Here it is necessary to point out that the New Testament—St. Paul in particular—uses "law" (*nomos*) in several differing contexts. Often he does not delineate clearly between these contexts, which in part is cause for some confusion. On occasion, it can refer to Mosaic law, at times to Levitical law, and at times to moral law. Both Jesus and the New Testament writers agree concerning the moral law: in its nature it is "good" and "holy," abiding, and therefore compatible with authentic faith.[9] For this reason the Psalmist can praise it unceasingly, declaring that the human heart delights in it.[10]

48

What is the relationship between the "cardinal virtues" and the natural law?

From Aristotle to Aquinas, virtue has been understood in much the same way. Virtue is a habit (*habitus*) that accords with our fundamental nature and with reason. A well-lived life, a life of happiness, is a virtuous life. For the purposes of our present discussion, we may say that the virtues provide "mediating principles between a basic teleological conception of human nature and the properly moral norms of the natural law."[1] For the natural lawyer, however, to speak of "well-being" and "happiness" is to severely qualify these terms in light of contemporary culture, since they are imbued with substantive moral content.

As a habit, virtue is thus a stable disposition that expresses itself through particular actions that are oriented toward the good.[2] Such actions, by nature, stand in bold contrast to vicious actions, or vice, which is in conflict with nature and right reason.[3] The natural law, then, dictates to human reason that virtue must be sought and that vice is to be avoided. The "cardinal" or "hinge" or "principal" virtues—wisdom (prudence), justice, temperance, and courage—are acquired elements of moral goodness that concern themselves with the main aspects of human existence, much "like a hinge on which a door turns."[4] According to Aristotle, the cardinal virtues are "chief" because they are of *greatest service* to others.[5] With this, Aquinas agrees: these virtues are central to the conduct of human affairs.[6] These four are particularly important because of their role in uniting human society and preserving the common good. Even when in the historic Christian tradition they are distinguished from the theological virtues of faith, hope, and charity, Aquinas notes that charity inhabits and expresses itself in *all* of the virtues, thereby helping us to see their unity.

In its essence, wisdom (or prudence)[7] instructs us in terms of those actions that are profitable or edifying and those that are harmful. Not insignificantly, the genre of "wisdom literature" was common among ancient Near Eastern cultures, including Israel of old. For this reason, wisdom is saluted and praised in the Old Testament, as the book of Proverbs demonstrates. In wisdom literature, wisdom stands in opposition to foolishness or ignorance. It bears not only on what is to be done (or avoided) but also *when and how* it is to be done. Aspects of wisdom, whether among the ancients or in wisdom literature *per se*, include insight, foresight, perception, and understanding, all of which contribute to humans' ability to foresee the end as well as the proper means to the end. The prudent person, according to Aristotle, "is able to deliberate finely about things that are good and beneficial"; such people "calculate well to promote some excellent end."[8] Wisdom can be said to suffuse the other virtues.

The virtue of justice traditionally is depicted as a blindfolded woman holding equally balanced scales. In designating justice as "blind," we are simply acknowledging that its judgments are not impaired or colored by prejudice. Justice classically understood is concerned to guard the common good. It serves as a guide for social relations at all levels, underpinning duty or obligation and rendering to all their due—that is, what is "rightfully" owed, based on the natural law—and allowing people to flourish as individuals and as social groups. In its essence, justice guards human integrity and moral principle.[9] Justice is so important that Aristotle can say, "neither the evening star nor the morning star is so marvelous,"[10] while Cicero calls it the "queen of all the virtues."[11] Its foundations are truth, constancy, and trustworthiness.[12] Significantly, though a Stoic, Cicero considers the role of religion to be central to the establishment of justice. The reason for this is quite simple: religion inculcates within human beings an attitude of reverence, and when this foundational element is absent, justice is severely undermined.[13] Significantly, Thomas Aquinas agrees.[14]

From Aristotle to Aquinas, most discussions of justice distinguish between at least two types or species: distributive and commutative.[15] As noted in Question 14, Aristotle uses the language of "mediating" (i.e., distributive), "rectifying," and "reciprocal" to distinguish the applications and character of justice. Distributive justice, based on the natural law, is directed toward the ordering of duties in public life based on proportion and not mere numbers. It concerns itself with functions that vary—for example, based on allocation, opportunity, social location, means, etc. Commutative justice, by contrast, suggests that persons receive what is their due based on the principle of entitlement. This bears, for example, on the exchange of goods in the marketplace, the fulfillment of legal or financial contracts, as well as social obligations that comprise "criminal justice" and "restitution.[16] At bottom, reciprocity is underscored by this element; every person receives what is his or her due, i.e., what is owed. Aquinas helpfully compares distributive and commutative justice in this way: the latter concerns the *relations between individuals within a given community*, whereas the former concerns *the relationship of the community as a whole to individuals*.[17] Justice, in its character, is always other-regarding. Just or unjust acts, at bottom, are voluntary in nature, and therefore either praiseworthy or blameworthy. Involuntary acts are coincidental or accidental, done in ignorance.[18]

Temperance (or self-control), as Aristotle describes it, has a "protecting" character; it "preserves" prudence or wisdom. That is to say, it guards wisdom from being corrupted by pleasure or pain, but particularly the dulling effects of pleasure.[19] It offers restraint over wrongful impulses or excesses. Such appetites or inclinations which temperance must moderate can be material or nonmaterial, physical or soulish, in nature. Here, as with the other virtues, humans distinguish themselves from animals. While appetites and desires are "natural," and hence in accord with human design, their excess is not. Clearly, an excess of pleasures is intemperate, and thus blameworthy. The intemperate person chooses pleasures or desires "at the cost of other [good] things."[20] Vices such as pride, anger, incontinence, lust, and gluttony stand in opposition to this virtue. Precisely here temperance sheds light on the fourth "cardinal" virtue, courage, since as it concerns the enduring of pain, displeasure, and what we ordinarily would not choose.

A useful definition of the virtue courage is the following: courage consists in "a reflective undertaking of dangers" and "the endurance of toil"; in many ways, this important virtue might be viewed as the "protector" of justice.[21] Aquinas observes that courage mirrors a certain "firmness of mind" which copes with weakness of the flesh, which is the task of endurance; it "wages war" against all of the vices. This firmness of mind is required both in doing good and in enduring evil, especially with regard to goods or evils that are difficult.[22] In avoiding the opposites of trepidation and recklessness, courage honors duty regardless of the consequences. Perseverance is at its heart; it endures, voluntarily and permanently, for the sake of what is true and right (and hence what is just), resisting timidity, dread of evil, and that which might be threatening.[23]

In the manifestation of the "cardinal" or "hinge" virtues, so named because they accord with human nature and the natural law, there arises "a most pleasing symphony of the faculties of the soul in man."[24] By these virtues, human beings are served and human society is sustained.

49

Why is "wisdom literature" universal, and how does it mirror the natural law?

THE RELEVANCE TO DAILY LIFE of the natural law, which in theological terms is part of "general revelation,"[1] is evidenced among other things in the fact that various people-groups and cultures around the globe have access to wisdom. Wisdom, of course, was viewed by ancient classical culture as a "cardinal virtue." As previous Questions have observed, wisdom is universal in its accessibility. It is the possession of no one people-group, society, or culture. All people are able to observe physical nature as well as human nature and draw inferences for life. Wisdom is the possession of any and all who seek it.[2]

Although the subject of wisdom receives relatively little attention in the modern world,[3] it is significant that many of the peoples of the ancient Near East, including Israel of old, developed and chronicled particular insights into living proverbial wisdom and enshrined them in a corpus of "wisdom literature." Hebrew examples of this are found in the Old Testament—for example, in the book of Job, Proverbs, and Ecclesiastes. Wisdom proceeds from observations made about the surrounding world as well as human nature. What is striking about the writings associated with this literary genre embedded in Hebrew scriptures is that *inter alia* they mirror not only the faith of Israel herself but also the treasures of other cultures and civilizations.[4] Consider, by way of example, these intuitions collected from African proverbial wisdom:

- No polecat ever smelled his own stink.
- When it rains, the roof always drips the same way.
- He has the kindness of a witch.
- It is patience that gets you out of a net.
- A butterfly that flies among the thorns will tear its wings.
- The strength of a crocodile is in the water.
- When you marry a beautiful woman, you marry problems.
- The sons of a king do not need to be taught about power.[5]

These insights, it goes without saying, would be regarded as universally true by anyone at any time and in any cultural context. As would the following insights, which come from the Old Testament book of Proverbs:

- As vinegar to the teeth and smoke to the eyes, so is a sluggard to those who send him.
- He who scorns instruction will pay for it, but he who respects a command is rewarded.
- Better a dry crust of bread with peace and quiet than a house full of feasting with strife.
- Starting a quarrel is like breaching a dam; so drop the matter before a dispute breaks out.
- A king's rage is like the roar of a lion, but his favor is like dew on the grass.

- Like a bad tooth or a lame foot is reliance on the unfaithful in times of trouble.[6]

No one, regardless of culture or social location, would need explanations for these proverbial statements; they are patent to *all* who hear or read them. Wisdom, then, can be seen as constituting a common mode of discourse for all people, the world over.

The "wise" person, moreover, is one who *desires* knowledge of and *pursues* the truth. In wisdom literature, what is conspicuous is the "profound and indissoluble unity between the knowledge of reason and the knowledge of faith."[7] The symbiosis capturing the "wisdom" perspective can be expressed in the following manner: "The world and all that happens within it, including history and the fate of peoples, are realities to be observed, analyzed and assessed with all the resources of reason, but without faith ever being foreign to the process."[8]

In a very practical sense, wisdom shows itself to be a necessary and universally accessible foundation for ethics, and hence an important—and practical—mirror of the natural law. The way in which proverbial wisdom bridges morality and social interactions between cultures and eras is on display in the fascinatingly relevant wisdom sayings recorded in the Old Testament book of Proverbs as well as in the philosophical complexities expressed in the book of Ecclesiastes. In both are found innumerable contrasts of ethical and practical importance—virtue versus vice, sloth versus industry, discretion versus indiscretion, straight versus crooked paths, uprightness versus wickedness, integrity versus dishonesty, lying lips versus truthful speech, prudence versus perversion. These observations, framed in proverbial style, are cross-cultural in character, arising from human nature and human tendencies. They challenge the hearer or reader toward a verdict, pointing in the direction of "the good." What is distinct about the wisdom genre of the Old Testament is that wisdom is anchored in the fear of God.

An important subtheme in the book of Ecclesiastes is that patterns of human behavior and questions about the meaning of life are recurring, intergenerational, and transcultural in nature. Accordingly, there is a time and place—a proper "season"—for everything that occurs in life—including suffering, misfortune, making moral judgments, grieving, and death.[9] The end product of Qoheleth's philosophical musings—the "conclusion of the matter" and "the whole duty of man"[10]—is twofold: nothing in life has meaning and purpose *outside* of a theistic outlook, and there is a moral accounting for all human deeds, whether good or evil. This philosophical "bottom line" is intended to express universal truth and have universal application; it is true wisdom, in accordance with the natural law.

For that reason, Ecclesiastes remains an invaluable, though much neglected, part of the biblical canon.[11] In neglecting this book we rob ourselves of much needed insights into the complexities of the human experience as we struggle with the vicissitudes of life and find our way among competing world- and life-views in a pluralistic culture. Such is the character of wisdom: it expresses universal truth, it is accessible to all who seek it, and it is eminently practical in its application.

50

What was C. S. Lewis's argument for the natural law?

C. S. Lewis presses his argument regarding the "law of nature," which he also calls the "law of oughtness" and the *Tao*, in his two classic works *Mere Christianity* and *The Abolition of Man*. He insists that the natural law not only does not contravene the ethics of Christ, but as an ethical standard simply cannot be contravened insofar as it is the source from which *all* moral judgments spring. Basic virtues such as reliability, faithfulness, justice, mercy, and generosity, he observes, form the backbone of all "civilized" societies and are intuited as true, independent of human or religious experience. There is, then, common moral ground on which *all* people stand and by which we may engage in moral persuasion with *all*.

In several previous Questions we noted the argument for natural law that Lewis develops in his essay "Right and Wrong as a Clue to the Meaning of the Universe," which is the introductory chapter of *Mere Christianity*.[1] The importance of this particular essay is the manner in which Lewis raises basic questions about human moral sentiments. He appeals to logic and asks his readers to consider the evidence of the universality of these sentiments. Why do all people wrestle with issues of justice and injustice? Why do we protest in the context of unjust treatment? And why is this reaction consistent among human beings irrespective of time and location, despite their theoretical attempts at denying moral absolutes? Based on this "law of nature" or "law of oughtness," Lewis concludes that people live out their lives *as if* a moral law indeed exists in the universe.

Lewis, of course, was well aware that many Christians—Protestants, in particular—object to the natural law precisely because they believe it to detract from Christianity's emphasis on the need for grace. But Lewis rejected this view. Far from contradicting Christian social ethics, natural law is presupposed by it. And Lewis himself leaves little room for misunderstanding, offering the reader further rationale in the volume *Christian Reflections*:

> The idea...that Christianity brought an entirely new ethical code into the world is a grave error. If it had done so, then we should have to conclude that all who first preached it wholly misunderstood their own message: for all of them, its Founder, His precursor, His apostles, came demanding repentance and offering forgiveness, a demand and an offer both meaningless except on the assumption of a moral law *already known* and *already broken*.[2]

Notably in *The Abolition of Man*, Lewis presses the argument further regarding objective moral truths:

> This thing which I have called for convenience the *Tao*, and which others called the Natural Law..., is not one among a series of possible systems of value. It is the sole source of all value judgment. If it is rejected, all value is rejected. If any value is retained, it is retained. The effort to refute it and raise a new system of value in its place is self-contradictory.[3]

The conclusion, for Lewis, is patent: "It is no more possible to invent a new ethics than to place a new sun in the sky. Some precept from traditional morality always has to be presumed. We never start from a *tabula rasa*: if we did, we should end, ethically speaking, with a *tabula rasa*."[4] Lewis would surely agree with the Roman poet

Horace: *Naturam expellas furca, tamen usque recurret* ("You may drive out nature with a pitchfork, yet it will always return!").[5] There is wisdom in what Lewis, in concert with natural lawyers of any age, is insisting—a wisdom that counters not only the autonomy and intractability of militantly secular culture but the false dichotomies that at times are lodged at the heart of religious (and particularly Protestant) ethical thinking.[6]

Endnotes

Chapter 1

1 Marcus Tullius Cicero, *On the Commonwealth* III:XXII, trans. George Holland Sabine and Stanley Barney Smith (Indianapolis and New York: Bobbs-Merrill Co., 1960), 215. The Loeb Classical Library series gives this volume the title *On the Republic*.

2 Heinrich A. Rommen, *The Natural Law: A Study in Legal and Social History and Philosophy*, trans. Thomas R. Hanley (Indianapolis: Liberty Fund, 1998), 57.

3 John Locke, *Questions concerning the Law of Nature*, ed. and trans. Robert Horwitz et al. (Ithaca: Cornell University Press, 1990), no. I, 101.

4 For example, Hugo Grotius, in *The Rights of War and Peace* I.1.10.

5 Locke, *Questions concerning the Law of Nature* no. I, 101.

6 J. Budziszewski, *What We Can't Not Know: A Guide*, 2nd ed. (San Francisco: Ignatius Press, 2011).

7 Steven A. Long, "God, Teleology, and the Natural Law," in Christopher Wolfe and Steven Brust, eds., *Natural Law Today: The Present State of the Perennial Philosophy* (Lanham: Lexington Books, 2018), 4.

8 Rom. 2:14–15.

9 I derive this basic, though slightly edited, definition from Russell Hittinger, in his essay "Liberalism and the American Natural Law Tradition," *Wake Forest Law Review* 25, no. 3 (1990): 429–99.

10 Here we may distinguish between "intuition" and "instinct." The latter does not lead us or guide us in any way to do what we *ought*, only what we *desire*. Instincts vary, whereas intuitions tend to be ordered to a higher purpose and thus have an obligatory character. Instinct, moreover, is not directed toward posterity or the future preservation of the species; it is present-oriented and raw need-driven.

11 So Thomas Aquinas, *Summa Theologica* [hereafter *S.T.*] I-II Q. 91.3.

12 Aquinas famously writes that human beings' rational "participation" in divine, eternal law is called the "natural law" (*S. T.* I-II Q. 91.2; cf. Q. 94.1).

13 These expressions are used by the writer C. S. Lewis in "Right and Wrong as a Clue to the Meaning of the Universe," which is chapter one of *Mere Christianity* (New York: Macmillan, 1960), 15–39. Elsewhere, in *The Abolition of Man*, Lewis refers to this "law of nature" as the *Tao* (by which he is *not* promoting the Eastern philosophy of Taoism).

14 Rom. 1:20.

15 Perhaps the most concise definition of natural law is provided by William E. May, "Bioethics and Human Life," in David F. Forte, ed., *Natural Law and Contemporary Public Policy* (Washington, DC; Georgetown University Press, 1998), 43: it consists in "ordered sets of true propositions about what is to be done."

16 C. S. Lewis, *The Abolition of Man* (repr.; New York: HarperOne, 2000 [1944]), 18.

17 Budziszewski, *What We Can't Not Know*, xix.

18 Ralph McInerny, "Are There Moral Truths That Everyone Knows?" in Edward B. McLean, ed., *Common Truths: New Perspectives on Natural Law* (Wilmington: ISI Books, 2000), 1 (emphasis added).

19 *Catechism of the Catholic Church* [hereafter *CCC*] no. 1956.

Chapter 2

1 Josef Fuchs, *Natural Law: A Theological Investigation*, trans. Helmut Reckter and John A. Dowling (New York: Sheed and Ward, 1965), 7.

2 Aquinas, *S. T.* I-II Q. 94.4.

3 The fact that all possess a basic awareness of moral principle, right from wrong, is not to argue that human beings have a detailed knowledge of moral matters.

4 Locke, *Questions concerning the Law of Nature* no. VIII, 213.

5 This is true even when the natural law implies the existence of a Creator and Lawgiver and when faith sheds greater light on the natural law, based on human design.

6 The fact of an imperfect justice system such as our own does nothing to undermine this claim or deny the natural law's existence. Nor the fact that injustice can be done masquerading as "criminal" or "state" justice (as, for example, in a totalitarian state). The latter, to illustrate, only demonstrates the degree to which human beings can choose evil in order to justify

power. The same may be said of the manner in which the Mafia, terrorists, and pirates go about their business.

7 For a concise and very helpful summary of penology as developed by Thomas Aquinas, who thought deeply about matters of justice in the human community, see Charles P. Nemeth, *Aquinas on Crime* (South Bend: St. Augustine's Press, 2008), esp. chapter 8.

8 We find these priorities of Aristotle laid out in both *Politics* and *Nicomachean Ethics.*

9 Rom. 2:15.

10 "Accident" is used here not to mean "mistake" but, in its philosophical sense, meaning a feature or property of a substance that is not essential to its existence. Hadley Arkes, in *First Things: An Inquiry into the First Principles of Morals and Justice* (Princeton: Princeton University Press, 1986), 51–54, helpfully develops this sort of thinking.

11 According to Aquinas, the fundamental principle of the natural law is that good is to be done and evil avoided (*S.T.* I-II Q. 94.2).

12 Denial of our basic design results in untold suffering and trauma—both to individuals and to wider society. Writer C. S. Lewis describes this phenomenon as no less than "the abolition of man."

13 So Niels Hemmingsen, *On the Law of Nature*, ed. and trans. E. J. Hutchinson (Sources in Early Modern Economics, Ethics, and Law; Grand Rapids: CLP Academic, 2018), 32.

14 Locke, *Questions concerning the Law of Nature* no. V, 161.

Chapter 3

1 Locke, *Questions concerning the Law of Nature* no. I, 117. *Questions* was written in Latin, since Latin was the language of theology and philosophy which Locke studied at Oxford.

2 This is the language of the New Testament; see, for example, Rom. 2:15.

3 Natural lawyer and just war theorist Francisco de Vitoria compared our nature to the light exuded by the sun. Thus, we would do "an injustice" against the sun by shutting ourselves off from its light and denying it; see Francisco de Vitoria, *Reflections in Moral Theology. De Indis Et De Jure Bells Reflectiones.* (Washington, DC: Carnegie Institution, 1917), 248. Hadley Arkes, "The Natural Law—Again, Ever," in Christopher Wolfe and Steven Brust, *Natural Law Today: The Present State of the Perennial Philosophy* (Lanham: Lexington Books, 2018), 134, n. 6, notes that this

analogy stems from a lecture by Vitoria delivered in 1539 at the University of Salamanca.

4 For this reason Jacques Maritain can write that the rejection of natural-law thinking "proves nothing..., any more than a mistake in addition proves anything against arithmetic"; see *Man and the State* (Chicago: University of Chicago Press, 1951), 90.

5 Of course, the terms "nature" and "law" mean different things to different people and are used in a variety of contexts. "Nature" in natural law reasoning refers to human design or constitution—the human *essence*; in the words of philosopher Étienne Gilson, *Moral Values and the Moral Life*, trans. L. R. Ward (Hamden: Shoe String Press, 1961), 55, "nature" is "the inner and direct source of the activity and doings of any being." "Law," though it can be used descriptively (for example, human law or positive law), is understood in natural law reasoning to indicate what is normative, that is, what *ought* to be done and what Thomas Aquinas calls "an ordinance of reason for the common good," which is "promulgated by him who has the care of the community" (*S. T.* I-II Q. 90.4).

6 Few have presented a case for design as moral knowledge as persuasively as Budziszewski, *What We Can't Not Know*, 93–102.

7 Locke, *Questions concerning the Law of Nature* no. II, 135.

8 Locke, *Questions concerning the Law of Nature* no. VIII, 213.

9 Arkes, *First Things*, 84.

10 Lewis, *The Abolition of Man*, 41.

11 James W. Ceaser helpfully addresses the political implications of this outlook in "The Doctrine of Political Nonfoundationalism," in idem, ed., *Designing a Polity: America's Constitution in Theory and Practice* (Lanham and Plymouth, UK: Rowman & Littlefield, 2011), 3–21. Ceaser notes that what variously goes by "anti-foundationalism," "political deconstruction," or "deliberative democracy" is often a product of criticism of the past. Such voices, in any case, find common ground in "seeking to erect a high wall of separation between [moral] foundations and politics" (4).

12 Locke, *Questions concerning the Law of Nature* no. II, 119.

13 For Locke, the human conscience is a primary "proof" of the natural law (*Questions concerning the Law of Nature* no. I, 111–13). The conscience, which is part of human nature, is not the ultimate seat of moral authority. It witnesses to the natural moral law as the ultimate seat of authority, the awareness of which, in theistic terms, has been implanted by the Creator (Rom. 2:14–15).

14 "Right and Wrong" constitutes the first chapter of Lewis's classic work *Mere Christianity*.

15 Even the noted Emory University primatologist Frans de Waal, famous for his work on the behavior and social intelligence of primates, has not been able to find the great apes wrestling with issues of fairness, justice, dignity, or the problem of evil, his valiant attempts notwithstanding. In his work, de Waal attempts to draw parallels between primate and human behavior, from peacemaking and morality to culture. His scientific work has been published in hundreds of technical articles in journals such as *Science, Nature,* and *Scientific American.* Among his books are *Chimpanzee Politics* (1982), *Good Natured* (1997, with the subtitle *The Origins of Right and Wrong in Humans and Other Animals*), *Our Inner Ape* (2006), *The Age of Empathy* (2009), *The Bonobo and the Atheist* (2013), and *Are We Smart Enough to Know How Smart Animals Are?* (2017), as well as two edited volumes, *The Primate Mind* (2012) and *Evolved Morality* (2014).

16 For Aquinas, a "first principle" of natural law is in fact the "Golden Rule": "do unto others as you would have them do unto you; do not unto others as you would not have them do unto you" (*S. T.* I-II Q. 94.4 and Q. 95.2). Hereon see Damiano Simoncelli, "From Natural Law to the Golden Rule: Aquinas Revisited," *Ethics, Politics & Society* 1 (2018): 261-75.

Chapter 4

1 To say that moral principle is "indemonstrable" is not to say that its effects cannot be observed. It is only to say that law cannot legislate against internal motivations. Metaphysics is not mathematics.

2 Aquinas, *S. T.* I-II Q. 91.3.

3 Aquinas, *S. T.* I-II Q. 94.4.

4 Aristotle, *Politics: A New Translation*, trans. C. D. C. Reeve (Indianapolis: Hackett Publishing Co., 2017), 2 (1252a).

5 This is *not* to argue, however, that every decision has moral significance. In wishing to travel to New York City or Washington, DC, I have the choice of driving by car, taking a bus, or flying in an airplane. All of these options can be justified as "good." If, however, my boarding a plane is to serve the terrorist goal of hijacking the flight and then flying into buildings in New York City or Washington, DC, my decision is unjustified according to the ends toward which it is directed.

6 Arkes, *First Things*, 3.

7 Aquinas, *S.T.* I-II Q. 21.1; 90.1; 91.1; 94.2. "Reason" here might best be described as "right reason," since all of us manage on occasion—perhaps regularly—to "rationalize" wrong decisions or choices.

Chapter 5

1 On the matter of human dignity, see also Questions 16 and 21; on the common good, see as well Question 7.

2 The Greek term *apologia* may be defined as a defense, justification, explanation, or vindication.

3 J. Budziszewski, *Written on the Heart: The Case for Natural Law* (Downers Grove: InterVarsity Press, 1997), 184–85, distinguishes between these three varieties.

4 Thus, for example, despite the controversy that surrounds these issues today, natural law reasoning will have us seek to protect the unborn so that human life *in utero* is not destroyed; it will argue against granting same-sex activity and relationships the same legal equivalence and protection as marriage; and it will move us to care for the sick, the elderly and the infirm rather than pressuring them in the direction of euthanasia. These basic ethical positions have their grounding in natural law reasoning.

5 Two opposite "apologetic" ways of thinking are to be avoided, even when they are exceedingly common. On the one hand, it is erroneous to think that the natural law is obliterated or does not exist because of human fallenness, wickedness, or the effects of "sin." Despite the human condition, human fallenness does not eradicate our designed nature and the image of God within. Otherwise, we would need to give up our feeble attempts to work for criminal justice, to hold people accountable for their action, or to preserve civil society. On the other hand, we must avoid attempting to demonstrate through mere philosophical method the fact of the natural law, since reason and faith are the two "wings," as it were, that work harmoniously in the pursuit of truth.

6 See Questions 16 and 21.

7 Christian ethicist Gilbert Meilaender, in *Neither Beasts nor God: The Dignity of the Human Person* (New York and London: Encounter Books, 2009), 9–18, identifies the pairs of preservation and purpose, procreation and sacrifice, and love and worship as those elements unique to the human species and thus constitutive of human dignity.

8 *Gaudium et Spes* no. 27; the encyclical is accessible at https://www.vatican.va/archive/hist_councils/ii_vatican_council/documents/vat-ii_const_19651207_gaudium-et-spes_en.html.

9 I refer here to Peter Singer, the Ira W. DeCamp Professor of Bioethics at Princeton University. This is an underlying theme in *Animal Liberation: A New Ethics for Our Treatment of Animals* (New York: Random House, 1975) and in Chapter 3 of *Practical Ethics* (Cambridge and New York: Cambridge University Press, 1980). Re-titled *Animal Liberation: The Definitive Classic of the Animal Movement*, the former volume appeared in 2015 in its fortieth anniversary edition.

10 The expression *lebensunwertes Leben* ("life unworthy of living"), referring to such individuals, initially appeared among German academics and became "mainstreamed" in the two decades leading up to World War II, culminating in Nazi extermination camps.

11 Singer, *Animal Liberation*, 19.

12 What is telling—and immensely instructive for our purposes—is the fact that Singer's mother has suffered as a result of Alzheimer's in a manner that would require her to be euthanized, based on what Singer himself has argued so stridently. Singer, however, did not call for her elimination. This contradiction was observed in an essay written by Michael Specter titled "The Dangerous Philosopher," published in the September 6, 1999 issue of *The New Yorker*. When Specter pressed Singer on the inconsistency—indeed the contradiction—between the theory in his books and his actions as they affected his mother, Singer could only weakly reply, "I think this has made me see how the issues of someone with these kinds of problems are really very difficult...Perhaps it is more difficult than I thought before, because it is different when it's your mother" (p. 55). Indeed, it is more difficult to eliminate people when we know them. In a later response to a moral theologian who had written Singer to inquire about his inconsistency, Singer responded, disappointingly, "No, that doesn't mean my rules are wrong, it only means that I disobeyed them in the case of my mother, and acted unethically" (Peter J. Colosi, "What's Love Got to Do with It: The Ethical Contradictions of Peter Singer," *Godspy* [February 25, 2005], republished by the Catholic Education Resource Center and accessible at https://www.catholiceducation.org/en/health/euthanasia-and-assisted-suicide/what-s-love-got-to-do-with-it-the-ethical-contradictions-of-peter-singer.html). Notice here the use by Singer of the language of "wrong" and "disobedience." This is telling, for it simply demonstrates how even utilitarians parasitically employ the categories of natural law reasoning—right and wrong, obey and disobey. Whence come moral obligations?

13 As a philosophical "utilitarian," Singer's position is that we have a duty—a *moral* duty?—to increase the amount of pleasure and decrease the amount

of pain and suffering for the most people possible. The implication is that moral absolutes do not—should not—govern moral choices; killing fellow human beings is thus justifiable.

14 The Christian view of personhood is distinct in that it anchors our understanding of human nature in the *imago Dei*, the image of God, by which it is understood that human beings have special status and superior rank—and hence special worth—in the created order.

15 Aquinas, *S.T.* I-II Q. 29.1, 3, 4.

16 This is not to argue that they are not to be cared for and cherished as part of the created order by human beings who are stewards of that order. It is only to point out, contra "animal rights" activists, that "animal rights" has the unintended (or perhaps intended) consequence of demeaning human personhood and undermining the very notion of human dignity.

17 Locke, *Questions concerning the Law of Nature* no. IX, 215.

18 Already several generations ago C. S. Lewis warned against this tendency in *The Abolition of Man*.

19 At most, the secular materialist, for whom there is no transcendent good, can only speak of "biological complexity"—of genes and appetites and instincts and stimuli.

20 As evidence thereof, some spoke of a "third wave" of democratization that had spread around the globe; see, for example, Samuel P. Huntington, *The Third Wave: Democratization in the Late Twentieth Century* (Norman: University of Oklahoma Press, 1991).

21 Yet it would seem that greater human rights violations exist today worldwide than ever before, despite the conspicuous accent on "rights" since the Second World War.

22 See, in this regard, David Gelernter, "The Irreducibly Religious Character of Human Dignity," in Edmund D. Pelegrino et al. eds., *Human Dignity and Bioethics: Essays Commissioned by the President's Council on Bioethics* (Washington, DC: President's Council on Bioethics, 2008), 387–405.

23 See Question 28.

24 A case in point is the German lawyer Heinrich Rommen, whose two important books written in the mid-1930s—*Der Staat in der katholischen Gedankenwelt* ("The State in the Catholic Thought-World") and *Die ewigie Wiederkehr des Naturrechts* ("The Perennial Return of Natural Law")—resulted in his imprisonment by the Nazis. The reason for that imprisonment was his role in calling for robust Catholic social action

during the years of the Weimar Republic's dissolution and Nazism's rapid entrenchment. Rommen was able to flee Germany for the United States in 1938. In the words of Russell Hittinger, "Rommen watched with alarm as the Nazi party deftly used German legislative, administrative, and judicial institutions to impose totalitarian rule. 'Our modern dictators,' he remarked, 'are masters of legality.' 'Hitler,' Rommen concluded, 'aimed... at a legal grasp of power according to the formal democratic process.'" See Russell Hittinger, "Introduction," in Rommen, *The Natural Law* (see Chapter 1, n. 2), xi. *The Natural Law* is an English translation of the 1936 volume *Die ewige Wiederkehr des Naturrechts*.

25 In this vein, Rommen writes, "totalitarianism has opened the eyes of more and more thinking people to the ultimate consequences to which the denial of the natural law must lead" (*The Natural Law*, 136).

26 Hittinger, "Introduction," xii.

Chapter 6

1 Heraclitus, *Fragments* 112–14, reproduced in Charles M. Bakewell, *Source Book in Ancient Philosophy* (New York: Scribner's, 1907), 34.

2 In the end, we might call Aristotle, with his emphasis on the priority of the *polis* (the political community), a "state socialist"; so, correctly in my view, Rommen, *The Natural Law*, 17.

3 Aristotle, *Nicomachean Ethics* 5.7 (1134b-1135a).

4 Aristotle, *Nicomachean Ethics* 10.9 (1179b-1180b).

5 Cicero, *On the Commonwealth* III:XX, 215–16.

6 John Lawrence Hill, *After the Natural Law: How the Classical Worldview Supports Our Modern Moral and Political Values* (San Francisco: Ignatius, 2016), 55.

7 Matthew Hale, *Of the Law of Nature*, ed. David S. Sytsma (Grand Rapids: CLP Academic, 2015), 61.

8 Matt. 5:17–18.

9 This is evidenced in his "Golden Rule" ethic (Matt. 7:12; Luke 6:31; Luke 10:37).

10 Rom. 1:20.

11 Rom. 2:15.

12 Acts 14:15–17.

13 See as well Question 11.

14 Acts 17:18–30. Since the mid-third century BCE, the Council of the Areopagus had functioned as an authoritative body in civil-legal and educational matters. The Council consisted of about thirty members and was presided over by the president of the assembly. During the Roman era it was comprised of several committees that adjudicated on civil, legal and educational matters.

15 See in particular Question 13.

16 Thomas Aquinas, *S. T.* I-II Q. 94.4.

17 Hereon see as well Questions 43 and 44.

18 Martin Luther, "Table Talk," no. 3911 (July 7, 1538), in *Luther's Works* [hereafter *L. W.*] vol. 54, ed. T.G. Tappert (Philadelphia: Fortress, 1967), 293; also see Martin Luther, *Lectures on Genesis 6–14* (1536), in *L. W.* 2:160.

19 *L. W.* 35:168.

20 Philip Melanchthon, *Loci Communes* (1543), trans. J.A.O. Preus (St. Louis: Concordia Publishing House, 1992), Locus 6 ("The Divine Law"), 70.

21 Melanchthon, *Loci Communes*, Locus 6, 70.

22 John Calvin, *Institutes of the Christian Religion* 2.8.1, ed. John T. McNeill and trans. Ford Lewis Battles (LCC; Philadelphia: Westminster Press, 1960), pp. 367–68; cf. 2.2.22.

23 Calvin, *Institutes* 2.2.22.

24 Calvin, *Institutes* 2.2.22.

25 Hale, *Of the Law of Nature*.

26 On the role of Vitoria and Suárez, see Question 27.

27 Grotius, *The Rights of War and Peace*, xii; I am reliant here on the English translation edited by Richard Tuck (Indianapolis: Liberty Fund, 2005), 91.

28 Richard Hooker, *Of the Laws of Ecclesiastical Polity*, ed. John Keble et al., 3 vols. (Oxford: Clarendon Press, 1888), 1:285.

29 Nathaniel Culverwel, *Elegant and Learned Discourse of the Law of Nature*, ed. Robert A. Greene and Hugh MacCallum (Toronto: University of Toronto Press, 1971), 36.

30 Locke, *Questions concerning the Law of Nature* no. XI, 237.

31 See John Locke, *Two Treatises of Government*, ed. Peter Laslett (New York: Cambridge University Press, 1960), esp. sections 6 and 12.

32 Among the more prominent of Roman Catholic natural law thinkers of the 20th century are Étienne Gilson, Heinrich Rommen, Yves Simon, Jacques Maritain, John Courtney Murray, Germain Grisez, John Finnis, and Joseph Boyle; more recent exponents include Robert George, Russell Hittinger, and J. Budziszewski. Although it is by no means widespread, there has been renewed interest in the last two decades in natural law thinking among some Protestant evangelical types. See, for example, Stephen J. Grabill, *Rediscovering the Natural Law in Reformed Theological Ethics* (Grand Rapids and Cambridge, UK: Eerdmans, 2006); J. Daryl Charles, *Retrieving the Natural Law: A Return to Moral First Things* (Grand Rapids and Cambridge, UK: Eerdmans, 2008), *Natural Law and Religious Freedom* (London and New York: Routledge, 2018), and *The Idea and Importance of Natural Law: Fifty Questions and Answers* (Stone Tower Press, forthcoming); David VanDrunen, *Natural law and the Two Kingdoms* (Grand Rapids: Eerdmans, 2010), and *Divine Covenants and Moral Order: A Biblical Theology of Natural Law* (Grand Rapids and Cambridge, UK: Eerdmans, 2014); and Andrew T. Walker, *Faithful Reason: Natural Law Ethics for God's Glory and Our Good* (Nashville: B & H Academic, 2024). On the general suspicion toward natural law thinking among Protestants during the last century, see Questions 44 and 45.

Chapter 7

1 Aquinas, *S.T.* I-II Q. 90.1. Aquinas reasons here that "'lex' [law] is derived from 'ligare' [to bind], because it binds one to act."

2 Perhaps the two best representatives of both respectively are Aristotle, in his *Politics* and *Nicomachean Ethics*, and the Protestant reformation scholar Philip Melanchthon, who, more than any of the magisterial reformers, wrote on the matter of law.

3 Aquinas, *S.T.* I-II Q. 91.2 and 94.1.

4 Aquinas, *S.T.* I-II Q. 94.2.

5 Aquinas, *S.T.* I-II Q. 96.2.

6 For this reason, the writer of the book of Ecclesiastes asserts that God the Creator has set "eternity" in the hearts of men (Eccl. 3:11)—a formulation that corresponds with what the apostle Paul calls the law "written on their hearts" (Rom. 2:15). The natural law, then, gives a basic awareness of our moral obligations to God and to others.

7 Whether this reality is in fact *demonstrated* in every nation—or people-group—is not the issue at hand.

8 Aquinas, *S.T.* I-II Q. 90.3.

9 Aquinas, *S.T.* I-II Q. 91.3. At this point, Aquinas notes that the guidance of human law requires the natural law and transcendent divine law, and this for several reasons (*S.T.* Q. 91.4).

10 Aquinas, *S.T.* I-II Q. 96.3.

11 John Paul II, *Veritatis Splendor* no. 101, accessible at https://www.vatican.va/content/john-paul-ii/en/encyclicals/documents/hf_jp-ii_enc_06081993_veritatis-splendor.pdf.

Chapter 8

1 One relatively recent volume that takes up this very project is Owen Anderson, *The Natural Moral Law: The Good after Modernity* (Cambridge and New York: Cambridge University Press, 2012).

2 Representative of the positivist outlook is H. L. A Hart, *The Concept of Law*, 2nd ed. (Oxford: Clarendon Press, 1994). A helpful approach of the present-day legal and wider culture can be found in Charles E. Rice, "Natural Law in the Twenty-First Century," in Edward B. McLean, ed., *Common Truths: New Perspectives on Natural Law* (Wilmington: ISI Books, 2000), 293–318.

3 Few have analyzed the anatomy of conscience and guilt with more insight than Budziszewski, *What We Can't Not Know*, 149–68.

4 A helpful theoretical critique of modernity and post-modernity as it relates to the concept of the "good" is Owen Anderson, *The Natural Moral Law: The Good After Modernity* (New York: Cambridge University Press, 2012).

Chapter 9

1 Here Aquinas, *S.T.* I-II Q. 94.4 is being cited.

2 Budziszewski, *What We Can't Not Know*, 3.

3 (New York: Sheed and Ward, 1960).

4 Anderson, *The Natural Moral Law*, 42.

5 John T. Noonan, Jr., "The Natural Law Banner," in David F. Forte, ed., *Natural Law and Contemporary Public Policy* (Washington, DC: Georgetown University Press, 1998), 382.

6 Noonan, "The Natural Law Banner," 381–82.

7 Many academics in our time mirror the Sophists of past eras, who set nature (*physis*), with its universality, against law (*nomos*).

8 When John Locke writes that the duties of life do not "arm men against one another" (*Questions concerning the Law of Nature* no. XI, 247), he seems to be dissenting from the view of Thomas Hobbes, namely, that all men under "the law of nature" are in "a state of war." But he rejects this assumption, despite human fallenness; "the virtues themselves are not in conflict with one another nor do they compel men [to conflict]," he responds.

9 So Arkes, *First Things*, 7.

10 *Veritatis Splendor* ("The Splendor of Truth") no. 99; the encyclical is accessible at https://www.vatican.va/content/john-paul-ii/en/encyclicals/documents/hf_jp-ii_enc_06081993_veritatis-splendor.html.

11 John Paul II, *Veritatis Splendor* no 96.

Chapter 10

1 The argument here for "integration" as opposed to separation has literal merit, inasmuch as the English word "religion" stems from the Latin term *religare*, "to bind together." All people place "good faith" in their own view of ultimate reality, whether or not that view is (traditionally) considered to be "religious."

2 See Jürgen Habermas and Joseph Ratzinger (Pope Benedict XVI), *The Dialectics of Secularization: On Reason and Religion*, trans. Brian McNeil (San Francisco: Ignatius Press, 2007); the German original is titled *Dialektik der Säkularisierung: Über Vernunft und Religion* and was published by Verlag Herder in 2005.

3 *Fides et Ratio*, introduction; accessible at https://www.vatican.va/content/john-paul-ii/en/encyclicals/documents/hf_jp-ii_enc_14091998_fides-et-ratio.html.

4 *Veritatis Splendor* no. 4.

5 *Fides et Ratio* no. 77.

6 *Fides et Ratio* no. 14.

7 *Fides et Ratio* no. 77.

8 *Fides et Ratio* no. 48.

9 *Fides et Ratio* no. 46.

10 *Fides et Ratio* no. 53. In this regard, John Paul writes: "It is the same God who bestows faith and kindles within human understanding the light of reason; God cannot deny himself, nor can truth contradict itself."

11 The nature and role of philosophy, at least in the academy, has changed dramatically—and quite visibly—in more recent history. It has migrated

from its literal meaning, the "love of wisdom," to an embrace of nihilism. In fact, contemporary philosophy can be said to be in explicit *opposition* to faith and revelation. One might argue that this phenomenon reached a zenith in the 19th century, with its effects being felt in the 20th century, by means of unprecedented death and destruction underpinned by the atheistic humanism of totalitarian regimes.

Chapter 11

1 The two poets are Epimenides the Cretan and Aratus of Cilicia.

2 Acts 17:18.

3 In fact, elsewhere Paul notes that conscience might condemn a person for something that is not necessarily wrong (1 Cor. 8:7).

4 1 Tim. 4:2.

5 See also Question 17.

6 C. S. Lewis, *Mere Christianity*, rev. ed. (New York: Macmillan, 1960), 19.

7 For more on wisdom, see Question 46.

8 For a concise but thoughtful examination of the role of general revelation, see Ted M. Dorman, *A Faith for All Seasons: Historic Christian Belief in Its Classical Expression* (Nashville: Broadman & Holman, 1995).

Chapter 12

1 That is, those comprising the first generation of Protestant reform—for example, Luther, Melanchthon, Calvin, Zwingli, Bucer, and Bullinger.

2 Rom. 1:18–20 and 2:14–15; cf. as well Paul's preaching in the cities of Lystra (Acts 14: 15–17) and Athens, specifically the Areopagus address (Acts 17:22–34).

3 Rom. 10:4.

4 Rather than "goal," most translations of *telos* render it "end," which is unfortunate, given the suggestion thereby that moral law is somehow superseded or terminated, no longer remaining in the new covenant era. Quite the contrary: the moral law endures for all time. In a similar vein, Paul observes that the law is holy, righteous, and good (Rom. 7:12).

5 Whether they usually do or don't perform this duty justly is, of course, a different question.

6 The term *diakonos* is applied twice in Rom. 13:4 while *leitourgos* appears once in 13:6.

7 Rom. 13:1–7.

8 Through the ages, Christian interpreters of Scripture have distinguished between three types of law: ceremonial, judicial, and moral. The former two were specific to—and ended with—theocratic Israel of the Old Testament; the latter is enduring.

9 Jesus appears to be waging a war on two fronts: against Pharisaism, which distorts the law on the one hand, and against antinomianism, which discards it on the other. Without the law there is no moral standard; without *nomos*, one is left with *anomia*.

10 For example, 1 Cor. 5:11; 6:9; 1 Pet. 4:3; 2 Pet. 2:6–7; Jude 7; and Rev. 2:14.

11 For example, Matt. 19:4–6 and Mark 10:6–9.

12 See Question 13. While readers of this volume may or may not have explicit theological interests, my purpose here is simply to demonstrate the considerable inconsistency that exists even in standard religious thinking. Moreover, both secular and religious alike are inclined to pit love against justice. This unfortunate state of affairs in religious thinking indicates that many religious believers (a) are often taught that love has priority over all other virtues, including justice; (b) tend to be ethically deficient, given this lack of theoretical (and theological) foundation; and (c) consistently lack the tools to apply their faith in terms of responsible social and public policy. What's more, these deficiencies tend to afflict both "liberal" and "conservative" types, with both being inclined to "spiritualize" the ethical demands of justice by means of the "priority of love."

13 Stephen Charles Mott, *Biblical Ethics and Social Change*, 2nd ed. (Oxford and New York: Oxford University Press, 2011), 45, 53.

14 On this essential unity, see J. Daryl Charles, "The Moral Underpinnings of Just Retribution: Justice and Charity in Symbiosis," *Providence: A Journal of Christianity and American Foreign Policy* 3 (2016): 5–16, and "The Natural-Law Underpinnings of Religious Freedom—A Closer Look," in *Natural Law and Religious Freedom* (London and New York: Routledge, 2018), 177–228.

15 Elsewhere I offer an overview of representative fathers on moral law—from Justin, Tertullian, and Clement of Alexandria to John Chrysostom, Ambrose, and Augustine—as well as Aquinas. See J. Daryl Charles, *Retrieving the Natural Law: A Return to Moral First Things* (Grand Rapids and Cambridge, UK: Eerdmans, 2008), 85–90. See as well the following two summaries of patristic understanding of natural law: Stanley Berke, *The Possibility of Invincible Ignorance of the Natural Law* (SST 58;

Washington, DC: Catholic University of American Press, 1941), 5–11, and Matthew Levering, "Christians and Natural Law," in Anver Emon, Matthew Levering, and David Novak, *Natural Law: A Jewish, Christian, and Islamic Trialogue* (Oxford: Oxford University Press, 2014), 66–110.

16 Tertullian, *De Corona* 6; I am dependent here on the translation accessible at https://www.newadvent.org/fathers/0304.htm.

17 Irenaeus, *Against Heresies* IV.16.3–4.

18 Origen, *Contra Celsum* 7.2.

19 Ambrose, *Letter* no. 73 ("To Irenaeus").

20 Augustine, *On the Trinity* XIV.15.21.

21 Jean Porter, *Natural and Divine Law: Reclaiming the Tradition for Christian Ethics* (Grand Rapids and Cambridge, UK: Eerdmans, 1999), 15.

22 It is true that not everyone will come to the same conclusion about what constitutes "civil society." And it is true that most of our contemporaries will have a phobia about the place of "religious" values in the public sphere. The question, therefore, is not whether moral values will be tolerated but rather *whose* values in the end will prevail—after all, *someone* must draw the moral line. How will people of faith enter the public arena, and what will be our ethical resources? As it informs some of the more contentious ethical issues of the day, if one assumes a commitment to both natural law realities and the historic Christian moral tradition, ethical and bioethical challenges such as abortion, artificial reproductive technologies, gender-dysphoria, same-sex orientation, and euthanasia will necessitate that we argue on the basis of design and "respecting nature." According to both moral traditions, our nature *is* our design, and human design requires that we respect *both legitimate ends and legitimate means.*

23 *CCC* nos. 1954–1960.

24 Braaten, "Protestants and Natural Law," 25.

Chapter 13

1 Aquinas, *S. T.* I–II Q. 99.2–5.

2 Aquinas, *S. T.* I–II Q. 94.5.

3 Aquinas, S.T. I–II Q. 91.2 and Q. 94.1.

4 Aquinas, *S. T.* I–II Q. 94.4.

5 Aquinas, *S. T.* I–II Q. 6.4, 5 and Q. 92.1, 2.

6 Aquinas, *S.T.* I–II Q. 94.2. In this context, Aquinas observes: "All inclinations of human nature, to whatever part they belong…, all come under natural law so far as they can be charged with intelligence."

7 Aquinas, *S.T.* I–II Q. 93.2.

8 Aquinas, *S.T.* I–II Q. 90.

9 Aquinas, *S.T.* II–II QQ. 23–46, 58.

10 *City of God* 14.9.

11 *City of God* 15.22.

12 Aquinas, *S.T.* I-II Q. 62.2–4 and II–II Q. 23.8.

13 To state the obvious, no one wishes another to covet his goods or his spouse; no one wishes to be deceived or robbed; no one wishes to be physically attacked, mutilated or murdered.

14 Aquinas, *S.T.* II–II Q. 25; the question of war is discussed in II–II Q. 40.

15 Aquinas, *S.T.* II–II Q. 58.9.

Chapter 14

1 So Aristotle, *Nicomachean Ethics* 5.3–5 (1131a-1134a).

2 Aristotle, *Nicomachean Ethics* 5.1 (1129a) and 7 (1134b-1135a); I am reliant here on *Nicomachean Ethics*, 2nd ed., trans. Terence Irwin (Indianapolis: Hackett Publishing Co., 1999), 68, 78.

3 Aquinas, *S.T.* I–II Q. 58.5.

4 Hale, *Of the Law of Nature*, 25.

5 Of course, much of human history—at least in the Western cultural tradition—acknowledges that an almighty God has determined and revealed these standards, based on providential care of the universe. Perhaps the most obvious is the "American experiment." However, one need *not* be a theist to acknowledge, in all honesty, that justice—if it is truly *just*—transcends individuals, sub-cultures, people-groups, and nations.

6 Aquinas, *S.T.* I–II Q. 95.2.

7 Augustine, *On Free Choice* 1.5.

8 Not every law, of course, represents a moral norm. "Law enforcement"—think traffic regulations, for example—will vary city to city, region to region, and state to state and is established based on approximations of public safety; such regulations have no intrinsic moral content. The same could be said of many laws that help regulate society.

9 See John Rawls, *A Theory of Justice* (Cambridge: Belknap Press, 1971), *Political Liberalism* (New York: Columbia University Press, 1993), and *Justice as Fairness: A Restatement*, ed. Erin Kelly (Cambridge: Belknap Press, 2001).

10 Three useful—and in many ways penetrating—critiques of Rawls' thought are to be found in Christopher Wolfe, *Natural Law Liberalism* (Cambridge: Cambridge University Press, 2006); Christopher Wolfe and Robert P. George, eds., *Natural Law and Public Reason* (Washington, DC: Georgetown University Press, 2000); and Robert P. George, ed., *Natural Law, Liberalism, and Morality* (Oxford: Clarendon, 1996).

11 Estimates as to the exact number of deaths remain to this day somewhat disputed and imprecise.

12 This was the result of the Budapest Memorandum, signed by all four nations.

13 In Question 16 I address the matter of humanitarian intervention further.

14 After all, those regimes that massively violate these basic human rights in the end forfeit their own right to be shielded by international law. On the duty to intervene in cases of catastrophic need, see Michael Walzer, "The Politics of Rescue," chapter 5 of *Arguing About War* (New Haven and London: Yale University Press, 2004), 67–81; this essay was originally published in the journal *Dissent* (Winter 1995): 35–41.

15 Since no war is perfectly "just," it is more accurate to speak of "justified war," by which both whether or not to intervene and how to proceed in that intervention are subjected to severe moral qualification.

16 So Nigel Biggar, *In Defence of War* (Oxford and New York: Oxford University Press, 2013), 214.

17 On the unity of justice and charity in justifying intervention, see Paul Ramsey, *Basic Christian Ethics* (New York: Scribner's, 1950), and *The Just War: Force and Political Responsibility* (New York: Scribner's, 1968).

18 Ramsey, *Basic Christian Ethics*, 166–71.

19 Ramsey, *The Just War*, 35.

20 The transcript of this address appeared under the title "Healing Wounded People" in *The Washington Post* (February 2, 1997), C4.

21 Cicero, *On the Laws* I:XVI.

Chapter 15

1 Matt. 19:16–22; Mark 10:17–22; and Luke 18:18–23.

2 Matt. 19:19.

3 Aquinas, *S.T.* I–II Q. 96.4.

4 Aquinas, *S.T.* I–II Q. 100.8.

5 John Murray, *Principles of Conduct: Aspects of Biblical Ethics* (repr.; Grand Rapids: Eerdmans, 1991 [1957]), 7–8.

6 John Locke writes that "there exists nowhere a race so barbarous, so far removed from all humanity, that it does not take joy in the use of the senses [and] is not superior to brute beasts in the privilege of reasoning and the faculty of argumentation" (*Questions concerning the Natural Law* no. V, 165). In a similar vein, philosopher Peter Kreeft insists, "No culture in history has thought that love, kindness, justice, honesty, courage, wisdom, or self-control was evil—or that hate, cruelty, injustice, dishonesty, cowardice, folly, or uncontrolled addiction was good" ("What Is Natural Law and Why Is It Important?" in *Religion & Philosophy*, accessible at https://www.catholiceducation.org/en/religion-and-philosophy/philosophy/what-is-natural-law-and-why-is-it-important.html).

7 Precisely this was the argument of C. S. Lewis in his 1944 work *The Abolition of Man*.

8 One of the chief assumptions of America's founders and framers was that religion is necessary to the advancement of morality, and thus, to the advancement of genuine freedom. See in this regard, for example, Mark David Hall and Daniel L. Dreisbach, eds., *Faith and the Founders of the American Republic* (Oxford and New York: Oxford University Press, 2014), and Daniel L. Dreisbach, Mark David Hall, and Jeffrey H. Morrison, eds., *Forgotten Founders on Religion and Public Life* (Notre Dame: University of Notre Dame Press, 2009).

Chapter 16

1 See as well Question 5.

2 Locke, *Questions concerning the Law of Nature* no. VIII, 205.

3 Locke, *Questions concerning the Law of Nature* no. VIII, 207.

4 Locke, *Questions concerning the Law of Nature* no. VIII, 212–14.

5 For helpful commentary that examines the interplay between these three factors, see Robert P. George, *Conscience and Its Enemies: Confronting the Dogmas of Liberal Secularism* (Wilmington: ISI Books, 2013), 3–6.

6 So Thomas S. Kidd, "Epilogue," in Thomas S. Kidd, ed., *God of Liberty: A Religious History of the American Revolution* (New York: Basic Books, 2010), 255.

7 See https://www.un.org/en/udhrbook/pdf/udhr_booklet_en_web.pdf. The Second World War was a turning point insofar as up to that point, most governments around the world assumed that international law did not remove their sovereignty, and hence prevent what later were viewed as massive human rights violations.

8 The volume consists of 700–800 pages.

9 Contributor Gilbert Meilaender, however, cares to disagree, noting that "an attentive reader [of the *Human Dignity* volume] who genuinely seeks clearer understanding and insight may sometimes find it" (Meilaender, *Neither Beast Nor God*, 80).

Chapter 17

1 For further reflections on "principled pluralism," see the next Question.

2 We can acknowledge that "the common good" must be guided by the intuition of what is *universally right*—whether that measurement is, for example, the "Ten Commandments" or "self-evident truths" or Kant's "categorical imperative" or the U.N.'s definition of "inalienable rights." These elements, however formulated, derive from nature's dictates and constitute the foundations of any free and ordered society.

3 The exception to this is behavior flowing out of "deeply held convictions"—or, more accurately, deeply-entrenched malevolent behavior—which threatens or undermines the broader common good. Thus, for example, public authorities in our day are *required*, based on "the good," to restrict and punish terrorists who, for deeply held reasons, wish to kill human beings and destroy Western culture.

4 Although subsidiarity is typically identified with Catholic social thought, it is not in its essence a religious principle. In fact, one might argue that its secular version is advanced by people as diverse as Tocqueville and, more recently, political philosopher Michael Walzer; see John A. Coleman, "A Limited State and a Vibrant Society," in John A. Coleman, ed., *Christian Political Ethics* (Princeton and Oxford: Princeton University Press, 2008), 22–53.

5 So *Catechism of the Catholic Church* nos. 1882–1885.

6 "Spheres of creation" has traditionally been associated with a Reformed theological outlook. "Sphere sovereignty" has often been associated with the early 20th-century Dutch theologian (and former Prime Minister) Abraham Kuyper.

7 James W. Skillen, in his essay "Pluralism as a Matter of Principle," in John A. Coleman, ed., *Christian Political Ethics* (Princeton and Oxford: Princeton University Press, 2008), 148, says it well: human beings "are always more than citizens, and thus equal civil rights entails government's equal, [namely] nondiscriminatory protection of every nongovernment sphere of life (friendship, family, church, education, and so forth), each of which has its own nonpolitical jurisdiction." Catholic social thought and Reformed thinking have generally been more robust in terms of their understanding of the contributions of Christian faith to the public sphere and "civil society" than other theological traditions.

8 See the recent opinion piece by former Nebraska Senator Ben Sasse, "America's True Divide: Pluralists vs. Zealots," *Wall Street Journal* (January 3, 2023), A17, in which the pluralist argument is set forth succinctly with contemporary application. On the concept of "principled pluralism" more generally, see James W. Skillen, *Recharging the American Experiment: Principled Pluralism for Genuine Civic Community* (Grand Rapids: Baker, 1994).

9 Already 35 years ago, author Allan Bloom, in *The Closing of the American Mind* (New York: Simon & Schuster, 1987), 25, famously made the observation that relativism was "the only virtue" to which "all primary education for more than fifty years has dedicated itself." It is difficult to disagree.

10 It needs reiterating that both claims—human nature and "the good" are not knowable and "the good" varies—are metaphysical claims, that is, *ultimate* claims.

11 Budziszewski, *What We Can't Not Know*, 7.

12 This sort of logic is helpfully developed, with considerable insight, by Arkes, in *First Things*, 51–84.

13 Joseph Cardinal Ratzinger (Pope Benedict XVI), *Values in a Time of Upheaval*, trans. Brian McNeil (San Francisco: Ignatius Press, 2006), 56.

14 Budziszewski, *What We Can't Not Know*, 178–80.

15 See Question 33.

16 As this volume goes to press, mass killings are rampant in the U.S., cities are reeling because of violence and homicide rates, law-enforcement on all levels is broadly hindered, and lawlessness abounds. How, then, do we argue? Utilitarian thinking fails inasmuch as it lacks a fixed center, a foundation of ethical norms, from which human beings can then reason; it is biased against "moral absolutism." Further undermining our attempts to protect the common social good are biological explanations of criminal behavior—blame it on biology, or my criminal brain.

17 Hereon see the next Question.

18 In Question 33 I address various of these problems further in examining secularism as a worldview.

Chapter 18

1 On the modern history of this term, see the fascinating volume by A. J. Conyers, *The Long Truce: How Toleration Made the World Safer for Power and Profit* (Dallas: Spence, 2001).

2 Joseph Cardinal Ratzinger (Pope Benedict XVI), in *Values in a Time of Upheaval* (San Francisco: Ignatius Press, 2006), 55, states it in this way: "The concept of 'truth' has in fact moved into the zone of antidemocratic intolerance."

3 Here the greater threat comes not from the religious viewpoint but from a militant secularism.

4 As such, we can distinguish between people as human beings—whose humanity and dignity we affirm—and their distorted views.

5 John Attarian, "In Dispraise of Tolerance, Sensitivity and Compassion," *The Social Critic* (Spring 1998): 16.

6 Attarian, "In Dispraise," 18.

7 In our day, the argument is quite often proffered by social activists that the religious voice (usually meaning the *Christian* voice) upbraids social cohesion. This argument, however, is contrived solely in the interests of those wishing to set aside "traditional"—and hence, natural law—norms.

8 On this distinction, see J. Budziszewski, "The Illusion of Moral Neutrality," *First Things* 35 (August/September 1993): 34.

9 Hence, despite the literature of the last several decades to the contrary, the metaphor of "culture wars" is no mere metaphor. At stake is the clash of competing, all-encompassing visions for humanity and society.

10 Attarian, "In Dispraise," 22.

11 In this Question I have adapted material from J. Daryl Charles, *The Unformed Conscience of Evangelicalism: Recovering the Church's Moral Vision* (repr.; Dallas: Fontes Press, 2020 [InterVarsity Press, 2002]), 42–48.

12 Elsewhere I have developed the difference between tolerance properly and improperly construed in J. Daryl Charles, "Truth, Tolerance, and Christian Conviction: Reflections on a Perennial Question," in *Christian Scholars Review* 36, no. 2 (Winter 2007): 185–218, and *Natural Law and Religious Freedom*, chapter 4 ("Second Thoughts on 'Pluralism,' 'Neutrality,' and 'Tolerance'"), 124–52.

Chapter 19

1 Gen. 1: 10, 12, 18, 21, 25, and 31.

2 This sanction concerns the shedding of *innocent* blood, and that in *private* association, not killing in the context of a just war or capital punishment executed by civil authorities; see in this regard Rom. 12:9–13:7 for clarification.

3 Gen. 9:6.

4 The New Testament reinforces the fact that the image of God remains intact, despite human fallenness; see, for example, 1 Cor. 11:7.

5 See, for example, statements in the Psalms such as "The Law of the Lord is perfect…" (19:7) and "Oh, how I love your law…" (119:97). This "law," for the Psalmist, has a transcendent character.

6 In the book of Proverbs, law guides and guards the way of the wise.

7 It is noteworthy that the writer of Ecclesiastes, consistent with the "wisdom literature" perspective, observes: "There is a time for everything, and a season for every activity under heaven" (3:1)—an observation repeated in 3:17. What distinguishes the Old Testament "wisdom" perspective is that it is anchored in creation and divine sovereignty. Without transcendence and the natural law, wisdom cannot be distinguished from and compared to folly. Wisdom was part of the very creation of the world (Proverbs 8), yet she is part of daily life and decision-making (Proverbs 1:5–7:27 and 9:1–18).

8 The fact that the Old Testament prophets venerate the moral law finds confirmation in Jesus's statements concerning "the law and the prophets" (for example, Matt. 5:17; 11:13; 22:40; Luke 16:16).

9 Jesus's frequent conflict with the scribes and Pharisees, mirrored in all four gospel narratives but in particular the focus of Matthew, well illustrates this tension. Much of the argument found in the epistle to the Hebrews mirrors the reality of the Old Testament serving as a shadow of (permanent) things to come.

10 Matt. 5:17; 17:12; and 22:40; cf. Luke 24:44; Acts 13:15; and Rom. 3:21.

11 Matt. 5:43; 19:19; 22:40; Mark 12:31; 12:33; Luke 10:27; Rom 13:9; Gal. 5:14; and James 2:8.

12 See also Q. 15 .

13 Luke 10:25–37.

14 Luke 10:27. On natural law and the parable of the "Good Samaritan," see Q. 29.

15 *CCC* no. 1959, accessible at https://www.vatican.va/archive/ENG0015/_INDEX.HTM.

Chapter 20

1 See Matt. 19:3–12 and Mark 10:2–12; cf. Gen. 1:27 and 5:2.

2 See as well the discussion in Question 12.

3 Matt. 5:17. Jesus appears to be waging a war on two fronts: against Pharisaism, which distorts the law on the one hand, and against antinomianism, which discards it on the other. Without the law there is no moral standard; without *nomos*, one is left with *anomia*.

4 The enduring nature of the commandments is affirmed elsewhere in the New Testament—for example, James 2:8–12.

5 See, in this regard, J. Daryl Charles, "The Greatest or the Least in the Kingdom? The Disciple's Relationship to the Law (Matt. 5:17–20)," *Trinity Journal* 13 Ns (1992): 139–62, and "'Do Not Suppose That I Have Come…': The Ethic of the 'Sermon on the Mount' Reconsidered," *Southwestern Journal of Theology* 46, no. 3 (Summer 2004): 47–70.

6 For a helpful background discussion, see Morris J. Fish, "An Eye for an Eye: Proportionality as a Moral Principle of Punishment," *Oxford Journal of Legal Studies* 28, no. 1 (Spring 2008): 57–71.

7 See, for example, Exo. 21:24; Lev. 24:20; and Deut. 19:21.

8 In fact, Lev. 19:18 expressly forbids revenge, which is prevented by an exact compensation. Elsewhere in the Old Testament revenge is expressly forbidden in Prov. 20:22 and Prov. 24:29.

9 For this reason, although rabbinic interpretation and application of the *lex talionis* was throughout history non-literal and monetary in nature (after all, how does one compensate for damages short of death?), one exception to this was the murder (i.e., intentional killing) of another human being. Because a person's life is sacred and mirroring the *imago Dei*, it is without any material equivalent.

10 Fish, "An Eye for an Eye," 61 (emphasis added).

11 By contrast, Babylonian society would have interpreted law based on the victim's social status.

12 On Jesus's affirmation of moral law while chastening private applications of "justice," see Charles, " 'Do Not Suppose That I Have Come…,'" 47–70.

13 Note the language here: Jesus says "Do not resist an evil person," not "Do not resist evil." The issue here clearly concerns *personal* matters, not civil society or protecting the common social good.

14 Moreover, the injuries incurred in the Pentateuch are permanent; they are not a matter of insult or personal "injury," which is the context of Matthew 5:38–42.

15 Augustine's letter to Marcellinus, a Roman official in Carthage, is instructive in the way that its addresses the subject of punishment. Marcellinus had previously written to ask for help in answering objections to Christian faith by non-Christians. One of their charges was based on a misreading of Matt. 5:38–42. Augustine attacks this common distortion by insisting that Jesus's teaching was intended to address *personal attitudes*: "these precepts refer to a disposition of the heart" (*Epistle* 138; I am reliant here on the translation provided in Michael W. Tkacz and Douglas Kries, eds., *Augustine: Political Writings* [Indianapolis: Hackett, 1994], 205).

16 Augustine, *Contra Faustum* XIX.25; accessible at http://www.ccel.org/ccel/schaff/npnf104.html.

17 Augustine, *Contra Faustum* XIX.25.

Chapter 21

1 See Questions 5, 14, and 16.

2 Representative is Jeremy Waldron, "The Irrelevance of Moral Objectivity," in Robert P. George, ed., *Natural Law Theory* (Oxford: Clarendon Press, 1992), 158–87.

3 On the latter, see Jacques Maritain, *The Rights of Man and Natural Law*, trans. Doris C. Anson (New York: Charles Scribner's Sons, 1943); idem, *Man and the State* (Chicago: University of Chicago Press, 1951); and John Finnis, *Natural Law and Natural Rights* (Oxford: Clarendon, 1980).

4 Natural law does not tell us—or require—that *democratic* government be the sole form of political organization; however, it does tell us that any mode of political rule that denies a transcendent authority and does not recognize the inherent "natural" rights of the human person and the family is tyrannical and should be resisted.

5 Consider the language of Article 1 of the Universal Declaration of Human Rights, adopted and proclaimed on December 10, 1948, by the General Assembly of the United Nations: "All human beings are born free and equal in dignity and rights. They are endowed with reason and conscience and should act towards one another in a spirit of brotherhood." In its preamble, the UDHR refers to "the inherent dignity" of "all members of the human family."

6 Goldstone, "Healing Wounded People," C4.

Chapter 22

1 See David Novak, "Judaism and Natural Law," *American Journal of Jurisprudence* 43, no. 1 (1998): 117–34. An extended version of this essay appears in Anver M. Emon, Matthew Levering, and David Novak, *Natural Law: A Jewish, Christian, and Islamic Trialogue* (Oxford: Oxford University Press, 2014), 4–44.

2 Mishneh Torah: Yesodei ha-Torah, 1.1; cited by Novak, "Judaism and Natural Law," 119.

3 Novak, "Judaism and Natural Law," 134.

4 Novak, "Judaism and Natural Law," 134.

5 This is the conclusion of Tamar Rudavsky, "Natural Law in Judaism," in Jonathan A. Jacobs, ed., *Reason, Religion, and Natural Law* (Oxford: Oxford University Press, 2012), 83–105, who is in broader agreement with David Novak.

Chapter 23

1 While this reality is changing in our day, with a militantly secular outlook pervading gate-keeping institutions in Western culture, such is beyond the scope of the present volume.

2 Thus, for example, Qur'an 3:83.

3 The "spiritual jihad" is viewed by most Muslims as the "great jihad," while violent jihad—literally, "jihad by the sword" (so Surah 9:5 and 9:29, for example)—is said to be the "lesser jihad."

4 Tragically, "Middle Eastern" departments in many colleges and universities have become far more radicalized in the last two decades than anyone might have imagined. Thus, even to represent the views that I am presenting in this volume is to be guilty of "Islamophobia." Elsewhere I have addressed this trend in two essays; see J. Daryl Charles, "Regensburg Left Behind," *Touchstone* (September/October 2009), accessible at https://www.touchstonemag.com/archives/article.php?id=22–07–034-f, and idem, "Islamophobia Unveiled: Unsympathetic Reflections on a New Watchword," *Providence: A Journal of Christianity and American Foreign Policy* (April 3, 2018), accessible at https://providencemag.com/wp-content/uploads/J-Daryl-Charles-Islamophobia-Unveiled-Unsympathetic-Reflections-on-a-New-Watchword.pdf. Two resources offering up-to-date critiques of the 'Islamophobia' charge—a charge that often originates in the academy—are the Middle East Forum and the National Association of Scholars.

5 For a thoughtful analysis of the jihadist mindset and in the context of emerging global trends (including policy analysis), see Devin R. Springer, James L. Regens, and David N. Edger, *Islamic Radicalism and Global Jihad* (Washington, DC: Georgetown University Press, 2009).

6 Here the argument is *not* that the Judeo-Christian tradition, as evidenced in the Western context, has *always and everywhere* mirrored these priorities—only that a metaphysical commitment to "right reason," moral reflection, and voluntarism have *generally* resulted in human, political, and religious freedom.

7 Thus, one finds absolutely stunning the words of two Western Muslims, Hamza Yusuf Hanson and Mahan Hussain Mirza, who were invited to respond to the question of "Religious Freedom Supports the Common God: Three-Non-Christian Voices," in Stephen V. Monsma and Stanley W. Carlson-Thies, *Free to Serve: Protecting the Religious Freedom of Faith-Based Organizations* (Grand Rapids: Brazos, 2015), 157–159. Two of their most basic claims defy credulity and are patently false. The first: "Historically, Islamic civilization has always been a multiethnic, multilingual, and multireligious entity" (157). This claim would come as news to most people. Perhaps some peoples were "multiethnic" to the extent that Islam has always grown via conquest of other people groups (and hence a "multiethnic composition post-conquest). The second: "Even cursory readings of the Qur'an indicate that 'there is no compulsion in religion' and that 'the truth is clear from your Lord, so let him who will, believe, and let him who will, disbelieve.'" The truth is that virtually nowhere in the Muslim world today could Muslims believe, much less speak out, this claim. It is a rare phenomenon in the 21st century to find authentic religious freedom in Muslim-majority countries. Much more common is radicalized terrorism and persecution of non-Muslims, and, on occasion, death-threats based on "apostasy."

8 Not infrequently, these "moderates"—if and where they choose to speak out with regard to Islamic extremism, rigidity, or terrorist tendencies—pay a price. This "price" often requires that such individuals adopt a pseudonym (with more prominent "moderates" at times receiving government protection), given the frequently violent responses to public criticism of Islam.

9 Holding a very different view is Anver M. Emon, *Islamic Natural Law Theories* (Oxford: Oxford University Press, 2010). Emon argues on the basis of two assumptions: a "resurgence" of interest in pre-modern Islamic legal traditions and increased efforts among "Abrahamic faith

communities" to search for common ground. Emon, however, does not examine the faith-and-reason, non-compulsion argument I present here in this Question; nor does he give an account of Islam's overwhelmingly violent history—from the beginning—a history that would seem to repudiate a proper understanding of "natural law."

10 In his address, titled "Faith, Reason, and the University: Memories and Reflections," Benedict combined personal reflections on teaching theology at the University of Bonn decades earlier with his assessment of the state of contemporary academic discourse.

11 According to the letter, "the Unity of God, the necessity of love for Him, and the necessity of love of the neighbor" are "common ground" between Muslims and Christians and "the basis for all future interfaith dialogue." This is a remarkable claim, given the differences between the two faiths that originate with the proclamations and practice of Muhammad himself and extend to our day, in which *jihad* ("struggle") is advanced—often violently—against any who oppose or resist Islam.

12 It was unfortunate and misguided that the Yale document presumed to speak for all of Christendom, as well as for policy-makers, not only because of its theological error but for its asking for "forgiveness" for both the Crusades and the current "war on terrorism," while failing to account for widespread and egregious human rights violations around the globe that are committed by militant expressions of Islam.

13 It needs reiterating that the speech was designed to address the interaction—rather than the divorce—of faith and reason. That Muslim leaders could not/cannot acknowledge this reality is instructive.

14 "'Harassment' is much too weak a word" to describe what converts suffer in Middle Eastern countries, writes Paul A. Marshall, in "The Range of Religious Freedom," in Paul A. Marshall, ed., *Religious Freedom in the World* (Lanham and Plymouth, UK: Rowman & Littlefield, 2008), 10. See in this regard as well Paul Marshall, Lela Gilbert, and Nina Shea, *Persecuted: The Global Assault on Christians* (Nashville: Thomas Nelson, 2013), in which four of ten chapters are devoted to persecution in the Muslim world.

15 Elsewhere I have examined the lecture by Benedict XVI, the Muslim response "A Common Word," and the unwitting Christian response at https://www.touchstonemag.com/archives/article.php?id=22–07–034-f&readcode=&readtherest=true. See as well the very perceptive essay by Adam S. Francisco, "Natural Law: A Basis for Christian-Muslim Discourse," in *Natural Law: A Lutheran Appraisal*, ed. Robert C. Baker (St. Louis: Concordia Publishing House, 2011), 235–47.

Chapter 24

1 While the death sentence is still applied in some states, it is growing less frequent. As I write, a jury in Florida has just recommended a life sentence (without parole) for the man who murdered seventeen—seventeen!—people in the Marjory Stoneman Douglas High School shooting in 2018.

2 See Question 26.

3 Robert P. George, *Conscience and Its Enemies: Confronting the Dogmas of Liberal Secularism* (Wilmington: ISI Books, 2013), 166.

4 George, *Conscience and Its Enemies*, 166–67.

5 While the amount of literature on embryonic and fetal development as it relates to the ethics of abortion is massive, two useful presentations of the natural-law argument can be found in Patrick Lee and Robert P. George, "The Wrong of Abortion," in Andrew I. Cohen and Christopher Wellman, eds., *Contemporary Debates in Applied Ethics* (New York: Blackwell Publishers, 2005), 13–26, and George, *Conscience and Its Enemies*, 155–201.

Chapter 25

1 This is the burden of Hugo Grotius, considered the father of international law, in *The Rights of War and Peace* (1625).

2 Hereon see Question 30.

3 See Questions 26 and 27.

4 Paul Ramsey, "The Ethics of Intervention," in *The Just War: Force and Political Responsibility* (New York: Scribner's, 1968), 23.

5 Ramsey, "The Ethics of Intervention," 22.

6 John P. Hittinger, "Just War and Defense Policy," in David F. Forte, ed., *Natural Law and Contemporary Public Policy* (Washington, DC: Georgetown University Press, 1998), 342.

7 Jean Bethke Elshtain, "The Responsibility of Nations: A Moral Case for Coercive Justice," *Daedalus* (Winter 2003): 67.

8 Thomas G. Weiss and Cindy Collins, *Humanitarian Challenges and Intervention*, 2nd ed. (Boulder: Westview, 2000), 19.

9 Elshtain, "The Responsibility of Nations," 67–68.

10 Prov. 24:10–12.

Chapter 26

1 *City of God* 19.12–13.

2 Significantly, Thomas Aquinas discusses the idea of just war in the context of his wider discussion of *caritas*. Francisco Suárez, too, grounds his discussion of war similarly, in *De Caritate*, disputation 13 in his work *De Triplici Virtute Theologica*. See, as well, Question 13, where the interaction of justice and charity is also discussed.

3 *S.T.* II–II Q. 40.

4 While *post bellum* considerations and responsibilities are the subject of more recent just war theorizing, one might contend that they are resident—and assumed—in traditional *ad bellum* and *in bello* reasoning.

5 So argues John Finnis in "The Ethics of War and Peace in the Catholic Natural Law Tradition," in John A. Coleman, ed., *Christian Political Ethics* (Princeton: Princeton University Press, 2008), 200.

6 Anthony Coates, "Is the Independent Application of *Jus in Bello* the Way to Limit War?" in David Rodin and Henry Shue, eds., *Just and Unjust Warriors* (Oxford: Oxford University Press, 2008), 181.

7 *De Iure Belli ac Pacis* III.1.2

8 Indeed, military necessity justifies a resort to all measures that are necessary for securing submission of the adversary, provided that these measures are not inconsistent with moral criteria of discrimination and proportionality. Moral obligations in military service entail both to act and to refrain from acting. We may say that proportionality includes and extends the notion of military necessity.

9 So C. A. J. Coady, "The Status of Combatants," in David Rodin and Henry Shue, eds., *Just and Unjust Warriors* (Oxford: Oxford University Press, 2008), 158.

10 Augustine's discussions of the priority of charity are scattered, found in *Confessions*, *City of God*, and various letters. Perhaps familiar to most people are his famous words "Love, and do what you will" (*Homilies on the First Letter of John* 7.8).

11 "To Count Boniface" (#189), in St. Augustine, *Letters—Volume IV* (Washington, DC: Catholic University of America Press, 1955), 269. Aquinas, in his treatment of right intention, will repeat the admonition of Augustine given to Boniface (*S.T.* II–II Q. 40, a. 1).

12 *S.T.* II–II Q. 64, a. 7; I am here reliant on St. Thomas Aquinas, *Summa Theologiae*, vol. 38 (New York and London: McGraw-Hill and Eyre & Spottiswoode, 1964), 41–42. A most useful assessment of the importance of right intention in Aquinas's understanding of war is that of Darrell Cole, "Thomas Aquinas on Virtuous Warfare," *Journal of Religious Ethics*

27, no. 1 (Spring 1999): 57–80. Cole argues that Aquinas's approach to warfare, with its emphasis on justice wed to charity, assists us in providing a coherent moral account of war to which even Christians can subscribe. In Aquinas we find the melding of justice and charity.

13 So William V. O'Brien, *The Conduct of a Just and Limited War* (New York: Praeger, 1981), 33–35. O'Brien, accurately in my view, calls this criterion "elusive but important" (338).

14 This tragic divorce characterizes both secular and religious approaches to ethics. Consider, for example, a representative case of the latter: Timothy P. Jackson, *The Priority of Love: Christian Charity and Social Justice* (Princeton and Oxford: Princeton University Press, 2003).

15 The just war tradition, it needs reiterating, gives an account of *comparative* rather than absolute or perfect justice, as Jean Bethke Elshtain, *Just War Against Terror: The Burden of American Power in a Violent World* (New York: Basic Books, 2003), 53, reminds us.

16 Benedict XVI, in his 2009 encyclical *Caritas in Veritate*, expresses well the resultant calamity when love is divorced from truth and justice: "Without truth, charity degenerates into sentimentality. Love becomes an empty shell, to be filled an arbitrary way. In a culture without truth, this is the fatal risk facing love. It falls prey to contingent subjective emotions and opinions, [and] the word 'love' is abused and distorted, to the point where it comes to mean the opposite" (no. 3).

17 Elsewhere I have developed the argument for the unity of justice and love more extensively. See, for example, J. Daryl Charles, "Justice, Neighbor-Love and the Just-War Tradition: Christian Reflections on Just Use of Force," *Cultural Encounters* 1, no. 1 (Winter 2004): 47–67, and idem, "The Natural-Law Underpinnings of Religious Freedom—a Closer Look: Justice and Neighbor-Love in Symbiosis," in *Natural Law and Religious Freedom* (London, and New York: Routledge, 2018), 177–228 (Chapter 6).

Chapter 27

1 Francisco Suárez, *Three Theological Virtues* 3.8.1. I am here dependent on the English translation of James B. Scott, *The Spanish Origin of International Law: Lectures on Francisco de Vitoria (1480–1546) and Francisco Suárez (1548–1617)* (Washington, DC: Georgetown University Press, 1929), 77.

2 Suárez, *Three Theological Virtues* 3.8.2.

3 Grotius, *On the Law of War and Peace* I.1.10 and I.3.16.

4 So Paul Christopher, *The Ethics of War and Peace*, rev. ed. (Upper Saddle River: Prentice-Hall, 1999), 81–103.

5 A common objection among religious thinkers is that natural law thinking is autonomous to a so-called Christian ethics and to the authority of Scripture. This view is utterly mistaken and mirrors a fundamental misunderstanding both of law as an entity and of the natural law as the basis of human moral intuition. The Hebrew and Christian scriptures *presuppose* natural law. Consider, for example Rom 2:14–15, which describes this phenomenon as a "law written on the [human] heart." Moreover, the Ten Commandments simply define the wider contours of the natural moral law as a moral code that applies to all of humanity and not exclusively to any particular culture or society. There is no disagreement or discord between the Ten Commandments and the natural law.

Chapter 28

1 William Lee Miller, "The Moral Project of the American Founders," in James Davison Hunter and Os Guinness, eds., *Articles of Faith, Articles of Peace: The Religious Liberty Clauses and the American Public Philosophy* (Washington, DC: Brookings Institution, 1990), 37. Miller is correct to note that unlike Europe, the U.S. over time would not divide politically and systematically along religious fault-lines. There were not two Americas—a Catholic and a Protestant. This, then, would contribute, in important ways to the creation and preservation of a "principled pluralism."

2 We can readily grant, however, that the problem is not *that* religious arguments enter the public square; the question is *how* they are utilized.

3 Alexis de Tocqueville, *Democracy in America*, ed. and trans. Harvey C. Mansfield and Delba Winthrop (Chicago and London: University of Chicago Press, 2000), I.2.9, p. 275.

4 This is the essence of Benedict XVI's encyclical *Religious Freedom, the Path to Peace*; accessible at https://www.vatican.va/content/benedict-xvi/en/messages/peace/documents/hf_ben-xvi_mes_20101208_xliv-world-day-peace.html.

5 United Nations, "Universal Declaration of Human Rights," accessible at https://www.un.org/sites/un2.un.org/files/2021/03/udhr.pdf.

Chapter 29

1 Luke 10:30–37.

2 Consider as well the story recounted in John 4:4–26, 39–42, which ever so slightly mirrors the racial and social tensions between Jews and Samaritans. What Jesus is doing here is nothing short of scandalous.

3 Prior to his ascension, Jesus declared that following the giving of the Holy Spirit, his disciples would be his witnesses "in Jerusalem, and in all Judea *and Samaria*, and to the ends of the earth" (Acts 1:8, emphasis added).

4 Paul Ramsey, *The Just War: Force and Political Responsibility* (New York: Scribner, 1968), 35–36.

5 Ramsey, *The Just War*, 142.

6 Ramsey, *The Just War*, 143.

Chapter 30

1 Hugo Grotius, *The Rights of War and Peace* II.20.8, observes that the natural law "remains still in force [even] where there are no courts of justice."

Chapter 31

1 We are not bound to help meet the needs of all people; such would be impossible. Rather, we are to apply charity to the needs of others to the extent that we are able. The issue here is stewardship and charity as directed.

2 Habermas and Ratzinger, *The Dialectics of Secularization*, 51–52.

3 Habermas and Ratzinger, *The Dialectics of Secularization*, 58.

4 Habermas and Ratzinger, *The Dialectics of Secularization*, 60.

5 Habermas and Ratzinger, *The Dialectics of Secularization*, 61.

6 Habermas and Ratzinger, *The Dialectics of Secularization*, 68.

7 Habermas and Ratzinger, *The Dialectics of Secularization*, 69.

Chapter 32

1 This theme underscores Madison's *Memorial and Remonstrance Against Religious Assessments*.

2 Tocqueville, *Democracy in America*, 280.

3 Tocqueville, *Democracy in America*, 275.

4 Locke, *Questions concerning the Law of Nature* no. XI, 237.

5 See John Locke, *Two Treatises of Government*, ed. Peter Laslett (New York: Cambridge University Press, 1960), esp. sections 6 and 12.

6 Alexander Hamilton, "Federalist no. 31," in *The Federalist* (New York: Random House, 2000), 188; cited as well as in Arkes, "The Natural Law—Again, Ever," 122.

7 Whether and to what extent various founders actually modeled this standard, by our standards, is clearly beyond the concerns of the present discussion.

8 Gen. 1:26–27; 5:1; 9:6–7; Ps. 8:5–6; 2 Cor. 3:18; and Col. 3:10; cf. Eccl. 3:11.

9 George Washington to John Jay (15 August 1786), Founders Online, accessible at https://founders.archives.gov/documents/washington/04–04-02–099.

10 George Washington to John Jay (15 August 1786), Founders Online, accessible at https://founders.archives.gov/documents/washington/04–04-02–099.

11 A delegate to the Second Continental Congress and an important thinker and statesman in his own right, Witherspoon served as the sixth President of the College of New Jersey (to become Princeton University) from 1768 until 1794.

12 *The Federalist* No. 51, accessible at www.constitution.org/fed/federa51.htm.

13 William Lee Miller, *The First Liberty: America's Foundation in Religious Freedom* (Washington, DC: Georgetown University Press, 2003), 129–30.

14 Author and social philosopher Michael Novak uses this language to depict the American founding; see his *On Two Wings: Humble Faith and Common Sense at the American Founding* (San Francisco: Encounter Books, 2002).

15 Michael Novak, "Foreword: Religious Liberty," in Daniel L. Dreisbach, Mark David Hall, and Jeffry H. Morrison, eds., *The Founders on God and Government* (Lanham: Rowman & Littlefield, 2004), xi.

Chapter 33

1 See Question 17.

2 It might well be argued that a third worldview, that of Islam, is ascendant in the West.

3 For a helpful discussion of secularism as a world-view and as a "religion," see Brendan Sweetman, *Why Politics Needs Religion: The Place of Religious Arguments in the Public Square* (Downers Grove: IVP Academic, 2006), 59–84.

4 Christian Smith, ed., *The Secular Revolution: Power, Interests, and Conflict in the Secularization of American Public Life* (Berkeley: University of California Press, 2003), esp. 1–12.

Chapter 34

1 Aquinas, *S.T.* I-II Q. 94.2; cf. Q. 80.1.

2 Hale, *Of the Law of Nature*, 6–7.

3 This is found in Aquinas's discussion of "the good" in *S. T.* I-II Q. 94.

4 On the matter of human inclinations, see Michael Pakaluk, "Natural Inclinations in Aquinas's Account of Natural Law," in Christopher Wolfe and Steven Brust, eds., *Natural Law Today: The Present State of the Perennial Philosophy* (Lanham: Lexington Books, 2018), 19–32.

5 Budziszewski, *What We Can't Not Know*, 115.

6 From a Christian standpoint, the natural law represents the wisdom of the Creator. It is immutable inasmuch as it is participation in the divine nature and divine law.

7 Matthew Hale identifies four internal modes or faculties by which human awareness of the natural law is sensed: the intellect, the exercise of reason, conscience, and implanted inclinations; see Hale, *Of the Law of Nature*, 121–75.

Chapter 35

1 See Question 33.

2 Charles Darwin, *The Origins of Species and the Descent of Man* (New York: The Modern Library, 1936), 914.

3 Michael Ruse and E.O. Wilson, "The Evolution of Ethics," *New Scientist* 108, no. 1478 (October 17, 1985): 51–52.

4 One of the more enlightening—and succinct—assessments of metaphysical naturalism can be found in chapter 5 of J. Budziszewski, *The Line Through the Heart: Natural Law as Fact, Theory, and Sign of Contradiction* (Wilmington: ISI Books, 2009), 79–95 ("Accept No Imitations: Natural Law vs. Naturalism").

5 Hence the utterly remarkable statement by preeminent sociobiologist E.O. Wilson, who insists: "The great questions—'Who are we?' 'Where did we come from?' 'Why are we here?'—can be answered *only, if ever*, in the light of scientifically based evolutionary thought"; see Edward O. Wilson, Foreword to Michael Ruse and Joseph Travis, eds., *Evolution: The First Four Billion Years* (Cambridge, MA, and London: Harvard University Press, 2009), viii (emphasis added). Consider as well the claim by "primate philosopher" Frans de Waal, in *Good Natured: The Origins of Right and Wrong in Humans and Other Animals* (Cambridge: Harvard University Press, 1996), 218: "We seem to be reaching a point at which science can wrest morality from the hands of philosophers."

6 See Question 13.

7 If this were so, then the so-called "brightest" human beings among us would be the most moral.

8 Aquinas, *S.T.* I–II Q.2.3.

Chapter 36

1 Budziszewski, *What We Can't Not Know*, xix.

2 Thus Question 3.

3 Budziszewski, *What We Can't Not Know*, 173–95.

4 Thomas Sowell, *Intellectuals and Society* (New York: Basic Books, 2009).

5 Heraclitus, *Fragments* 112–14, reproduced in Charles M. Bakewell, *Source Book in Ancient Philosophy* (New York: Scribner's, 1907), 34.

Chapter 37

1 Robert James Bidinotto, "Crime and Moral Retribution," in Robert James Bidinotto, ed., *Criminal Justice? The Legal System Versus Individual Responsibility* (Irvington on Hudson: Foundation for Economic Education, 1994), 183.

2 Bidinotto, "Crime and Moral Retribution," 187.

3 The plea bargain, in truth, falsifies the criminal's actual record by reducing the sentence and thereby creating a less dangerous impression.

4 This language has been used by Eugene H. Methvin, in "Mugged by Reality," *Policy Review* (July/August 1997): 37. This, however, is not to suggest that most people coming from broken or fatherless homes choose crime.

Chapter 38

1 Consider the following rather remarkable claim by one self-professing "criminologist": "Christian doctrine has contributed so much to the rise of a system of crime control *so unjust, malevolent, and ineffective* as the present punitive system" (Herman Bianchi, *Justice as Sanctuary: Toward a New System of Crime Control* [Bloomington and Indianapolis: Indiana University Press, 1994), vii [emphasis added]). In this volume the author wishes both to examine "the distorted Christian roots of the punitive model" of criminal justice and to present "a well-grounded draft for a nonpunitive but effective system of controlling criminality, based on conflict resolution" (ix-x). Surely, his views are today somewhat representative.

2 C. S. Lewis, "The Humanitarian Theory of Punishment," in *God in the Dock: Essays on Theology and Ethics*, ed. Walter Hooper (Grand Rapids: Eerdmans, 1970), 287–94.

3 Here for the sake of the immediate argument, I will leave aside growing interest in brain structure.

4 Whether these "root causes" are perceived as psychological, sociological, biological, or genetic, they all mirror a form of determinism. For the determinist, human actions are explained by antecedent factors and not moral agency. For a penetrating (indeed, withering) critique of the "root causes" orientation, see Stanton E. Samenow, "The Futility of Focusing on the Causes of Crime," in *Inside the Criminal Mind*, rev. ed. (New York: Crown, 2022), 3–14 (Chapter 1).

5 Karl Menninger, *The Crime of Punishment* (New York: Viking Press, 1968). Menninger's argument was that society needs "the crime and punishment ritual" as part of our collective lives, that as a society we "need" and "desire" crime to the extent of needing scapegoats to bear the burdens of our own guilt and iniquities. Menninger concludes his book with these words: "The public will grow increasingly ashamed of its cry for retaliation, its persistent demand to punish. This is its crime, our crime against criminals—and incidentally our crime against ourselves. For before we can diminish our sufferings from the ill controlled aggressive assaults of fellow citizens, we must renounce the philosophy of punishment, the obsolete, vengeful penal attitude. In its place we would seek a comprehensive, constructive social attitude—therapeutic in some instances, restraining in some instances, but preventive in its total social impact" (p. 280).

6 In addition, plenty of studies show that within a relatively short time following release on parole, most (as opposed to few) released prisoners continue their criminal behavior. Paroled inmates have very high rates of recidivism.

7 The address eventually was published in *The American Scholar* 62, no. 1 (Winter 1993): pp. 17–30.

8 A decade later, one sociologist and author who applauded Moynihan's thesis was Anne Henderschott, in *The Politics of Deviance* (San Francisco: Encounter Books, 2002).

9 Stanton E. Samenow, "The Basic Myths about Criminals," in Robert James Bidinotto, ed., *Criminal Justice? The Legal System Versus Individual Responsibility* (Irvington-on-Hudson: Foundation for Economic Education, Inc. 1994), 57.

10 Karol Wojtyla, *Sign of Contradiction* (New York: Seabury Press, 1979).

11 Here we can observe the clash of oppositional worldviews with their basic assumptions about human nature. One criminologist—surely representative of many today—denies the need for purification: "The suffering inflicted on criminals in the punitive model is not only avoidable; it *ought* to be avoided for the benefit of all, including victims and offenders" (Bianchi, *Justice as Sanctuary*, 35 [emphasis present]). *How* both victims and offenders "benefit" from his proposed nonpunitive model he does not tell us. Punishment according to one worldview is cruel and intolerable; according to another it is humane and in accordance with our fundamental design. Both cannot be right.

12 This is a reiteration of what is stated in Gen. 9:6.: "Whoever sheds the blood of [an innocent] man, by man shall his blood be shed..."

13 Francisco de Vitoria, *De Iuri Belli* 1, in *Vitoria: Political Writings*, ed. Anthony Pagden and Jeremy Lawrance (Cambridge Texts in the History of Political Thought; Cambridge: Cambridge University Press, 1991), 298.

14 See as well Question 20, where Jesus's attitude toward moral law and the *lex talionis*, mirrored in Matthew 5, is examined in more detail.

15 As I write, I read that San Quentin State Prison, located in the San Francisco Bay area and containing some of the more notorious serial killers in recent U.S. history such as Charles Manson, "Night Stalker" Richard Ramirez, and "Freeway Killer" William Bonin, will become the most enlightened, innovative facility in the state of California. California's governor Newsom has announced that the facility will henceforth be named "San Quentin Rehabilitation Center" (as reported in the *Wall Street Journal*, March 18–19, 2023, A3). As of the end of 2022, San Quentin contained over 500 "death row" prisoners, although the last execution occurred in 2006.

16 John J. DiIulio and Charles H. Logan, "Ten Deadly Myths about Crime and Punishment in the U.S.," in Robert James Bidinotto, ed., *Criminal Justice? The Legal System versus Individual Responsibility* (Irvington-on-Hudson: Foundation for Economic Education, 1994), 174–75.

17 DiIulio and Logan, "Ten Deadly Myths about Crime and Punishment in the U.S.," 175.

18 Not all wrongs, of course, are "criminal" or matters of justice. As individuals we endure—or should endure—personal insults, injuries or criticisms. These are not matters of the "common good," public law or "the law." Tragically, in a litigious society, the line distinguishing the personal from the public often gets blurred.

19 DiIulio and Logan, "Ten Deadly Myths about Crime and Punishment in the U.S.," 175.

Chapter 39

1 Take, for example, the just war theorists Francisco de Vitoria, in *De Juri Belli*, and Francisco Súarez, in *De Bello.*

2 Retributive justice does not deny the possibility of an offender being rehabilitated; however, it understands that punishment is part of, rather than being in opposition to, the work of inner change and transformation.

3 That injustice might take the form of consequences that are either too lenient or too severe.

4 Here again we distinguish between the widespread "rehabilitative" model advocated for decades by social scientists—a model that has already been critiqued above and for which evidence has been broadly lacking—and a severely qualified understanding of rehabilitation as *part of*, rather than being *opposed to*, the repertoire of punishment.

5 Oliver O'Donovan, "Payback: Thinking about Retribution," *Books & Culture* (July/August 2000): 16–21.

6 Retributive justice is particularly important as an international mechanism such as criminal tribunals—where, that is, they have teeth.

7 The term "harsh," of course, will be leveled against punishment that is just or unjust in nature. Hence, as a descriptor it is unhelpful. Proportionality and just desert should measure how we understand "harshness."

8 Bidinotto, "Crime and Moral Retribution," 194–95.

Chapter 40

1 Mass shootings for 2022 up through September are listed at https://www.gunviolencearchive.org/reports/mass-shooting?page=22; the homicide mortality rate for the U.S. through 2020 can be found at https://www.cdc.gov/nchs/pressroom/sosmap/homicide_mortality/homicide.htm.

2 https://www.themarshallproject.org/2022/07/06/what-you-need-to-know-about-the-rise-in-u-s-mass-shootings.

3 A common feature of much of the literature is to decry the "punitive" and "retributive" character of criminal justice in the U.S. However, this viewpoint does not represent the wider citizenry; it is generally confined to those in the academy who work in the social sciences or who are activists operating on the margins of the criminal justice system.

4 For a very concise summary of the most frequent abolitionist arguments, with appropriate responses, see Robert Blecker, *The Death of Punishment* (New York: Palgrave Macmillan, 2013), 273–78 ("Appendix A").

5 *Summa Contra Gentiles* 146; cf. as well *S.T.* II–II q. 64, a. 2 and 3.

6 *CCC* no. 2266, emphasis added.

7 This is the teaching of Romans 13:1ff.

8 This rationale, especially for the most vulnerable and innocent lives, undergirds Christians' commitment to fight against the evil of abortion—at *any* stage of human life development. See Question 42.

9 See David Gelernter, "What Do Murderers Deserve?" *First Things* (April 1998): 21–24.

10 Not insignificantly, Aquinas places the topic of war in the context of his wider discussion of *caritas*.

11 By taking a murderer's life, we affirm the dignity of the victims and their kin. But we also affirm the murderer's dignity by holding him morally accountable and punishing him in accordance with the highest value, namely, human life.

12 Here it needs reiterating that the present argument concerning capital punishment is only being applied to *one* crime, namely, premeditated murder.

13 A version of the answer to Question 40 appeared in the online journal *Public Discourse* (March 13, 2023); see https://www.thepublicdiscourse.com/2023/03/88061/.

Chapter 41

1 George, *Conscience and Its Enemies*, 3–8.

2 I am citing in what follows from Jürgen Habermas and Joseph Ratzinger (Pope Benedict XVI), *The Dialectics of Secularization: On Reason and Religion*, trans. Brian McNeil (San Francisco: Ignatius, 2006).

Chapter 42

1 So William E. May, "Bioethics and Human Life," in David F. Forte, ed., *Natural Law and Contemporary Public Policy* (Washington, DC: Georgetown University Press, 1998), 41.

2 Aquinas, *S.T.* I-II Q. 4.2.

3 As Skillen, "Pluralism as a Matter of Principle," 149, notes, the debate over whether the fetus is a "person" is beside the point; sexual intercourse leads to the propagation of human life, generation upon generation, and any human law must protect human sanctity. With relatively few exceptions, all humans *in utero* become full-fledged persons *ex utero*.

4 Peter Singer, "The Choice of a Pregnant Woman Always Outweighs the Life of the Fetus," in *Ethics: Opposing Viewpoints* (Farmington Hills: Greenhaven Press, 2015), 82–83.

5 This question is raised by Christopher Wolfe, in "Judicial Review," in David F. Forte, ed., *Natural Law and Contemporary Public Policy* (Washington, DC: Georgetown University Press, 1998), 181.

6 In the U.S., states currently vary in terms of law in this regard.

7 William E. May, "Bioethics and Human Life," in David F. Forte, ed., *Natural Law and Contemporary Public Policy* (Washington, DC: Georgetown University Press, 1998), 48.

8 So Meilaender, *Neither Beast Nor God*, 103.

9 Few have argued this point with greater force than G.E.M. Anscombe in her classic essay "War and Murder," in Robert Wasserstrom , ed., *War and Morality* (Belmont: Wadsworth, 1970), 42–53.

10 Few have presented the natural law position on end-of-life matters as succinctly and accurately as May, "Bioethics and Human Life," 41–54, esp. 46–48.

11 See Question 5.

12 The year 1938 marked the founding of the National Society for the Legalization of Euthanasia, later to be renamed the Euthanasia Society of America. According to *TIME* magazine, this society was the result of "a sizable group" of influential individuals who believed "so strongly in the right of an incurably diseased individual to have his life terminated." The society's trustees included Clarence Cook Little of the American Society for the Control of Cancer and of the American Birth Control League and Leon Fradley Whitney of the American Eugenics Society." See https://euthanasia.procon.org/historical-timeline/.

13 None has stated this more succinctly and forcefully than May, "Bioethics and Human Life," 41–54.

14 Skillen, "Pluralism," 151.

15 The very same rationale applies to incest, transexuality and other deviant forms of normative sexuality, which are being forced upon American

society in our day. It bears remembering that nations have been exterminated because of their violation of moral law as mirrored in sexual relationships; see in this regard Leviticus 18.

Chapter 43

1 See Question 14.

2 The primary sources here are Rawls, *A Theory of Justice* (1971), *Political Liberalism* (1993), and *Justice as Fairness* (2001); see n. 9 on p. 268 for full bibliographical data.

3 Richard John Neuhaus, *The Naked Public Square: Religion and Democracy in America* (Grand Rapids: Eerdmans, 1984), ix.

4 Richard John Neuhaus, "Why We Can Get Along," *First Things* (February 1996):27.

5 This phenomenon, not widespread but extremely vocal, harkens back to Puritan views of religion and politics as a "covenant" before God.

6 Hereon see Question 32.

7 Rom. 13:1–2.

8 Matt. 22:21 and Mark 12:17.

9 Michael Gerson and Peter Wehner, *City of Man: Religion and Politics in a New Era* (Chicago: Moody Publishers, 2010), 31.

10 It is curious that secularists' argument in our day, strangely, only seems to apply to confessional *Christians* and not, say, to *Muslims*. Why is this? Such selective exclusion needs to be examined. Is it perhaps possible that secularists sense that Muslims, in having their religion excluded from the public sphere, will react violently—a reaction that is on display in many parts of world?

11 Writing from the standpoint of faith, Gerson and Wehner (see previous note) suggest five principles to guide the concerned citizen in public persuasion: (1) distinguish between private duties and duties of the state; (2) distinguish between responsibilities of individuals and those associated with the institutional church; (3) recognize that Scripture does not offer a blueprint for how to participate in public affairs; (4) realize that the precise nature of political involvement will depend on the particular type of society in which one lives; and (5) realize that how God dealt with theocratic Israel in the "old covenant" differs from how God deals with nations today (32–45).

12 See in this regard Robert P. George, "Public Reason and Political Conflict: Abortion and Homosexuality," in *In Defense of Natural Law* (Oxford and

New York: Oxford University Press, 1999), 196–227, and more generally, Robert P. George and Christopher Wolfe, eds., *Natural Law and Public Reason* (Washington, DC: Georgetown University Press, 2000).

13 Richard John Neuhaus, "Afterword," in Christopher Wolfe, ed., *The Naked Public Square Reconsidered: Religion and Politics in the Twenty-First Century* (Wilmington: ISI Books, 2009), 191.

Chapter 44

1 Aristotle, *Nicomachean Ethics* 1.2 (1094b).

2 So Hemmingsen, *On the Law of Nature*, 80–81.

3 This is the argument of Richard John Neuhaus in "Private Morality, Public Virtue," in *The Naked Public Square: Religion and Democracy in America* (Grand Rapids: Eerdmans, 1984), 129–43. The concept and contours of a "natural law liberalism" are helpfully developed in Christopher Wolfe, *Natural Law Liberalism* (New York: Cambridge University Press, 2006).

4 As an example, one need only recall the discussions in the early 2000s as leaders of the European Union were proposing a new constitution: it was to contain no reference to God the Creator or to the Christian heritage to which most European nations were, in fact, indebted.

5 John Finnis describes this understanding of public reason as "unprincipled exception-making" in his essay "Telling the Truth about God and Man in a Pluralist Society," in Christopher Wolfe, ed., *The Naked Public Square Reconsidered: Religion and Politics in the Twenty-First Century* (Wilmington: ISI Books, 2009), 122.

6 Question 33.

7 In two previous Questions, we noted the example of John Rawls' influence.

8 Sweetman, *Why Politics Needs Religion*, 115–60, has examined these (and more) arguments in considerable detail.

9 Here it needs emphasizing that the natural law position does *not* require democracy *per se*. Other political structures can exist within a natural law framework, inasmuch as the *moral* and not legal-political component is paramount.

10 The Christian position is not that human beings are always as bad as they can be; they are a mix of good and potential evil. In the words of Aquinas (very loosely paraphrased), human beings are simultaneously "the crown jewel of creation" and "the scum of the earth."

11 So Sweetman, *Why Politics Needs Religion*, 159.

12 This argument, however, in no way excludes or denies the secularist "right" to moral arguments in the public sphere; it is only to point out that conventional stereotypes of religion and politics are exclusionary at best and false at worst.

13 Neuhaus, *The Naked Public Square*, 155.

14 Neuhaus, *The Naked Public Square*, 144.

15 Neuhaus, *The Naked Public Square*, 113.

Chapter 45

1 In Question 6, n. 32, I identify prominent natural lawyers of the 20th century who were Roman Catholic.

2 Carl E. Braaten, "Protestants and Natural Law," *First Things* 19 (January 1992): 20–26.

3 Tireless in his efforts to apply Christian faith to every realm of life, Kuyper was the founder of the Free (Reformed) University of Amsterdam in 1880, and from 1901 to 1905 he served as prime minister of the Netherlands.

4 Abraham Kuyper, *Christianity and the Class Struggle* (Grand Rapids: Piet Hein, 1950), 14, cited as well by Braaten, p. 20.

5 Abraham Kuyper, *Lectures in Calvinism*, rev. ed. (Grand Rapids: Eerdmans, 1987), 183.

6 Braaten, "Protestants and Natural Law," 25.

7 John T. McNeill, "Natural Law in the Teaching of the Reformers," *Journal of Religion* 26 (1946): 168.

8 *CCC* no. 9.

9 Braaten, "Protestants and Natural Law," 25.

Chapter 46

1 Elsewhere I evaluate natural law thinking in the magisterial Protestant reformers in J. Daryl Charles, *Retrieving the Natural Law: A Return to Moral First Things* (Grand Rapids and Cambridge, UK: Eerdmans, 2008), 111–25; in "Burying the Wrong Corpse: Evangelicals and Natural Law," in Jesse Covington, Bryan McGraw and Micah Watson, eds., *Natural Law and Evangelical Political Thought* (Lanham: Lexington Books, 2013), 3–34; reproduced in Christopher Wolfe and Steven Brust, eds., Natural Law Today: The Present State of Perennial Philosophy (Lanham: Lexington Books, 2018), 87–110, and in "The Protestant Reformers and the Natural Law Tradition," *Public Discourse* (August 23, 2021), accessible at https://www.thepublicdiscourse.com/2021/08/77349/.

2 Brad S. Gregory, *The Unintended Reformation: How a Religious Revolution Secularized Society* (Cambridge: Belknap Press, 2012), 208. This claim is found in the chapter titled "Subjectivizing Morality." Gregory's historiography, while impressive in scope, is sadly predicated on misguided—if not outright false—assumptions. Three stand out: for example, that late-medieval Europe and the Roman Catholic Church were characterized by a fundamental unity; that fragmentation was the result of 16th-century Reformation developments and not an evolving phenomenon with roots in the previous centuries; and that the doctrine of *sola scriptura* was novel—invented by the reformers—and the cause of an eventual hyper-pluralism in the West. Significantly, four historians of note are quite critical of Gregory's thesis: Euan Cameron, Carlos Eire, Bruce Gordon, and Alexandra Walsham; see "The Unintended Revolution: A Forum," *Historically Speaking* 13, no. 3 (June 2012): 5–15. To their credit, more recently E. J. Hutchinson and Korey D. Maas, in the "Introduction" to Neils Hemmingsen, *On the Law of Nature*, take Gregory to task for the false view (1) that the reformers rejected traditional "teleological Christian morality"; (2) that they "denied the free, rational exercise of the virtues in pursuit of the good"; and (3) that they rejected "morality's natural law as traditionally conceived" (xxii, n. 79, xxxii, n. 83, and xxxiv, n. 90). Gregory, of course, is not the only Roman Catholic to hold such distorted views of the magisterial reformers. It is shared by others—for example, Josef Fuchs, *Natural Law: A Theological Investigation*, 42, 49.

3 Philip Melanchthon, however, *does* treat the matter of law and natural law systematically.

4 While the reformers affirmed the "total depravity" of human nature, they did not mean thereby that humans are always as bad as they can possibly be, nor did they understand the problem of human fallenness to eliminate the image of God in humans and hence our design.

5 Martin Luther, *Against the Heavenly Prophets*, in *Luther's Works* [hereafter *L. W.*], vol. 40, ed. Conrad Bergendorff (Philadelphia: Fortress Press, 1958), 97.

6 Luther, *Against the Heavenly Prophets*, 97.

7 Martin Luther, "Table Talk no. 3911: Difference between Natural and Positive Law," in *L. W.*, vol. 54, ed. T.G. Tappert (Philadelphia: Fortress Press, 1967), 293.

8 Martin Luther, *How Christians Should Regard Moses*, in *L. W.*, vol. 35, ed. Theodore Bachmann (Philadelphia: Muhlenberg, 1960), 168.

9 Martin Luther, *Against the Sabbatarians*, in *L.W.*, vol. 47, ed. Franklin Sherman (Philadelphia: Fortress, 1971), 89.

10 Luther, *Against the Sabbatarians*, 94.

11 Luther, *How Christians Should Regard Moses*, 165.

12 Martin Luther, *Against the Heavenly Prophets*, 97.

13 Martin Luther, *Temporal Authority: To What Extent It Should Be Obeyed*, in *L.W.*, vol. 45, ed. Walther I. Brandt (Philadelphia: Muhlenberg Press, 1962), 128.

14 Luther, *Temporal Authority*, 127.

15 Luther, *Temporal Authority*, 127.

16 Generally, Melanchthon tends to be overlooked in many discussions of the magisterial Protestant reformers, disappearing in Luther's shadow. This is borne out alone in the titles of best known volumes that describe his life and work—e.g., *Melanchthon: The Quiet Reformer, Philip Melanchthon: Reformer without Honor, Der unbekannte Melanchthon* ("The Unknown Melanchthon"), or *Melanchthon: Alien or Ally?*. This broader neglect is tragic, an injustice that *should not* be, since *inter alia* Melanchthon was "the chief teacher and instructor, the scholarly publicist, and the theological diplomat of early Lutheranism"; moreover, it was he who was responsible for "the education of the new theological generation and for the formulation of all official utterances" (Robert Stupperich, *Melanchthon*, trans. Robert H. Fischer [Philadelphia: Westminster Press, 1965], 151). Despite our unfamiliarity with him, Melanchthon wrote the very first systematic treatise of Protestant theology, the *Loci Communes*, some fifty-one editions of which were printed *during* his lifetime. And, as the main public defender of Luther's cause, he had a hand in the officially adopted confessional writings of the Lutheran Reformation such as the Augsburg Confession (1530) and the Apology of the Augsburg Confession (1531), with The Book of Concord (1580) acknowledging its supreme debt to Melanchthon. And while, in the eyes of many, the "confessor" (Luther) was greater than the "professor" (Melanchthon), the Protestant Reformation could not have been established or carried through without the latter. As it was, the "forgotten Reformer" participated in almost every major theological colloquy of his day. For a more extended evaluation of Melanchthon's influence, see J. Daryl Charles, "Natural Law and Protestant Reform: Lessons from a Forgotten Reformer," *Pro Ecclesia* 28, no. 3 (2019): 301–19; this essay is reproduced in J. Daryl Charles, *Wisdom's Work: Essays on Ethics, Vocation, and Culture* (Grand Rapids: Acton Institute Press, 2019), 61–87.

17 Thus Wilhelm Dilthey, *Gesammelte Schriften* (Leipzig and Göttingen: Teubner and Vandenhoeck & Ruprecht, 1921–1974), 21:193, cited as well by John Witte, Jr., *Law and Protestantism: The Legal Teachings of the Lutheran Reformation* (Cambridge and New York: Cambridge University Press, 2002), 122.

18 Melanchthon's discussion of law and the natural law are found chiefly in Locus 6 of *Loci Communes*.

19 Melanchthon, *Loci Communes,* Locus 6, 70.

20 Luther had developed two uses of the law: (1) it restrains human nature and (2) it functions theologically to reveal human fallenness.

21 Hereon see John Witte, Jr., and Thomas C. Arthur, "The Three Uses of the Law: A Protestant Source of the Purposes of Criminal Punishment?" *Journal of Law and Religion* 10, no. 2 (1993/4): 433–65.

22 John Calvin, *Institutes of the Christian Religion* 2.8.1. Where I am citing Calvin, I am reliant on the translation of *Institutes* found in the LCC series, vols. 20 and 21, ed. John T. McNeill and trans. Ford Lewis Battles (Philadelphia: Westminster Press, 1960).

23 Calvin, *Institutes* 2.2.22; cf. 4.10.3–4.

24 Calvin, *Institutes* 2.2.13.

25 Calvin, *Institutes* 2.2.13.

26 Calvin, *Institutes* 4.10.3.

27 Calvin, *Institutes* 4.10.3.

28 Huldrich Zwingli, *Zwinglis sämtliche Werke*, ed. Melchior Schuler and Johann Schulthess (Zürich: Schulthess, 1828–1842), 4.243 (my translation).

29 The English translation is drawn from sermons of Bullinger collected and edited by Thomas Harding. See *The Decades of Heinrich Bullinger* (4 vols.; Cambridge: The Parker Society, 1849) 2.194 (sermon 1).

30 Romanus Cessario, *Introduction to Moral Theology* (Washington, DC: Catholic University of America Press, 2001), 69 (emphasis added).

Chapter 47

1 See as well Question 43.

2 https://www.ekd.de/en/The-Barmen-Declaration-303.htm.

3 See Karl Barth, *Church Dogmatics* II/1, trans. Geoffrey W. Bromiley (Edinburgh: T.&T. Clark, 1961), and *Protestant Theology in the Nineteenth Century: Its Background and History*, rev. ed. (London: SCM, 2001); on Brunner's response to Barth's rejection of natural law, see Emil Brunner and Karl Barth, *Natural Theology*, trans. Peter Fraenkel (London: Jeffrey Bless/Centenary Press, 1946). Barth, it needs to be said, was by no means the only one who grappled with the dilemma of National Socialism and the totalitarian state. Heinrich Rommen, Yves Simon, Jacques Maritain, and Eric Voegelin were among European emigrés during the 1930s and 40s who contributed to a renewal of natural law thinking. What they shared in common, in contrast to Barth, was the conviction that a traditional metaphysics of natural law, consistent with traditional Christian moral philosophy, might be advanced without capitulating to the modernist, secularist or fascist *Zeitgeist*.

4 See Jacques Ellul, *The Theological Foundation of Law*, trans. Marguerite Wieser (London: SCM, 1961), and *To Will and to Do*, trans. C. Edward Hopkin (Philadelphia and Boston: Pilgrim Press, 1969).

5 Thielicke studied under Barth in the early 1930s.

6 All citations are taken from Helmut Thielicke, *Theological Ethics—Volume I: Foundations* (Philadelphia: Fortress Press, 1966).

7 Offering a helpful yet concise comparison between classical and contemporary versions of liberalism is Christopher Wolfe, "Thomas Aquinas's Natural Law," in idem and Steven Brust, eds., *Natural Law Today: The Present State of the Perennial Philosophy* (Lanham and London: Lexington Books, 2018), 139–49.

8 Whether this can be applied to rabbinic Judaism is an open question (and beyond the scope of the present discussion).

9 Matt. 5:17–18; Rom. 7:12; 10:4–5; and James 2:10–11 (implied in vv. 17 and 24).

10 For example, Psalm 19 and 119.

Chapter 48

1 Jean Porter, N*ature as Reason: A Thomistic Theory of the Natural Law* (Grand Rapids and Cambridge, UK: Eerdmans, 2005), 177–78.

2 So Aquinas, *S.T.* I-II Q. 49.3, 4.

3 Aquinas, *S.T.* I-II Q. 55.1.

4 Aquinas, *S.T.* II–II Q.123.11.

5 Aristotle, *Rhetoric* I.9 (1366b).

6 Aquinas, *S.T.* I-II Q. 61.5.

7 Here I am using wisdom and prudence interchangeably.

8 Aristotle, *Nicomachean Ethics* 6.5 (1140a).

9 In its character, just retribution eschews both indulgence on the one hand and savagery on the other.

10 Aristotle, *Nicomachean Ethics* 5.1 (1129b).

11 Cicero, *On Obligations* 3.28.

12 Aristotle, *Nicomachean Ethics* 5.1 (1129b).

13 Cicero, *On Invention* 2.161.

14 Aquinas, *S.T.* II–II Q. 81.

15 See, for example, Aristotle, *Nicomachean Ethics* 5.2–5 (1130a14–1134a16) and Aquinas, *S.T.* II–II Q. 61.

16 On the matter of restitution, see Aquinas, *S.T.* II–II Q. 62.

17 Aquinas, *S.T.* II–II Q. 61.1.

18 Aristotle, *Nicomachean Ethics* 5.8 (1135a-b).

19 Aristotle, *Nicomachean Ethics* 3.10–12 (1117b-1119b) and 6.5 (1140b).

20 Aristotle, *Nicomachean Ethics* 3.2 (1119a).

21 Hemmingsen, *On the Law of Nature*, 131.

22 Aquinas, *S.T.* II–II Q. 123.2.

23 Aquinas, *S.T.* II–II Q. 123.6.

24 Hemmingsen, *On the Law of Nature*, 69.

Chapter 49

1 See Question 11.

2 This is the theme, for example, of the first four chapters of the book of Proverbs.

3 This may be more a Western phenomenon, given the secularization of much its social life.

4 The latter part of the book of Proverbs, for example, is devoted to wisdom sayings of surrounding non-Israelite cultures.

5 These proverbs have been gathered in Ruth Finegan, *Oral Literature in Africa* (Oxford: Oxford University Press, 1970), 389–425, and reproduced

with commentary in Claus Westermann, *Roots of Wisdom: The Oldest Proverbs of Israel and Other Peoples*, trans. J. Daryl Charles (Louisville: Westminster John Knox Press, 1995), 145–46.

6 Prov. 10:26; 13:13; 17:1; 17:14; 19:12; 25:19.

7 John Paul II, *Fides et Ratio* no. 16.

8 John Paul II, *Fides et Ratio* no. 16.

9 Eccl. 3:1–17.

10 Eccl. 12:13–14.

11 See J. Daryl Charles, *Wisdom and Work: Theological Reflections on Human Labor from Ecclesiastes* (Eugene: Cascade Books, 2021).

Chapter 50

1 See Questions 3 and 11.

2 C. S. Lewis, "On Ethics," in *Christian Reflections*, ed. Walter Hooper (Grand Rapids: Eerdmans, 1967), 57 (emphasis added).

3 C. S. Lewis, *The Abolition of Man* (New York: Macmillan, 1947), 56.

4 Lewis, "On Ethics," 46.

5 Horace, *Epistles* I.X.24; cited as well in Rommen, *The Natural Law*, 237n.2.

6 See Question 44.

Bibliography

Ambrose, St. *Letter* 73 ("To Irenaeus"). Accessible at https://www.fourthcentury.com/ambrose-letter-73/.

Anderson, Owen. *The Natural Moral Law: The Good after Modernity*. Cambridge and New York: Cambridge University Press, 2012.

Aquinas, Thomas. *Summa Theologica*. 3 Vols. Trans. Fathers of the English Dominican Province. New York: Benziger Bros, 1947.

Aristotle. *Nicomachean Ethics*. 2nd ed. Trans. Terence Irwin. Indianapolis: Hackett Publishing Co., 1999.

________. *Politics: A New Translation*. Trans. C. D. C. Reeve. Indianapolis: Hackett Publishing Co., 2017.

________. *Rhetoric*. Trans. W. Rhys Roberts. Accessible at https://classics.mit.edu/Aristotle/rhetoric.html.

Arkes, Hadley. *First Things: An Inquiry into the First Principles of Morals and Justice*. Princeton: Princeton University Press, 1986.

________. "The Natural Law—Again, Ever." In Christopher Wolfe and Steven Brust, ed., *Natural Law Today: The Present State of the Perennial Philosophy*, 111–38. Lanham: Lexington Books, 2018.

Augustine, St. *City of God*. Book XIX. Accessible at https://www.newadvent.org/fathers/120119.htm.

Augustine, *St. Letters—Vol. IV*. Washington, DC: Catholic University of America Press, 1955.

________. *On the Trinity*. Acessible to https://www.newadvent.org/fathers/130101.htm.

Bakewell, Charles M., *Source Book in Ancient Philosophy*. New York: Scribner's, 1907.

Barth, Karl. *Church Dogmatics II/1*. Trans. Geoffrey W. Bromiley. Edinburgh: T.&T. Clark, 1961.

________. *Protestant Theology in the Nineteenth Century: Its Background and History*, rev. ed. London: SCM, 2001.

Benedict XVI, *Caritas in Veritate*. June 29, 2009. Accessible at https://www.vatican.va/content/benedict-xvi/en/encyclicals/documents/hf_ben-xvi_enc_20090629_caritas-in-veritate.html.

Berke, Stanley. *The Possibility of Invincible Ignorance of the Natural Law*. SST 58. Washington, DC: Catholic University of American Press, 1941.

Bidinotto, Robert James. "Crime and Moral Retribution." In Robert James Bidinotto, ed., *Criminal Justice? The Legal System Versus Individual Responsibility*, 182–200. Irvington-on-Hudson: Foundation for Economic Education, 1994.

Blecker, Robert. *The Death of Punishment*. New York: Palgrave Macmillan, 2013.

Braaten, Carl E. "Protestants and Natural Law." *First Things* 19 (January 1992): 20–26.

Brunner, Emil and Karl Barth. *Natural Theology*. Trans. Peter Fraenkel. London: Jeffrey Bless/Centenary Press, 1946.

Budziszewski, J. *What We Can't Not Know: A Guide*. 2nd ed. San Francisco: Ignatius Press, 2011.

________. *Written on the Heart: The Case for Natural Law*. Downers Grove: InterVarsity Press, 1997.

Calvin, John. *Institutes of the Christian Religion*. Ed. John T. McNeill. Trans. Ford Lewis Battles. LCC. Philadelphia: Westminster Press, 1960.

Catechism of the Catholic Church. Washington, DC: United States Conference of Catholic Bishops, 1994.

Ceaser, James W. "The Doctrine of Political Nonfoundationalism." In *Designing a Polity: America's Constitution in Theory and Practice*, 3–21. Lanham and Plymouth, UK: Rowman & Littlefield, 2011.

Cessario, Romanus. *Introduction to Moral Theology*. Washington, DC: Catholic University of America Press, 2001.

Charles, J. Daryl. "Burying the Wrong Corpse: Evangelicals and Natural Law." In Jesse Covington, Bryan McGraw and Micah Watson, eds., *Natural Law and Evangelical Political Thought*, 3–34. Lanham: Lexington Books, 2013.

________. "Capital Crimes and Capital Punishment." *Public Discourse* (March 14, 2023). Accessible at https://www.thepublicdiscourse.com/2023/03/88117/.

________. "The Moral Underpinnings of Just Retribution: Justice and Charity in Symbiosis." *Providence: A Journal of Christianity and American Foreign Policy* 3 (2016): 5–16.

________. "Natural Law and Protestant Reform: Lessons from a Forgotten Reformer." *Pro Ecclesia* 28, no. 3 (2019): 301–19 (reproduced in *Wisdom's Work: Essays on Ethics, Vocation, and Culture,* 61–87. Grand Rapids: Acton Institute Press, 2019).

________. *Natural Law and Religious Freedom*. London and New York: Routledge, 2018.

________. "The Natural-Law Underpinnings of Religious Freedom—A Closer Look." In *Natural Law and Religious Freedom*, 177–228. London and New York: Routledge, 2018.

________. "The Protestant Reformers and the Natural Law Tradition." *Public Discourse* (August 23, 2021). Accessible at https://www.thepublicdiscourse.com/2021/08/77349/.

________. *Retrieving the Natural Law: A Return to Moral First Things*. Grand Rapids and Cambridge, UK: Eerdmans, 2008.

Christopher, Paul. *The Ethics of War and Peace*, rev. ed. Upper Saddle River: Prentice-Hall, 1999.

Cicero, Marcus Tullius. *On the Commonwealth* III:XXII. Trans. George Holland Sabine and Stanley Barney Smith. Indianapolis and New York: Bobbs-Merrill Co., 1960.

Coates, Anthony. "Is the Independent Application of Jus in Bello the Way to Limit War?" In David Rodin and Henry Shue, eds., *Just and Unjust Warriors*, 176–92. Oxford: Oxford University Press, 2008.

Colosi, Peter J. "What's Love Got to Do with It: The Ethical Contradictions of Peter Singer." *Godspy* (February 25, 2005). Accessible at https://www.catholiceducation.org/en/health/euthanasia-and-assisted-suicide/what-slove-got-to-do-with-it-the-ethical-contradictions-of-peter-singer.html.

Culverwel, Nathaniel. *Elegant and Learned Discourse of the Law of Nature*, ed. Robert A. Greene and Hugh MacCallum. Toronto: University of Toronto Press, 1971.

Darwin, Charles. *The Origins of Species and the Descent of Man*. New York: The Modern Library, 1936.

Dilthey, Wilhelm. *Gesammelte Schriften*. Vol. 21. Leipzig and Göttingen: Teubner and Vandenhoeck & Ruprecht, 1921–1974.

DiIulio, John J. and Charles H. Logan. "Ten Deadly Myths about Crime and Punishment in the U.S." In Robert James Bidinotto, ed., *Criminal Justice"? The Legal System versus Individual Responsibility*, 156–80. Irvington-on-Hudson: Foundation for Economic Education, 1994.

Dorman, Ted M. *A Faith for All Seasons: Historic Christian Belief in Its Classical Expression*. Nashville: Broadman & Holman, 1995.

Ellul, Jacques. *The Theological Foundation of Law*. Trans. Marguerite Wieser. London: SCM, 1961.

________. *To Will and to Do*. Trans. C. Edward Hopkin. Philadelphia and Boston: Pilgrim Press, 1969.

Elshtain, Jean Bethke. "The Responsibility of Nations: A Moral Case for Coercive Justice." *Daedalus* (Winter 2003): 64–72.

Finegan, Ruth. *Oral Literature in Africa*. Oxford: Oxford University Press, 1970.

Finnis, John. *Natural Law and Natural Rights*. Oxford: Clarendon, 1980.

Forte, David F., ed. *Natural Law and Contemporary Public Policy*. Washington, DC: Georgetown University Press, 1998.

Francisco, Adam S. "Natural Law: A Basis for Christian-Muslim Discourse." In Robert C. Baker, ed., *Natural Law: A Lutheran Appraisal*, 235–47. St. Louis: Concordia Publishing House, 2011.

Fuchs, Josef. *Natural Law: A Theological Investigation*. Trans. Helmut Reckter and John A. Dowling. New York: Sheed and Ward, 1965.

Gelernter, David. "The Irreducibly Religious Character of Human Dignity." In Adam Schulman, ed., *Human Dignity and Bioethics: Essays Commissioned by the President's Council on Bioethics*, 387–405. Washington, DC: President's Council on Bioethics, 2008.

George, Robert P. *Conscience and Its Enemies: Confronting the Dogmas of Liberal Secularism*. Wilmington: ISI Books, 2013.

________. "Public Reason and Political Conflict: Abortion and Homosexuality." In *In Defense of Natural Law,* 196–227. Oxford and New York: Oxford University Press, 1999.

________, ed. *Natural Law Theory*. Oxford: Clarendon Press, 1992.

George, Robert P. and Christopher Wolfe, eds. *Natural Law and Public Reason.* Washington, DC: Georgetown University Press, 2000.

Gerson, Michael and Peter Wehner. *City of Man: Religion and Politics in a New Era*. Chicago: Moody Publishers, 2010.

Gilson, Étienne. *Moral Values and the Moral Life*. Trans. L. R. Ward. Hamden: Shoe String Press, 1961.

Grabill, Stephen J. *Rediscovering the Natural Law in Reformed Theological Ethics*. Grand Rapids and Cambridge, UK: Eerdmans, 2006.

Gregory, Brad S. *The Unintended Reformation: How a Religious Revolution Secularized Society*. Cambridge: Belknap Press, 2012.

Grotius, Hugo. *The Rights of War and Peace.* 3 Vols. Ed. Richard Tuck. Indianapolis: Liberty Fund, 2005.

Habermas, Jürgen and Joseph Ratzinger (Pope Benedict XVI). *The Dialectics of Secularization: On Reason and Religion*. Trans. Brian McNeil. San Francisco: Ignatius Press, 2007.

Hale, Matthew. *Of the Law of Nature*, ed. David S. Sytsma. Grand Rapids: CLP Academic, 2015.

Hamilton, Alexander, John Jay, and James Madison. *The Federalist*. New York: Random House, 2000.

Harding, Thomas, ed. *The Decades of Heinrich Bullinger*. Vol. 2. Cambridge: The Parker Society, 1849.

Hemmingsen, Niels. *On the Law of Nature*. Ed. and trans. E. J. Hutchinson. Sources in Early Modern Economics, Ethics, and Law. Grand Rapids: CLP Academic, 2018.

Hill, John Lawrence. *After the Natural Law: How the Classical Worldview Supports Our Modern Moral and Political Values*. San Francisco: Ignatius, 2016.

Hittinger, Russell. "Liberalism and the American Natural Law Tradition." *Wake Forest Law Review* 25, no. 3 (1990): 429–99.

Hooker, Richard. *Of the Laws of Ecclesiastical Polity*. 3 Vols. Ed. John Keble et al. Oxford: Clarendon Press, 1888.

Hutchinson, E.J. and Korey D. Maas. "Introduction." In Niels Hemmingsen, *On the Law of Nature*, xi-xlii. Ed. and trans. E. J. Hutchinson. Sources in Early Modern Economics, Ethics, and Law. Grand Rapids: CLP Academic, 2018.

Irenaeus, *Against Heresies*. Accessible at https://www.newadvent.org/fathers/0103.htm.

John Paul II. *Fides et Ratio*. September 14, 1998. Accessible at https://www.vatican.va/content/ john-paul-ii/en/encyclicals/documents/hf_jp-ii_enc_14091998_fides-etratio.html.

________. *Veritatis Splendor*. August 6, 1993. Accessible at https://www.vatican.va/content/john-paul-ii/en/encyclicals/documents/hf_jp-ii_enc_06081993_veritatis-splendor.pdf.

Kuyper, Abraham. *Christianity and the Class Struggle*. Grand Rapids: Piet Hein, 1950.

________. *Lectures in Calvinism*, rev. ed. Grand Rapids: Eerdmans, 1987.

Lee, Patrick and Robert P. George. "The Wrong of Abortion." In Andrew I. Cohen and Christopher Wellman, eds., *Contemporary Debates in Applied Ethics*, 13–26. New York: Blackwell Publishers, 2005.

Levering, Matthew. "Christians and Natural Law." In Anver Emon, Matthew Levering, and David Novak, *Natural Law: A Jewish, Christian, and Islamic Trialogue*, 66–110. Oxford: Oxford University Press, 2014.

Lewis, C.S. *The Abolition of Man*. New York: HarperOne, 2000 [1944].

________. "On Ethics." In *Christian Reflections*, ed. Walter Hooper, 54–69. Grand Rapids: Eerdmans, 1967.

________. "The Humanitarian Theory of Punishment." In *God in the Dock: Essays on Theology and Ethics*, ed. Walter Hooper, 287–94. Grand Rapids: Eerdmans, 1970.

________. "Right and Wrong as a Clue to the Meaning of the Universe." In *Mere Christianity*, 15–39. New York: Macmillan, 1960.

Locke, John. *Questions concerning the Law of Nature*. Ed. and trans. Robert Horwitz et al. Ithaca: Cornell University Press, 1990.

________. *Two Treatises of Government*, ed. Peter Laslett. New York: Cambridge University Press, 1960.

Long, Steven A. "God, Teleology, and the Natural Law." In Christopher Wolfe and Steven Brust, eds., *Natural Law Today: The Present State of the Perennial Philosophy*, 3–18. Lanham: Lexington Books, 2018.

Luther, Martin. *Against the Heavenly Prophets*. In *Luther's Works—Vol. 40*, 79–223. Ed. Conrad Bergendorff. Philadelphia: Fortress Press, 1958.

________. *Against the Sabbatarians*. In *Luther's Works—Vol. 47*, 65–98. Ed. Franklin Sherman. Philadelphia: Fortress, 1971.

________. *How Christians Should Regard Moses*. In *Luther's Works—Vol. 35*, 161–74. Ed. Theodore Bachmann. Philadelphia: Muhlenberg, 1960.

________. "Table Talk," no. 3911 (July 7, 1538). In *Luther's Works—Vol. 54*, 293. Ed. T.G. Tappert. Philadelphia: Fortress, 1967.

________. *Temporal Authority: To What Extent It Should Be Obeyed*. In *Luther's Works—Vol. 45*, 81–129. Ed. Walther I. Brandt. Philadelphia: Muhlenberg Press, 1962.

Maritain, Jacques. *Man and the State*. Chicago: University of Chicago Press, 1951.

Marshall, Paul A., ed. *Religious Freedom in the World*. Lanham and Plymouth, UK: Rowman & Littlefield, 2008.

The Marshall Project. "What You Need to Know About the Rise in U.S. Mass Shootings." July 6, 2022. Accessible at https://www.themarshallproject.org/2022/07/06/what-you-need-to-know-about-the-rise-in-u-s-mass-shootings.

May, William E. "Bioethics and Human Life." In David F. Forte, ed., *Natural Law and Contemporary Public Policy*, 41–54. Washington, DC: Georgetown University Press, 1998.

McInerny, Ralph. "Are There Moral Truths That Everyone Knows?" In Edward B. McLean, ed., *Common Truths: New Perspectives on Natural Law*, 1–18. Wilmington: ISI Books, 2000.

McNeill, John T. "Natural Law in the Teaching of the Reformers." *Journal of Religion* 26 (1946): 168–82.

Meilaender, Gilbert. *Neither Beast nor God: The Dignity of the Human Person*. New York and London: Encounter Books, 2009.

Melanchthon, Philip. *Loci Communes* (1543). Trans. J.A.O. Preus. St. Louis: Concordia Publishing House, 1992.

Menninger, Karl. *The Crime of Punishment*. New York: Viking Press, 1968.

Methvin, Eugene H. "Mugged by Reality." *Policy Review* (July/August 1997): 32–38.

Miller, William Lee. *The First Liberty: America's Foundation in Religious Freedom*. Washington, DC: Georgetown University Press, 2003.

________. "The Moral Project of the American Founders." In James Davison Hunter and Os Guinness, eds., *Articles of Faith, Articles of Peace: The Religious Liberty Clauses and the American Public Philosophy*, 17–39. Washington, DC: Brookings Institution, 1990.

Miller, Nicholas P. *The Religious Roots of the First Amendment: Dissenting Protestants and the Separation of Church and State*. Oxford and New York: Oxford University Press, 2012.

Mott, Stephen Charles. *Biblical Ethics and Social Change*, 2nd ed. Oxford and New York: Oxford University Press, 2011.

Moynihan, Daniel Patrick. "Defining Deviancy Down." *The American Scholar* 62, no. 1 (Winter 1993): 17–30.

Nemeth, Charles P. *Aquinas on Crime*. South Bend: St. Augustine's Press, 2008.

Neuhaus, Richard John. *The Naked Public Square: Religion and Democracy in America*. Grand Rapids: Eerdmans, 1984.

________. "Why We Can Get Along." *First Things* (February 1996): 27–34.

Noonan, John T., Jr. "The Natural Law Banner." In David F. Forte, ed., *Natural Law and Contemporary Public Policy*, 380–84. Washington, DC: Georgetown University Press, 1998.

Novak, David. "Judaism and Natural Law." *American Journal of Jurisprudence* 43, no. 1 (1998): 117–34.

________. "Foreword: Religious Liberty," in Daniel L. Dreisbach, Mark David Hall, and Jeffry H. Morrison, eds., *The Founders on God and Government*, 9–15. Lanham: Rowman & Littlefield, 2004.

O'Brien, William V. *The Conduct of a Just and Limited War*. New York: Praeger, 1981.

O'Donovan, Oliver. "Payback: Thinking about Retribution." *Books & Culture* (July/August 2000): 16–21.

Pagden, Anthony and Jeremy Lawrance, eds. Vitoria: *Political Writings*. Cambridge Texts in the History of Political Thought. Cambridge: Cambridge University Press, 1991.

Origen. *Contra Celsum*. Accessible at https://www.newadvent.org/fathers/0416.htm.

Paul VI. *Gaudium et Spes*. December 7, 1965. Accessible at https://www.vatican.va/archive/hist_councils/ii_vatican_council/documents/vat-ii_const_19651207_gaudium-et-spes_en.html.

Porter, Jean. *Natural and Divine Law: Reclaiming the Tradition for Christian Ethics*. Grand Rapids and Cambridge, UK: Eerdmans, 1999.

________. *Nature as Reason: A Thomistic Theory of the Natural Law*. Grand Rapids and Cambridge, UK: Eerdmans, 2005.

Ramsey, Paul. *Basic Christian Ethics*. New York: Scribner's, 1950.

________. *The Just War: Force and Political Responsibility*. New York: Scribner's, 1968.

Rommen, Heinrich A. *The Natural Law: A Study in Legal and Social History and Philosophy*. Trans. Thomas R. Hanley. Indianapolis: Liberty Fund, 1998.

Rudavsky, Tamar. "Natural Law in Judaism." In Jonathan A. Jacobs, ed., *Reason, Religion, and Natural Law*, 83–105. Oxford: Oxford University Press, 2012.

Ruse, Michael and E.O. Wilson. "The Evolution of Ethics." *New Scientist* 108, no. 1478 (October 17, 1985): 50–52.

Samenow, Stanton E. "The Basic Myths about Criminals." In Robert James Bidinotto, ed., *Criminal Justice? The Legal System Versus Individual Responsibility*, 47–58. Irvington-on-Hudson: Foundation for Economic Education, Inc. 1994.

Scott, James B. *The Spanish Origin of International Law: Lectures on Francisco de Vitoria (1480–1546) and Francisco Suárez (1548–1617)*. Washington, DC: Georgetown University Press, 1929.

Simoncelli, Damiano. "From Natural Law to the Golden Rule: Aquinas Revisited." *Ethics, Politics & Society* 1 (2018): 261–75.

Singer, Peter. *Animal Liberation: A New Ethics for Our Treatment of Animals*. New York: Random House, 1975.

________. "The Choice of a Pregnant Woman Always Outweighs the Life of the Fetus." In Noël Merino, ed., *Ethics: Opposing Viewpoints*, 82–83. Farmington Hills: Greenhaven Press, 2015.

Smith, Christopher, ed. *The Secular Revolution: Power, Interests, and Conflict in the Secularization of American Public Life*. Berkeley: University of California Press, 2003.

Sowell, Thomas. *Intellectuals and Society*. New York: Basic Books, 2009.

Specter, Michael. "The Dangerous Philosopher." *The New Yorker* (September 6, 1999). Accessible at https://www.michaelspecter.com/1999/09/the-dangerous-philosopher/.

Stupperich, Robert. *Melanchthon*. Trans. Robert H. Fischer. Philadelphia: Westminster Press, 1965.

Sweetman, Brendan. *Why Politics Needs Religion: The Place of Religious Arguments in the Public Square*. Downers Grove: IVP Academic, 2006.

Tertullian, *De Corona*. Accessible at https://www.newadvent.org/fathers/0304.htm.

Thielicke, Helmut. *Theological Ethics—Volume I: Foundations*. Philadelphia: Fortress Press, 1966.

Tocqueville, Alexis de. *Democracy in America*, rev. ed. Ed. and trans. Harvey C. Mansfield and Delba Winthrop. Chicago and London: University of Chicago Press, 2000.

Universal Declaration of Human Rights. United Nations. December 10, 1948. Accessible at https://www.un.org/sites/un2.un.org/files/2021/03/udhr.pdf.

VanDrunen, David. *Divine Covenants and Moral Order: A Biblical Theology of Natural Law*. Grand Rapids and Cambridge, UK: Eerdmans, 2014.

________. *Natural law and the Two Kingdoms*. Grand Rapids: Eerdmans, 2010.

Vitoria, Francisco de. *Reflections in Moral Theology. De Indis Et De Jure Bells Reflectiones*. Ed. Ernest Nys. Trans. John Pawley Bate. Washington, DC: Carnegie Institution, 1917.

Walker, Andrew T. *Faithful Reason: Natural Law Ethics for God's Glory and Our Good*. Nashville: B & H Academic, 2024.

Washington, George. "George Washington to John Jay." 15 August 1786. Accessible at https://founders.archives.gov/documents/washington/04–04-02–099.

Weiss, Thomas G. and Cindy Collins. *Humanitarian Challenges and Intervention*, 2nd ed. Boulder: Westview, 2000.

Westermann, Claus. *Roots of Wisdom: The Oldest Proverbs of Israel and Other Peoples*, trans. J. Daryl Charles.Louisville: Westminster John Knox Press, 1995.

Witte, John, Jr. *Law and Protestantism: The Legal Teachings of the Lutheran Reformation*. Cambridge and New York: Cambridge University Press, 2002.

Witte, John, Jr., and Thomas C. Arthur. "The Three Uses of the Law: A Protestant Source of the Purposes of Criminal Punishment?" *Journal of Law and Religion* 10, no. 2 (1993/4): 433–65.

Wojtyla, Karol. *Sign of Contradiction*. New York: Seabury Press, 1979.

Wolfe, Christopher. *Natural Law Liberalism*. Cambridge and New York: Cambridge University Press, 2009.

_________. "Thomas Aquinas's Natural Law." In Christopher Wolfe and Steven Brust, eds., *Natural Law Today: The Present State of the Perennial Philosophy*, 139–49. Lanham: Lexington Books, 2018.

Zwingli, Huldrich. *Zwinglis sämtliche Werke*. Band 4. Ed. Melchior Schuler and Johann Schulthess. Zürich: Schulthess, 1828–1842.

About the Author

J. Daryl Charles, PhD, is a 2024/25 Elshtain visiting fellow at the Institute on Religion & Democracy and a senior fellow of the Center for Religion, Culture & Democracy, serves as a contributing editor of *Providence: A Journal of Christianity and American Foreign Policy* and the journal *Touchstone*, and has served as the Acton Institute Affiliated Scholar in Theology and Ethics. Charles is author, co-author, editor or co-editor of 24 books, including *Virtue amidst Vice* (Sheffield Academic Press, 1997), *The Unformed Conscience of Evangelicalism* (InterVarsity Press, 2002), *Retrieving the Natural Law* (Eerdmans, 2008), *War, Peace and Christianity* (Crossway, 2010), *Natural Law and Religious Freedom* (Routledge, 2018), *America's Wars and the Just War Tradition* (University of Notre Dame Press, 2019), and most recently, *Just War and Christian Traditions* (University of Notre Dame Press, 2022), and *Our Secular Vocation* (B&H Academic, 2023). He is also the translator (German to English) of Claus Westermann's *Roots of Wisdom* (Westminster John Knox Press, 1995). Charles has taught at Taylor University and Union University and was a 2013/14 visiting professor in the honors program at Berry College. Has served as director and senior fellow of the Bryan Institute for Critical Thought and Practice, as the 2007/8 William E. Simon visiting fellow in religion and public life at the James Madison Program, Princeton University, and as the 2003/4 visiting fellow of the Institute for Faith and Learning, Baylor University. Charles's research interests include faith and public life, the natural law, the ethics of war and peace, and criminal justice ethics. Before entering the university classroom full-time he did public-policy work in criminal justice in Washington, D.C.